From Dissent to Democracy

From Dissent to Democracy

The Promise and Perils of Civil Resistance Transitions

JONATHAN C. PINCKNEY

OXFORD
UNIVERSITY PRESS

OXFORD
UNIVERSITY PRESS

Oxford University Press is a department of the University of Oxford. It furthers
the University's objective of excellence in research, scholarship, and education
by publishing worldwide. Oxford is a registered trade mark of Oxford University
Press in the UK and certain other countries.

Published in the United States of America by Oxford University Press
198 Madison Avenue, New York, NY 10016, United States of America.

© Oxford University Press 2020

Library of Congress Cataloging-in-Publication Data
Names: Pinckney, Jonathan C., author.
Title: From dissent to democracy : the promise and perils of civil resistance transitions /
Jonathan C. Pinckney. Description: New York : Oxford University Press, 2020. |
Includes bibliographical references and index.
Identifiers: LCCN 2019055838 (print) | LCCN 2019055839 (ebook) |
ISBN 9780190097301 (hardback) | ISBN 9780190097318 (paperback) |
ISBN 9780190097332 (epub)
Subjects: LCSH: Democratization. | Civil disobedience. | Democratization—Nepal. | Civil
disobedience—Nepal. | Democratization—Zambia. |
Civil disobedience—Zambia. | Democratization—Brazil. | Civil disobedience—Brazil.
Classification: LCC JC423 .P46 2020 (print) | LCC JC423 (ebook) | DDC 321.09—dc23
LC record available at https://lccn.loc.gov/2019055838
LC ebook record available at https://lccn.loc.gov/2019055839

1 3 5 7 9 8 6 4 2

Paperback printed by Marquis, Canada
Hardback printed by Bridgeport National Bindery, Inc., United States of America

To the ones who keep fighting.

Contents

Acknowledgments

THIS BOOK HAS benefited from more people than I can possibly name, yet the contributions of a few deserve special attention. This project began under the guidance of my advisor Erica Chenoweth, to whom I am deeply grateful and whose mentorship has shaped me into the scholar that I am today. I am also deeply grateful to Cullen Hendrix, Aaron Schneider, and Tim Sisk. Their guidance and comments from the earliest stages of this project have been invaluable. They were also generous in sharing contacts for my fieldwork.

The fieldwork I conducted in Nepal, Zambia, and Brazil would have been impossible had it not been for the kindness and generosity of many people. First, I would like to thank my interviewees in all three countries, who gave their time and attention to my project and answered my questions with honesty and detail.

I was able to conduct the fieldwork thanks to financial support from the International Center on Nonviolent Conflict, who honored me by making me a Research Fellow, gave me grant funding to support both the travel and hiring of research assistants, and offered me the chance to publish some of the findings in their monograph series. My sincere thanks to Hardy Merriman, Maciej Bartkowski, Amber French, and all the others at ICNC who believed in my research and supported me so generously.

In Nepal, particular thanks go to Subindra Bogati and all the wonderful staff at Nepal Peacebuilding Initiative who not only provided me with names and contact information and made many calls on my behalf but also gave me a desk in their office and let me join their community while I was in Kathmandu. Special thanks as well to Ches Thurber, who provided invaluable expertise on doing research in Nepal and provided me with an extensive list of contacts, and to Chiranjibi Bhandari, who shared many of his personal contacts and provided invaluable help in getting me settled in Kathmandu. Thanks as well to Chandan Amatya, whose home I stayed in during my time in Nepal and who was an excellent roommate, guide to life in Nepal, and sounding board for my ideas about Nepalese politics.

In Zambia, I owe particular thanks to Miles Larmer, Adrienne LeBas, Nic Cheeseman, and Marja Hinfelaar, all of whom were very kind in sharing both their insights on Zambia and the contacts of many of my eventual interviewees. Sishuwa Sishuwa at the University of Zambia was an invaluable resource, providing the bulk of my initial contacts in Zambia. I also owe special thanks to Akashambatwa Mbikusita-Lewanika, who gave me a lengthy interview on his front porch in Mongu one lovely evening and hosted me in his home that night, giving me a very warm welcome on my first day in Zambia. Thanks also to Mawano Kambeu, whose home in Lusaka I stayed in and who was kind enough to wake up early in the morning several times to drive me to the bus station or help me find my way around the city.

In Brazil, my thanks go to my research assistants: Karine Fernandes, Fabricio Freitas, Paula Moreira, and Isabela Ottoni. All four were model trainees during my trip to Brasilia to initiate the program, devoted themselves to the project, and worked tirelessly to ensure its success despite a very challenging environment. My thanks also go to Fernando Horta, who not only arranged my contacts with my research assistants but who also hosted me in his home while I was in Brasilia, drove me back and forth to the University of Brasilia to conduct my trainings there, and in many more ways was crucial to making my fieldwork in Brazil happen. Thanks as well to Dr. Ana Flavia Platiau at the University of Brasilia, who was kind enough to allow me to use space at the university to conduct the training of my research assistants.

I have had the privilege to present early versions of this research in many different forums, and the project has benefited immensely from the feedback I received there. I owe particular thanks to Luke Abbs, Consuelo Amat, Colin Beck, Felix Bethke, Charles Butcher, Mauricio Rivera Celestino, Killian Clarke, John Chin, Marianne Dahl, Indra de Soysa, Scott Gates, Kristian Skrede Gleditsch, Carl Henrik Knutsen, Milli Lake, George Lawson, Liesel Mitchell, Benjamin Naimark-Rowse, Sharon Erickson Nepstad, Håvard Mokleiv Nygård, Daniel Ritter, Bintu Sarah Sakor, Ole Magnus Thiessen, and Ches Thurber, who all either invited me to present the work or offered detailed comments on it at presentations. I'm also grateful to all of those who attended my panels at the 2017 meetings of the International Studies Association and the American Political Science Association, the Mobilization Conference on Nonviolent Strategies and the State, the Rethinking Revolutions workshop at the London School of Economics, and my book workshop at the Peace Research Institute of Oslo.

While working on this book I had the joy and the privilege to be part of two phenomenal communities of brilliant scholars in the PhD program at the Josef Korbel School of International Studies and the Department of Political Science and Sociology at the Norwegian University of Science and Technology

(NTNU). Every one of my colleagues at Korbel and NTNU has been kind, supportive, and encouraging. I would like to particularly thank Joel Day, Kyleanne Hunter, Pauline Moore, and Chris Shay.

Finally, my gratitude goes out to my family, particularly my parents, Coty and Beth Pinckney and Kandyce Pinckney, for their kindness, patience, and support.

Introduction

WHEN THE REVOLUTION DOESN'T DELIVER

> *Liberation may be the condition of freedom but by no means*
> *leads automatically to it. . . . The notion of liberty implied in*
> *liberation can only be negative, and hence, . . . even the inten-*
> *tion of liberating is not identical with the desire for freedom.*
> *Yet if these truisms are frequently forgotten, it is because liber-*
> *ation has always loomed large and the foundation of freedom*
> *has always been uncertain, if not altogether futile.*
> —HANNAH ARENDT, *On Revolution* (1963)

THE OLD ACTIVIST's description was unequivocal: "We thought Zambia was going to be a paradise, a heaven on earth. . . . The private sector would create jobs for people . . . people would have freedom of expression . . . and the government would create an enabling environment for them to do whatever they wanted to do."[1]

After a year and a half organizing protests and rallies against the country's single-party socialist government, his group, the Movement for Multiparty Democracy (MMD), had been on the verge of a democratic breakthrough. Their task was not easy. After only a brief period of democracy in the 1960s and early 1970s Zambia had become a single-party state in the hands of the United National Independence Party (UNIP). Power had become increasingly central-ized around the founding president, Kenneth Kaunda. UNIP encouraged a cult of personality for Kaunda, ascribing almost superhuman abilities to the man. The slogan was "In heaven, there is God. On earth, there is Kaunda."

Despite the strength of the government's opposition, the MMD had won several victories. They pressured the government first to legalize other parties, and then to hold presidential and legislative elections. The ruling party was still trying to use state resources as its personal election fund and hoping to continue its rule with only the trappings of democracy. Yet through careful campaigning, nationwide organization, and a strong network of local supporting organizations, the MMD slowly but surely began undermining UNIP's hold on the Zambian political system. As the election approached, UNIP's core structures began to collapse, with prominent figures defecting to MMD in droves. And finally, when the voting was over, MMD had not only won but had nearly swept the parliamentary elections and taken three-quarters of the presidential vote. It was a peaceful revolution, a dramatic overturning of the country's political system through civic pressure from below. The conditions were in place for the MMD to create the "paradise" that they had promised.

Yet as the conversation continued, the story rapidly turned from excitement and hope to frustration and disgust. New leaders used the privileges of office to foster their own interests and promote networks of corruption and patrimonialism. New jobs went to underqualified recipients based on kickbacks and tribal allegiance. The MMD government routinely obstructed the freedom of expression they had promised, using the repressive tactics of their old dictatorial opponents. A state of emergency and constitutional amendments a few years after the MMD came to power with the transparent goal of disenfranchising the opposition marked a definitive turn away from the democratic path.

This outcome is sadly all too frequent. Many of the transitions of democracy's "third wave" (Huntington, 1993) since the 1970s have failed to result in robust, high-quality democratic regimes. Countries have remained perpetually mired in "transition" (Carothers, 2002), established quasi-democratic institutions described in terms such as "competitive authoritarianism" (Levitsky & Way, 2010), "illiberal democracy" (Zakaria, 1997), or "hybrid regimes" (Diamond, 2002), or reverted to dictatorship after only brief open periods (Svolik, 2008). The map in Figure I.1 shows these trends' prominence. Out of the 71 countries that have experienced democratic transitions since Portugal's Carnation Revolution of 1974 (the typical starting point for the third wave of democratization), only 12 are liberal democracies today, 39 are minimally democratic, and 20 have returned to autocracy.[2]

The failure of many of these recent transitions connects intimately to another important global trend: what some have identified as a significant era of democratic decline (Diamond, 2015; Mechkova, Lührmann, & Lindberg 2017; Mounk, 2018). While the decline has multiple causes, including the erosion of democratic institutions in many formerly strong democracies, much of it can be explained by the failure of recent democratic transitions or democratic backsliding in new democracies.

What is puzzling about a case like Zambia is that its political transition had one key characteristic that scholarship would suggest might protect it from democratic reversal: its political breakthrough was initiated, led, and brought to fruition through a peaceful, organized campaign from the bottom up, a campaign

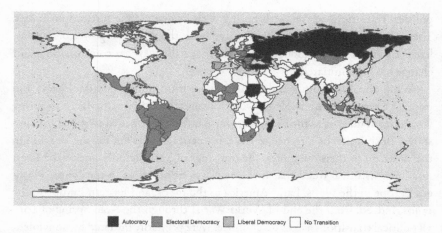

Autocracy   Electoral Democracy   Liberal Democracy   No Transition

FIGURE I.I Democracy after Third-Wave Transitions, 1974–2019

of nonviolent resistance.[3] While early democratization literature focused on the positive effects of elite-led transitions (Higley & Burton, 2006; O'Donnell & Schmitter, 1986), more recent work has found strong evidence that nonviolent revolutions are uniquely positioned to promote democracy in the political regimes that follow them (Celestino & Gleditsch, 2013; Johnstad, 2010; Karatnycky & Ackerman, 2005; Teorell, 2010).

Nonviolent resistance has numerous effects that should promote democracy. For instance, it involves ordinary people in political action, spreading norms of empowerment that diffuse influence from elites to the masses (Sharp, 1973). It creates networks of civic engagement that support strong democratic institutions (Putnam, Leonardi, & Nanetti, 1994). And it often brings to power inspiring leaders like Nelson Mandela and Vaclav Havel who use their moral authority to push their countries down the democratic path.

Yet often the nonviolent overthrow of a dictator is followed not by a smooth transition to democracy but instead by violence, instability, and a return to dictatorship. Why these patterns occur has been of particular salience in the scholarly and policy literature in the years since the 2011 uprisings across the Middle East typically referred to as the "Arab Spring" (Roberts, Willis, McCarthy, & Ash, 2016; Zartman, 2015). Popular, primarily nonviolent revolutions in a part of the world that had long been resistant to democratic change created a moment of hope and a seeming vindication for advocates of democracy even in the most difficult environments. Yet the following years brought chaos in Libya, civil wars in Syria and Yemen, and a new, even harsher authoritarian regime in Egypt. As of late 2019, Tunisia is the only country that appears to have emerged from the political transitions of the Arab Spring with its democratic institutions intact. These varying outcomes have highlighted both the potential power of nonviolent resistance to bring about change and the challenges that come once a major change has been initiated.

While the Arab Spring and its subsequent transitions focused scholarly and popular attention on nonviolent revolutions and their aftermath, the Arab Spring was far from unique, as the example from Zambia that opened this introduction shows. Both in the occurrence of large, primarily nonviolent revolutions and in the variation in their outcomes, the uprisings of 2011 are only one of the latest in a long historical trend that includes waves from Africa in the 1960s, southern Europe in the 1970s, Latin America in the 1980s, and Eastern Europe in the 1990s. Indeed, from the end of World War II through the Arab Spring of 2011, 78 political transitions across 64 countries were primarily initiated by nonviolent resistance.

The variation in these transitions' outcomes has been immense, emphasizing the importance of understanding their dynamics. When nonviolent revolutions go well, they can lead to high-quality democracies that transformatively improve the lives of their citizens, as in places like Portugal (Fernandes, 2015). Yet when they go badly, the effects can be devastating and deadly, as seen in Egypt, where two turbulent years of transition from 2011 to 2013 culminated in a military coup, bringing the authoritarian president Abdel Fattah el-Sisi to power and initiating a period of repression even worse than the one that preceded the revolution (Ketchley, 2017).

So why do nonviolent revolutions sometimes go so very wrong? Why do successful nonviolent revolutions sometimes lead to democracy and sometimes not? Few scholars have looked directly at the mechanisms that connect nonviolent resistance with democratization, meaning that we have little systematic knowledge of when these mechanisms are likely to successfully operate and when they are not. Thus, variation in the outcomes of transitions initiated by nonviolent resistance remains a major scholarly puzzle. In this book I take on this puzzle, proposing a theory of the connection between nonviolent resistance and democratization that builds on the disparate insights of the scholarly literature on these topics.

The Argument: Mobilization and Maximalism

My central argument is that while successful nonviolent resistance indeed sets up political transitions that are more likely to lead to democracy, for these advantages to carry through into a new democratic regime they must meet and overcome several unique challenges. The positive effects of nonviolent resistance on democracy, such as increased empowerment for ordinary people and spreading norms of consensus-based conflict resolution, are indirect. They operate at a temporal remove. For nonviolent resistance to lead to democracy these effects must carry through an uncertain political transition when the rules of the political game are in flux.

The unique characteristics of nonviolent revolutions set up transitions whose politics differ systematically from others', such as armed revolutions or top-down liberalizations. To answer the question of how and when nonviolent revolutions lead to democracy, we must investigate civil resistance transitions separately, analyzing how their patterns of political interaction lead to unique democratic challenges. What are these challenges? The theory that I develop in Chapter 1, building on what we know about democratic transitions in general and nonviolent resistance specifically, leads me to hypothesize that two patterns of political behavior are highly likely to influence the level of democracy at the end of a civil resistance transition.

First, the high levels of *mobilization* characteristic of a nonviolent resistance movement must carry through the transition. This holds new elites accountable and ensures that the masses maintain the temporary power advantage of a nonviolent revolution until new institutions are in place. Second, political actors must redirect the tools of nonviolent resistance from the revolutionary breakdown of power structures into institutionalized paths. If they fail to do so, then the political system is characterized by what I refer to as *maximalism*. The higher the degree of mobilization and the lower the degree of maximalism during a civil resistance transition (CRT), the greater the likelihood of democracy at the transition's end.

Patterns of mobilization and maximalism are influenced by earlier political, social, and economic structures but are not fully determined by them. Instead they arise from patterns of strategic interaction between major political actors during the transition. This means that we cannot fully predict a transition's level of mobilization and maximalism and that these patterns of behavior have their own independent effects rather than simply acting as the channels through which prior structural forces act upon politics.

Previewing the Evidence

The claims I have just presented are all empirical, subject to testing and falsification. The bulk of the book is devoted to this testing, involving an integrated set of quantitative and qualitative research methods. I leverage the strengths of both these approaches through a nested analysis research design (Lieberman, 2005), blending the scope and external validity of quantitative analysis with the in-depth examination of causal mechanisms provided by qualitative methods.[4]

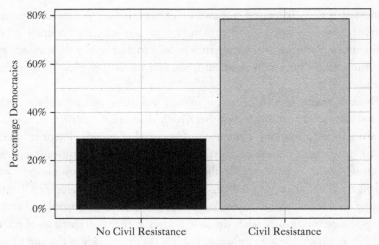

FIGURE I.2 Rates of Democracy by Transition Type

The evidence provides strong support for the book's hypotheses. I present the bulk of the statistical evidence in Chapter 2 and highlight some of the key findings here. First, following prior work in the nonviolent resistance literature, I find strong evidence that civil resistance transitions are indeed much more likely than other modes of transition to result in democratization. Figure I.2 shows this difference.[5] Nearly 80% of transitions initiated by nonviolent resistance ended with at least a minimal level of democracy, while fewer than 30% of transitions initiated by other means ended with the same minimal level of democracy.

This is unsurprising, given the growing consensus in the literature that civil resistance has a strong positive effect on democratization, but it provides further justification for my theoretical emphasis on civil resistance transitions. There is something distinctive about civil resistance and its relationship to democracy.

Second, I find strong and statistically robust evidence that mobilization during a CRT significantly improves democratic prospects, while maximalism during a CRT significantly harms them. Figure I.3 shows the levels of mobilization and maximalism across all CRTs from 1945 through 2011; the shape of the points is based on whether the regime at the end of the transition was at least minimally democratic.[6] There is a very clear distinction in the distribution of democracies and nondemocracies. The countries that ended as democracies tend to cluster in the upper-left-hand side of the graph, with high levels of mobilization and low levels of maximalism. Those countries that failed to become democratic cluster in the lower-right-hand side of the graph, with low levels of mobilization and higher levels of maximalism.

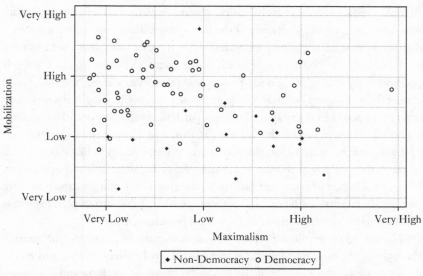

FIGURE I.3 Mobilization and Maximalism in Civil Resistance Transitions

Mobilization and maximalism during a civil resistance transition have strong effects both on the likelihood of achieving a minimal level of democracy and on the overall quality of the democratic regimes that they precede. Nor can these effects be explained by preexisting social, economic, or political structures. They both retain a significant effect on posttransition levels of democracy when controlling for the most common structural explanations of democratization and add significant explanatory power to purely structural democratization models.

Qualitative evidence from three in-depth case studies further bolsters these robust statistical findings. Following the logic of nested analysis, I selected three cases that my theory explains well but that are otherwise highly divergent from one another. This case selection strategy allows me to see whether the mechanisms of my theory occur across cases from a wide variety of backgrounds. The three cases, each of which I examine in their own chapter (Chapters 3–5), are the 1984 Diretas Ja (Direct Elections Now) movement against the military dictatorship in Brazil and the subsequent democratic transition, the 1991 Movement for Multiparty Democracy in Zambia, and the 2006 Second People's Movement against a resurgent monarchy in Nepal.

In Brazil I find that continued social mobilization, particularly around the writing of the 1988 Constitution, significantly pushed the country's democratic transition forward, undermining the elite hold on politics and ensuring the institutionalization of many important social and political protections. Furthermore, even formerly revolutionary actors, such as the country's communist party (the

PCdoB), redirected their mobilization toward institutional and electoral politics, strengthening the legitimacy of the new system. The result has been a robust democracy that has withstood many challenges in the decades since the transition.

In Zambia the absorption of much of the country's opposition into a single political party during the period of struggle led to very low levels of mobilization during the subsequent political transition. With few external checks, the new elites brought to power in the 1991 movement—particularly the new president and former trade unionist, Frederick Chiluba—returned to many of the worst practices of the regime that went before them, even increasing levels of political corruption while using state power to shut down attempts to organize political opposition. However, a legacy of resistance facilitated the emergence of a new movement to prevent the country's full return to autocracy when Chiluba attempted to change the Zambian Constitution to run for a third presidential term.

Nepal's 2006 revolution sparked over a decade of massive mobilization throughout the country as political movements, civil society groups, and ethnic minorities took the example of the successful ouster of the king and the uncertainties of the transitional period as lessons in how to advocate for their own agendas. However, this mobilization has been characterized by high levels of maximalism as movements and political parties have sought to employ the most powerful tools in the resistance toolkit to disrupt the creation of new institutions that might disadvantage them. The result has been a fractious politics and an ever-extending period of transition, tied to a gradual loss of faith in and support for democracy among a population who have largely failed to see any fruit from the 2006 revolution.

In brief, the three cases provide strong evidence that the two challenges of civil resistance transitions indeed operate in the way suggested by my theory and shown correlationally in my statistical testing. When mobilization is high and maximalism is low, as in Brazil, this facilitates a successful democratic transition. When mobilization and maximalism are both low, as in Zambia, this brings about an elite semi-democratic regime, characterized by low levels of democratic accountability. When mobilization and maximalism are both high, as in Nepal, new elites are kept in check, but democratic politics fails to institutionalize and is subject to constant breakdowns. The failure to successfully resolve these challenges has enduring effects on a country's posttransition political orders.

Placing the Argument in the Literature

This book sits at the intersection of two scholarly literatures that have been, for the most part, separate: the literature on democratization and the literature on nonviolent resistance. While I do not engage in a full review of either of these literatures, it is important to summarize some of the major discussions and trends in both in order to situate my argument and its contribution.

Two axes have characterized many of the debates over democratization (by far the larger of the two literatures) in the past several decades. Along one axis, scholars have argued about whether democratization is driven primarily by slow-moving structural factors or shorter-term contingent political dynamics. Along the second axis, scholars have disagreed over whether democratization is primarily a result of top-down decisions to liberalize or bottom-up pressure.

The debate over structural or contingent factors was jump-started by early work on democratization, most prominently by Seymour Martin Lipset (1959), which proposed that socioeconomic development was the core factor influencing the likelihood of democratization (so-called modernization theory).[7] The specific mechanisms through which development affected democratization, and the specific types of development most relevant for democratic prospects, varied depending on the scholar, but typical studies focused on economic growth, urbanization, and education. For example, Barrington Moore (1966, p. 418) intimately tied the possibility of democracy to the growth of the middle class, famously arguing, "No bourgeois, no democracy."

Many of the third-wave transitions beginning in the 1970s undermined scholarly confidence in the modernization theory story, giving rise to a much more contingent story of democratization based on political factors primarily during the transition period itself (Di Palma, 1990; O'Donnell & Schmitter, 1986; Rustow, 1970). The emphasis on the transition as a crucial period of examination gave rise to the somewhat ungainly label of "transitology" to describe this approach to democratization. Barbara Geddes (1999) critiqued monocausal explanations for democratization, such as modernization theory, arguing that there were many distinct causal paths to democracy that required disaggregation. And in a paradigmatic book, Adam Przeworski and his coauthors (2000) argued that modernization theory's findings on the relationship between development and democracy essentially reversed the causal arrow. Poverty was not a barrier to democratization; rather wealth was a defense against democratic backsliding. While Przeworski and his coauthors still emphasized the centrality of development, they made important space for contingency in the shocks that could spark initial democratic transitions.

The gradual waning and eventual reversal of the third wave brought structural stories of democratization back into prominence. A widely cited article by Thomas Carothers (2002) critiqued the transitology approach as overly teleological and not adequately taking into account the real challenges to democratization from underdevelopment. Such seminal scholarly touchstones as Daron Acemoglu and William Robinson's *Economic Origins of Dictatorship and Democracy* (2005) and Carles Boix's *Democracy and Redistribution* (2003) focused on the role of economic inequality and factor endowments in motivating both the demand for democratization from below and the decision to repress such demands from above. More recently Steven Levitsky and Lucan Way (2010) have emphasized the rise of "competitive authoritarianism" across many transitions and the frequent lack of democratic progress without significant "linkage and leverage" from democratic Western powers. And the strong causal relationship between economic development and democratization has been revived through in-depth work by Boix and Stokes (2003).[8]

Running orthogonally to debates over structure and contingency in democratization have been debates over whether the primary pressure for democracy tends to come from elites or nonelites. The early transitologists tended to focus on elite moves to liberalize as the crucial factor in bringing about democratization (O'Donnell & Schmitter, 1986). In a well-known article and book, John Higley and Michael Burton (1989, 2006) argued that elite consensus was the key factor leading to democratic stability. In contrast, other early influential works argued that pressure from below, often conceptualized in terms of economic class, was the key factor in driving democratic transitions (Rueschemeyer, Stephens, & Stephens, 1992). More recently, Stephan Haggard and Robert Kaufman (2016b) have emphasized the importance of "distributive conflict" in driving many democratic transitions forward.

My argument falls squarely in line with the *contingent* and *nonelite* sides of the democratization literature. I am skeptical of the ability of slow-moving structural factors to explain the dynamics of political transitions. Significant debate continues over even the most well-respected of these findings, leading Haggard and Kaufman (2016a, p. 11) to speculate in a recent review article that "although debates over the structural determinants of democratization and democratic stability will undoubtedly continue . . . attempts to anchor the rise and fall of democracy to underlying socio-economic factors are likely to remain incomplete at best." While economic development, education, and other structural factors influence democratization, they do a poor job of fully explaining its variation. Following the pattern of the transitologists, though, I argue that giving due respect to the contingency of political transition does not mean abandoning any hope of broad, generalizable theory. Instead, by carefully analyzing the power positions and incentives of central social actors, we can come up with consistent, operationalizable patterns of behavior that can give insight into how transitions are likely to unfold.

I also make the empirical claim that it is pressure from outside the elite, rather than elite consensus, that plays the crucial role in democratic progress. This is evidenced both by the finding that transitions driven by nonviolent resistance, rather than elite liberalization, are most likely to democratize and to remain stable democracies (Bayer, Bethke, & Lambach, 2016) and by my finding in this book, previewed earlier, that it is social and political mobilization and the character of that mobilization that drive democratization in civil resistance transitions.

While often studied in the broader literature on democratization (Linz & Stepan, 1996; O'Donnell & Schmitter, 1986), transitions specifically following nonviolent revolutions have been something of a black box. The democratization literature tends to group them with other transitions, obscuring their unique dynamics (Guo & Stradiotto, 2014; Haggard & Kaufman, 2016b). The literature on nonviolent revolutions tends to end its analysis with the success or failure of the nonviolent resistance campaign to oust the old regime and not look at what comes after the campaign ends (Chenoweth & Stephan, 2011; Nepstad, 2011; Ritter, 2015).

Scholars who focus on bottom-up transitions more generally, such as Elizabeth Wood (2000), Donatella Della Porta (2014), and Stephan Haggard and Robert Kaufman (2016b), have added significant and important insights to our understanding of democratization. Scholars such as George Lawson (2004) and Samuel Huntington (1993), who have included most of the CRTs in broader categories of "negotiated revolutions" or "transplacement," have also advanced our understanding of many of the processes at work in CRTs. Yet the unique character of nonviolent resistance and its effects on political order provides a useful analytical entry point for continuing to enhance our understanding of the many distinct paths whereby countries move or do not move from dictatorship to democracy (Geddes, 1999; Haggard & Kaufman, 2016a).

This book thus addresses a significant gap in the existing democratization literature by putting this unique subset of political transitions under its own distinct empirical investigation. It also contributes to these larger debates on the relative influence of structural or strategic factors and the power of elites or masses to shape political transformation.

The second literature this book's argument speaks to is the literature on nonviolent resistance. This literature is much newer and less developed. Early antecedents focused on the moral or ethical dimensions of nonviolent resistance, with little discussion of its empirical dynamics or strategic considerations.[9] The example of Mahatma Gandhi sparked a wave of interest in nonviolent resistance in the early and mid-20th century. Gandhi's own voluminous writings[10] reflected on both the ethical and strategic dimensions of nonviolent resistance and sparked several significant scholarly examinations of his thought and practice throughout the decades of the Indian independence struggle (Bondurant, 1958; Gregg, 1935; Iyer, 1973).

A growing literature in the decades after Gandhi sought to develop a comprehensive theory of nonviolent resistance and to examine its dynamics across a small number of case studies. Gene Sharp's (1973) book *The Politics of Nonviolent Action* was one of the most comprehensive efforts to provide a theoretical foundation for nonviolent resistance, drawing on thinkers as diverse as Gandhi and Machiavelli. Important empirical works on the subject in later decades include Kurt Schock's (2005) examination of "unarmed insurrections" that blends the nonviolent resistance literature with a sociological literature on social movements, and Sharon Erickson Nepstad's (2011) book on nonviolent revolutions, which identifies several of the important factors that determine nonviolent movements' success or failure.[11]

There was a major shift in the literature on nonviolent resistance in 2011 with the publication of Erica Chenoweth and Maria Stephan's book *Why Civil Resistance Works*, one of the first attempts to perform a cross-national statistical study of the relative effectiveness of nonviolent and violent resistance. Chenoweth and Stephan's core finding, that nonviolent campaigns succeeded twice as often as comparable violent campaigns, sparked significant interest in the subject. This interest, tied with the public availability of their data on nonviolent and violent campaigns, led to a wealth of new studies looking statistically at various aspects of nonviolent resistance.[12]

The theoretical link between nonviolent resistance and democracy has been a core part of that literature since its early days. Gene Sharp (1973) argued that nonviolent resistance was inherently democratizing, since it empowered those under systems of authority to change those systems. Several studies beginning in the early 2000s tested this relationship between nonviolent resistance and democratization. Adrian Karatnycky and Peter Ackerman (2005) conducted one of the first of these studies, showing that countries that had experienced a transition between 1972 and 2005 were much more likely to be "free" at the end of their transitions if the transition was initiated by civic forces without the use of violence (relative to transitions initiated by elites or by violent action). This general relationship has been replicated in studies that have adopted several varying approaches to operationalizing the key concepts in question (Celestino & Gleditsch, 2013; Chenoweth & Stephan, 2011; Johnstad, 2010; Teorell, 2010). Nonviolent resistance not only makes democracy more likely; it makes democracy more likely to endure over time (Bayer et al., 2016) and increases the quality of the democratic regimes it initiates (Bethke & Pinckney, 2019).

Yet the literature on nonviolent resistance, despite its significant insights, has given us little understanding to date on the variation in democratization outcomes after nonviolent resistance movements. This book's contribution to the nonviolent resistance literature is thus to extend the analysis beyond the success of nonviolent resistance in ousting dictators and initiating political change and ask what types of political change nonviolent resistance in fact brings about.

Setting the Terms

Having described my core puzzle and the argument I raise to answer it, previewed the evidence, and situated my argument in the existing literature, the final task in this introduction is to clearly lay out the concepts that will be underlying my arguments and evidence in the remainder of the book. I focus on four concepts here: civil resistance,[13] democracy, transitions, and civil resistance transitions.

What is civil or nonviolent resistance? These words conjure powerful historical images: Gandhi marching to the sea or Martin Luther King Jr. at the head of a column of protesters on the Edmund Pettus Bridge. Others may think of a lone figure standing in front of a column of Chinese tanks moving on Tiananmen Square. Still others may think of incidents from their own national histories: Russians surrounding the Duma in 1991 to stop a hard-liner coup, South Africans launching strikes and boycotts in the townships to bring down apartheid, or millions of Filipinos gathering on the EDSA Boulevard to prevent President Ferdinand Marcos from stealing an election.

What do these images share? First, they are actions undertaken by *unarmed civilians*. In nonviolent resistance individuals come together to create change using their force of personality, moral authority, and noncooperation rather than their direct ability to impose physical costs. Nonviolent resistance is something that people do without engaging in or threatening physical violence but also without bringing weapons.[14]

Scholars have rightly pointed out that violence goes well beyond its most direct physical manifestations (Galtung, 1969; May, 2015). Even if no direct physical force is involved, socioeconomic structures in unjust political systems can have negative effects that are accurately described as violent. Yet measuring the impact of these more diffuse forms of violence consistently across many different cases is challenging. To maintain consistency, I simplify the definition of nonviolent resistance to exclude only the most obvious and straightforward manifestations of violence: actual physical assaults upon persons and the plausible threat of such physical assaults.

Nonviolent resistance as I am discussing it is *political*. That is to say it involves a struggle over what David Easton (1954) called the "authoritative allocation of values," the ways in which communities define and distribute the things that they care about. Political targets are often governments but need not be so. They need only be an individual or collective actor that has some ability to affect this process of definition and distribution. Political action is a broad category. However, it

excludes aspects of purely personal discipline or moral character that may sometimes be included in the category of nonviolent resistance.

Nonviolent resistance is *resistance*. Actions that lack physical violence or the
threat of physical violence may be nonviolent, but they do not necessarily constitute nonviolent resistance. Nonviolent resistance as *resistance* stands in opposition to the normal modes of constituting and conducting politics. Actions that
are nonviolent but fall within the normal bounds of institutional politics are not
nonviolent resistance. As an action that stands in opposition to normal modes
of politics, nonviolent resistance is destructive to the current power structure
(Sharp, 1973; Vinthagen, 2015).

Because of this, context is important in defining nonviolent resistance.
The same action may not have the same meaning in different contexts.
A march supporting an electoral candidate in an advanced democracy is not
nonviolent resistance since such marches are a normal, accepted, and power-
reinforcing aspect of such countries' politics. However, the same march
undertaken in a country where the opposition is highly repressed or illegal
and such marches undermine the rule of the regime would clearly be nonviolent resistance.

Nonviolent resistance is not synonymous with any one action, method, or tactic such as protests, strikes, or boycotts. For an outside observer to know whether
nonviolent resistance is occurring requires some degree of familiarity with the
power structure in that society at that moment in time.[15]

There are two primary effects of nonviolent resistance on political order, the
first negative and the second positive. The negative effect follows logically from
the definition of nonviolent resistance. If nonviolent resistance is noninstitutional and disruptive of current patterns of political behavior, then by definition
it will be destructive of the existing order. One need only look at the metaphors
employed by scholars of nonviolent resistance to see this destructive character.
Robert Helvey (2004, p. 9) describes the goal of nonviolent resistance as to
"undermine, neutralize, or destroy . . . the pillars of support" that uphold a power
holder. It undermines current institutions, demanding their redefinition and
reconstitution.

The positive effect is also inherent in the disruptive character of nonviolent
resistance. Nonviolent resistance requires an act of agency, stepping outside the
routines and expectations of political life to envision a different order. This makes
it inherently creative, expressive, and empowering. It puts tools in its participants'
hands and practices them in engaging in politics. It spreads civic culture and
engagement, building social capital and investment in future outcomes.[16] This
in turn is likely to build the social trust and norms of civic engagement necessary
for a long-term sustainable political order (Putnam et al., 1994). For this reason,

nonviolent resistance—while destructive of individual political orders in the short term—will have a positive long-term effect.

Nonviolent resistance is also a tool of those who lack traditional avenues of power. This is almost tautological based on this definition. Those with power employ institutional means because they have designed such means to suit their ends. Institutional politics solidifies the set of players in power and excludes challengers. In Bruce Bueno de Mesquita's (2005) terms, institutional politics is the weapon of the winning coalition. As long as politics employs the same institutional mechanisms, the winning coalition will remain of a similar size and composition.

Regular nonviolent resistance challenges the boundaries of the winning coalition. The elite can never be entirely secure as the corridors of power are assaulted from outside. To avoid institutional arrangements' complete breakdown, elites must bargain with those who use nonviolent resistance, expanding institutional avenues of access to power (Tilly, 1978). Nonviolent challenger groups will then be incorporated into institutional arrangements, with a concurrent expansion in the size of the winning coalition.[17] With each instance of major nonviolent resistance from a challenger group there is likely to be an attendant increase in winning coalition size, gradually expanding the representativeness of the political order and making the system more democratic.

The second concept I use throughout this book is democracy. I define democracy in two ways: an ideal type and a binary characteristic. I use both definitions because both have insights to offer. There is a real sense in which democracy and nondemocracy are categorically different, for instance in the perpetual presence of the threat of violence in nondemocratic systems (Svolik, 2012), and thus simply looking at regimes along a spectrum of "more or less democratic" is limited. However, there are important distinctions between regimes that fall within these broad categories, and looking at these distinctions can also give insights.

As an ideal-type system, I follow Robert Dahl's (1973, p. 2) seminal definition of democracy as "a political system which is . . . almost completely responsive to all of its citizens . . . considered as political equals." This definition in turn implies that democracies give their citizens unimpaired opportunities to formulate their preferences, signify those preferences, and have those preferences weighted equally by the government. Political systems approximate democracy in this sense to greater or lesser degree. The closer a system comes to this ideal, the greater its degree of democracy. When the system changes from a form that poorly approximates this ideal to one that more closely approximates it we may describe the process as democratization.

I also examine democracy from the binary perspective as originally formulated by Joseph Schumpeter (1942). For Schumpeter, democracy is "that institutional arrangement for arriving at political decisions in which individuals acquire the power to decide by means of a competitive struggle for the people's vote" (p. 241). Democracy either fully obtains or fully fails to obtain for a political system at any point in time. Democratization is the movement from one side of the line to the other. Countries accomplish it wholesale.

The next concept to define is the political transition. Scholars of transitions have written a great deal on this subject,[18] and so I follow their lead. Political transitions are those periods of time when one regime has broken down and a new regime is not yet in place. Regimes are the basic set of rules and institutions that define who governs in a society and the primary means of political access (Geddes, Wright, & Frantz, 2014). Regimes include, but are not limited to, the set of formal written laws that legally set out these procedures and identities. For example, both Lebanon's constitutionally mandated religious power sharing (Aboultaif, 2019) and Nigeria's informal alternation of the presidency between north and south are important aspects of their country's regimes.

A transition begins when these basic rules and institutions are destabilized and become unclear to the major actors. This can occur because of any number of different impetuses and can be initiated by decisions from the top (Trimberger, 1978) or resistance from the bottom (Wood, 2000). Scholars have categorized these in several different ways, distinguishing them on the basis of their level of conflict (Guo & Stradiotto, 2014; Karl & Schmitter, 1991), primary actors (Collier, 1999; Della Porta, 2014; Huntington, 1993), or method of contention (Chenoweth & Stephan, 2011). No matter the impetus, routinized politics ceases to operate as it has in the past (O'Donnell & Schmitter, 1986).

Times of transition are inefficient for achieving political goals since actors do not have shared expectations of others' behavior. Because of this, those involved will tend to minimize the transition's duration as much as possible. A transition ends when a regime has come into place and has endured long enough to begin functioning as a regime, that is to say, when a temporary configuration of political power holders and rules for choosing them has persisted long enough that its actions become routinized and actors strategize about the future based around the assumption that this set of rules and power holders will continue.

Civil resistance transitions are that subset of political transitions in which civil resistance plays a crucial role in breaking down the prior regime. Had the civil resistance campaign not occurred, then either regime breakdown would have been highly unlikely or its dynamics would have been so radically different that it would be unrecognizable relative to the events that occurred.

Civil resistance need not be the only factor, or even the only necessary factor in initiating a transition for it to be a CRT. For one thing, to demonstrate such a strong condition would be exceedingly empirically difficult, perhaps impossible.

Even deep familiarity with particular cases will not free us from the difficulty of interpreting which factors were truly necessary in as complex a phenomenon as regime breakdown and transition.

For example, one of the cases I examine is the 2006 overthrow of King Gyanendra of Nepal in the so-called Jana Andolan II or Second People's Movement. The Jana Andolan II approximates the ideal type of a CRT. An autocrat stepped down after millions of people took to the streets to demand his ouster. His resignation initiated a major transformation in the political and social institutions of the country. This seems to be a clear example of a CRT.

Yet arguing that civil resistance was the *only* necessary factor in explaining the transition immediately becomes problematic. The civil resistance campaign came at the end of a 10-year civil war by Maoist revolutionaries. The civil war degraded state capacity and undermined the king's legitimacy (Adhikari, 2014). Furthermore, the civil resistance campaign was partially led by old elites who had been disenfranchised by the king's recent moves to consolidate power. It was also aided by the defection of the regime's former ally and regular Nepali behind the scenes consultant: the government of India. A careful observer could make a plausible argument that all these factors were necessary for the outcome of the Nepali transition.

A critical scholar could easily apply a similar analysis to any transition we might care to categorize as a CRT if we are attempting to justify a strong set of inclusion criteria. We might quickly find ourselves with no cases remaining to analyze. It is important to note that such elimination of cases upon close inspection is not unique to CRTs. Almost any strict classification that attempts a high standard of empirical necessity will quickly run into problems if the investigators are intellectually honest. Because of these difficulties, the lower standard of crucial but not sole contributing factor is both much more useful and ultimately more intellectually defensible.

A critic can still, of course, attack whether civil resistance was indeed crucial to regime breakdown in a case. But here we are on much more solid empirical ground and can have meaningful discussions about the plausibility of alternative scenarios. Such discussion is particularly warranted when civil resistance movements took place but their impact is unclear. In the cases that I examine in depth this is perhaps most prominent in Brazil, where scholars have argued that the primary impetus for change came from the military hierarchy, not from resistance from below (Stepan, 1989).

If civil resistance was crucial for the initiation of a transition, then the dynamics of transition approximate the theoretical model that I have described even if other factors have played an important role. We should still observe a balance of power in favor of more prodemocratic figures, higher levels of popular mobilization and awareness, and the dispersion of skills and knowledge of non-violent resistance among both elites and the general populace. In other words, all the mechanisms that move CRTs toward democracy should be present. These mechanisms should flow naturally from a crucial role for civil resistance, regardless of other precipitating factors. Hence, in identifying CRTs I rely on this definition of crucial contribution but not necessarily sole major contribution to transition initiation.

The Rest of the Book

The subsequent chapters move in detail through the argument that I have sketched in this introduction. Chapter 1 takes on the question of what makes civil resistance transitions unique and worthy of their own empirical investigation. I develop the theory of the power positions during CRTs that in turn generates my two hypotheses about the transitional behaviors that lead to democracy and discuss the implications of those hypotheses not just for the general level of democracy following a CRT but for the specific characteristics of regime likely to follow CRTs with different patterns of transitional politics. I propose four basic categories of regime that typically follow particular patterns of mobilization and maximalism. Countries where mobilization is high and maximalism is low tend to become democracies. Countries where mobilization is low and maximalism is high tend to return to autocracy.

Countries along the other diagonal both tend to result in quasi-democratic or hybrid regimes, but of distinct types. Countries where mobilization and maximalism are both low tend to become what I call "elite semi-democracies," having the forms of democracy but dominated by a small group of elites. Countries with high mobilization and high maximalism tend to become "fractious semi-democracies," in which no one group can reestablish an authoritarian regime but the constant back and forth of revolutionary competition prevents the institutionalization of democratic politics.

Having laid out the theoretical rationale for my hypotheses, in Chapter 2 I begin my empirical analysis with a large-n quantitative study. I analyze every political transition around the world from 1945 to 2011 and examine the characteristics of transitions that tend to end in democracy and those that do not. I first show—confirming the earlier literature on nonviolent revolutions—that CRTs tend to have much more democratic outcomes. I then show that measures of *mobilization* and *maximalism* during CRTs largely explain variation in democratization in these cases, both in terms of improving a country's overall level of democracy and in making it more likely that a country will at least meet a minimal standard of democratic rule.

The next step in the analysis is to confirm that the quantitative findings operate when examining individual cases. This is crucial to show that mobilization and maximalism are explaining democratization, not some outside unobserved factor that happens to correlate with them. I perform this qualitative analysis in Chapters 3 through 5, with a separate in-depth case study in each chapter.

I selected cases following the logic of nested research design, which calls for analyzing on-the-line cases. In other words, the researcher examines cases that the theory predicts well but that otherwise are extremely different from one another. Thus, I selected cases that varied in terms of region, time period, and prior regime but whose levels of mobilization and maximalism and their regimes at the end of the transition fit what my theory would predict.

The transitions that I examine are the transition in Nepal in the 2000s following the 2006 Second People's Movement (Chapter 3), the transition in Zambia in the 1990s following the overthrow of President Kenneth Kaunda by the Movement for Multiparty Democracy (Chapter 4), and the transition in Brazil in the 1980s away from military rule (Chapter 5). The research is based on original interviews with key actors during these countries' transitions, as well as in-depth examination of primary and secondary sources.

The studies are not comparative, except in the sense that they test the relevance of my proposed patterns of behavior in three contexts that are radically different and demonstrate the plausibility of three transitional paths implied by my theoretical framing. In each case, the transitional events and outcomes closely match the predictions of my theory. In Nepal, a case with high mobilization and high maximalism, the resulting regime is a fractious semi-democracy. In Zambia, a case with low mobilization and low maximalism, the resulting regime is an elite semi-democracy. And in Brazil, a case with high mobilization and low maximalism, the resulting regime is a democracy.

Chapter 6 concludes the study, summarizing the insights gained from the research and proposing new directions to continue examining this important question. While my research offers several insights, it also opens many questions. I dig into some of these questions and offer thoughts on the lessons of this research for scholars, activists, and policymakers.

I

The Challenges of Civil Resistance Transitions

WHY DO NONVIOLENT revolutions lead to democracy? I argue that a crucial factor in explaining this phenomenon is the pattern of political behavior during the transitions that follow nonviolent revolutions. High levels of mobilization and low levels of maximalism are two of these important patterns.

This chapter has four goals. First, I argue that transitions following nonviolent revolutions present political actors with incentives and a balance of power that pushes these transitions toward democracy. CRTs also have three unique mechanisms that help carry this pro-democratic position through the transition to a new regime. Second, I show that the nature of these mechanisms implies the two challenges of mobilization and maximalism. Third, I detail my predictions for the specific regimes to which different patterns of mobilization and maximalism lead. Fourth, I address some potential alternative explanations for democratization in CRTs.

Nonviolent Resistance, Democracy, and Transitions

Traditionally, scholars such as Guillermo O'Donnell and Philippe Schmitter (1986) and Adam Przeworski (1991) have modeled the transition to democracy as one in which different political forces have ordered preferences related to democratization and varying assets at their disposal. Hard-liners prefer a strong authoritarian regime, while soft-liners prefer a limited opening. Moderates in the opposition prefer limited democratization, and radicals want major transformative changes. The traditional argument has typically been that transitions are most likely to successfully lead to democracy when an alliance between the soft-liners and the moderates sidelines the extreme demands of both hard-liners and radicals. If the radicals push too far, the hard-liners are likely to respond with a coup d'état that reestablishes an authoritarian regime.

How does a nonviolent revolution change this picture? Two major differences are central: incumbent cohesion and balance of political force. First, nonviolent resistance has the potential to undermine the cohesion of the previous ruling coalition. Sharp (1973) points to the ability of nonviolent resistance to prevent a "rally 'round the flag" effect by providing figures from the regime the potential to defect and join, and even sometimes lead, the opposition. Such fragmentation of the ruling coalition was key in prominent civil resistance campaigns such as the Rose and Orange revolutions in postcommunist Georgia and Ukraine, respectively (Bunce and Wolchik, 2011), as well as in several of the movements for multiparty democracy across Africa in the early 1990s (Bratton & Van de Walle, 1997; Nepstad, 2011; Rakner, 2003).

In particular, civil resistance has superiority over violent resistance in fragmenting authoritarian control over state coercive forces. Chenoweth and Stephan (2011, 48–50) show that civil resistance campaigns commonly spark widespread security force defection, a point also emphasized by Nepstad (2011). If civil resistance has shown the military and other implements of state coercion to be unreliable, then the calculations of hard-liners on interrupting the transition with a coup must be tempered. Their control over the armed forces may be questionable.

Second, in contrast to the model in which fear of a coup is the overwhelming concern, nonviolent revolutions have a different type of possible defection that can affect democratization: a return to resistance. If democratizing reforms are not suitably extensive, the people may return to the streets and push for more. Costly defection in a nonviolent revolution is less likely to be a game of compromise between soft-liners and moderates to avoid overly threatening the core concerns of hard-liners than it is to be an attempt by soft-liners and moderates to as much as possible meet the demands of the revolution while still maintaining their own privileged position.

Simply stated, the coercive force in a CRT is much more likely to be in the hands of the radicals and less likely to be in the hands of the hard-liners. However, since the victory of the radicals has been nonviolent, forces of the ancien régime, both hard and soft, remain political players with points of leverage over the transition.

This balance of coercive force contrasts sharply with transitions initiated either by top-down liberalization or by violent revolutions. In the first case, the balance of force lies more closely with the ancien régime, and the strategic dynamics approximate those laid out in the original transitology literature. In the second case, military victory implies an overwhelming advantage of force on the part of the opposition, and democratization becomes a matter solely of bargains worked out among the moderate and radical victors.

Because of this unique balance of coercive force at the beginning of the transition it is important to distinguish CRTs from other types of transitions. A categorization, for instance, that groups CRTs with other bottom-up transitions is likely to overstate the level of coercive force available to the forces of change and also miss some of the democratizing mechanisms inherent in the practice of nonviolent resistance. A categorization that groups them in with top-down transitions is likely to understate the impetus for change and overstate the position of old regime figures.

What are the implications of the unique balance of coercive force in a CRT? The first is the most common contention in the literature on this subject: non-violent resistance as a force initiating a transition is likely to make democratization more likely and the democratic quality of the resulting regimes higher.[1] Nonviolent resistance can break down less representative political orders and create greater civic engagement that pushes regimes toward deeper democracy. In particular, the powerful example of nonviolent resistance having ousted the old regime will make it an attractive tool for challengers.

Not all these challenges will succeed. Their success will depend on any number of contingent factors, from their level of popular support (Chenoweth & Stephan, 2011) to the availability of resources and allies (McAdam, 1982), the strategic capacity and skill of the challengers (Ganz, 2009), and the cohesiveness of the winning coalition that has initially come to power during the transition (Lichbach, 1998). However, even if a small proportion of nonviolent challenges succeeds during the transition, it may have important spillover effects far into the future. Shifts in institutions to accommodate challengers will be more likely to occur in the more fluid time of a transition. Once these shifts have taken place, reinforcing institutional feedback mechanisms will make them more difficult to dislodge. Hence we may expect a general trend of more highly democratic and representative institutions to continue well into the future.

So nonviolent resistance opens the political system to challenges that expand the governing coalition. In addition, the unique balance of coercive force at the beginning of a CRT is in many ways the ideal situation for establishing democratic institutions. One crucial factor in the emergence of democracy is the inability of any political actor to rule unilaterally. Any actor able to fully monopolize the levers of power, even if they enter power with democratic aims, is unlikely to maintain these aims. Democracy is more likely to emerge when different actors with different goals can check one another. In a CRT, this is much more likely to be the case than in a transition initiated from above or through violent revolution. Multiple checking forces exist; there is the potential for challenges from without; and often the most powerful actors have greater democratic preferences.

In brief, we may expect that nonviolent resistance as a force initiating a transition will be likely to democratize politics by opening the bounds of competition. However, of course, in many cases we do not see this effect obtaining empirically. Why is this the case? To address that puzzle, we must focus not just on the nature of nonviolent resistance in initiating a transition but on what happens after the transition has been initiated: how this difference in the distribution of power and influence is translated through the transition into the following regime.

The Mechanisms of Civil Resistance Transitions: Leaders, Norms, Power

Transitions always end. The lack of shared expectations of appropriate behavior harms actors' interests and makes accomplishing any kind of policy agenda or even simply ensuring one's continued power position more difficult. Yet while transitions always end, they are never immediate. Even if one regime ends and as its closing act sets out a set of rules for the new political order, this does not constitute a fully formed regime. Regimes are constituted not just by the formal rules of political behavior but by actors' informal regular expectations (Helmke & Levitsky, 2004). Until the rules have been in place and generally followed for a period, expectations will still be uncertain.

This period of uncertainty means that the influence of a nonviolent revolution in initiating a transition upon the regime at the transition's end is necessarily indirect. It must operate through the transition's mediation. There are intermediate steps between nonviolent resistance initiating a transition and democracy at transition's end.

Three central mechanisms carry the positive influence of nonviolent resistance through the transition and into the following regime. These are the elevation of pro-democratic leaders, the spread of pro-democratic norms, and the diffusion of power from the elites to the masses.

The Leaders Mechanism

The first mechanism is the elevation of certain *leaders*. Transitions initiated through civil resistance are highly likely to elevate to positions of power those with preferences strongly against the old regime and with strong preferences for a democratic regime, relative to transitions initiated through other means (Ekiert & Kubik, 2001). The power advantages of these people with democratic preferences in turn push the transition toward democracy (McFaul, 2002). Initiating the transition through nonviolent resistance is also likely to create a broad-based mandate for radical, democratizing change (Bunce, 2003). In contrast, those with a preference for retaining the old regime are much more likely to remain in positions of power in transitions initiated by top-down liberalization, and the mandate for change is likely to be more moderate.

Nonviolent resistance movements are diverse, and people are elevated to leadership for any number of reasons. Yet the practice of resistance is likely to select for leaders who will have more democratic preferences, relative to how leaders come to power in other transitions. There are several reasons for this. Perhaps the most important is that resistance campaigns tend to involve high risk with a low probability of reward and few opportunities for personal enrichment along the way. Following a logic similar to Jeremy Weinstein's (2006) investigation of rebel movements in civil wars, nonviolent resistance movements are likely to attract individuals motivated by a normative desire to achieve positive change. When there is little to be materially gained by sticking your neck out you are likely to do so only if you have strong motivating beliefs. Many of the social movements that underlie nonviolent revolutions also de-emphasize the role of leaders and focus on consensus-based decision-making (Barker, Johnson, & Lavalette, 2001; Nepstad & Bob, 2006; Tufekci, 2017). They are unlikely on average to attract individuals with a strong attachment to power and desire for personal aggrandizement compared to authoritarian regimes or violent rebel groups.

Their positions of leadership in toppling the old regime often give these figures significant leverage to achieve positions of influence during the transition, either through formal negotiations with the regime or through more direct struggles during the transition. For instance, one of the biggest waves of nonviolent revolutions in the 20th century was the overthrow of communist regimes in Eastern Europe and the Soviet Union in the late 1980s and early 1990s (Ash, 2014). During the years leading up to the 1989 revolutionary earthquake, many cultural and social elites across Eastern Europe participated in countercultural movements against their communist regimes. When those regimes fell, many of these resistance figures entered major positions of influence. People like Lech Wałęsa in Poland and Lennart Meri in Estonia were elevated from ordinary professions, an electrician in Walesa's case and a filmmaker and writer in Meri's case, to the highest offices in their countries.

Another of these anticommunist activists, Vaclav Havel of Czechoslovakia, is an archetypal example of this mechanism at work.[2] From a young age, Havel, a writer and theater producer, was motivated by a desire for creative expression beyond the bounds of what was allowed under the Czechoslovak communist regime. Through repeated clashes with a state authority that repressed this expression, Havel developed a strong ideology of "living in truth," an avoidance of political chicanery, and support for freedom of action and expression. In normal circumstances Havel's profession as a playwright would have given him little exposure to or opportunity for political elevation. However, in the context of a nonviolent resistance movement Havel became, first, an ideological inspiration and, later, a major political leader.

Thus in 1989, when the Czechoslovak Velvet Revolution unseated the country's communist regime, the soft-spoken absurdist playwright found himself elected as Czechoslovakia's first postcommunist president. Havel was well known during his time in office for an informality and support for full-scale democratization. Furthermore, while he vigorously opposed the division of Czechoslovakia into two independent states (to the point that he resigned as president before the country's division), his leadership helped this division to happen peacefully. Havel's presidency was not without its difficulties, but throughout he maintained a commitment to the principles of personal liberty and moral politics that his many years of activism had forged.

This relationship is certainly not deterministic. Participation in civil resistance is neither a necessary nor a sufficient condition for democratic preferences. Ayatollah Ruhollah Khomeini played a critical leadership role in Iran's primarily nonviolent revolution and held extremely antidemocratic inclinations. Other leaders who hold democratic views may depart from them when political stimuli push them in different directions. As a student, Viktor Orban was a leader in the Hungarian movement against communism, but as prime minister several decades later, he rolled back several aspects of Hungary's democracy.

Yet for every Khomeini and Orban there are many more Havels, Wałęsas, and others whom both personal factors and their participation in resistance will make far more inclined to promote democracy. The policies put in place by these leaders, and perhaps more critically their attitude toward politics as informed by their participation in nonviolent resistance, will help carry through the more democratic power positions from the beginning of the transition to its conclusion.

The leaders mechanism is an important avenue that translates the democratizing effect of nonviolent resistance through the transition. Yet on its own the elevation of democratically inclined leaders is insufficient. For one thing, leaders' internal preferences are not fully stable. In changing circumstances and with access to greater power, leaders are likely to behave differently. Similarly, as described earlier, the character of nonviolent revolutions means that members of the old regime still play a significant role during the transition. There is often a high degree of continuity between the people in government before the transition and those in power during the transition (Pakulski, Kullberg, & Higley, 1996). The democratizing effects of nonviolent resistance require additional mechanisms to translate through the transition.

The Norms Mechanism

The second mechanism is the creation of new *norms* of political behavior. The practice of nonviolent resistance tends to spread norms of consensus-based decision-making and peaceful dispute resolution. This does not necessarily arise out of a commitment to principled nonviolence. Rather it arises through practice. Experience in nonviolent resistance and the example of nonviolent resistance as an avenue for resolving major issues gives political players the tools and experience needed to deal with real struggles without resorting to violence.

This combination of conflict and consensus is at the heart of democratic practice (Lipset, 1960). Scholars are increasingly skeptical of a model of democracy in which electoral outcomes simply reflect an idealized "will of the people" (Achen & Bartels, 2016). Instead, as theorists of agonistic democracy have emphasized, political struggles, including in democracies, involve inescapable clashes between differing group identities (Mouffe, 2013; Wenman, 2013). What democracy brings to the table is a set of norms and institutional practices that limit "antagonism" to "agonism" (Mouffe, 1999), that is to say, norms and practices that turn all-or-nothing struggles into regular, limited competition between rivals.

The practice of nonviolent resistance prefigures this normative arrangement. In a nonviolent resistance movement, participants engage in direct struggle with the goal of achieving a transformative change. Yet the practice of that struggle is limited. Most commonly these limitations are phrased in terms of practical appeals, not in terms of moral principles. Movement leaders and other participants discourage one another from escalating the conflict because they see such escalation as counterproductive. It undermines the particular mechanisms through which the "weapons system" of nonviolent resistance operates (Boserup & Mack, 1975).

As Barbara Deming (1971, p. 25) writes, nonviolent action at its core involves "solicitude for [the opponent's] person in combination with a stubborn interference with her actions." The norms communicated from the practice of nonviolent resistance are not passivity in the face of oppression, nor are they simply norms of getting along and avoiding conflict. Rather they communicate that conflict exists, but that engaging in conflict and seeking to resolve it productively requires self-limitation.

This normative structure is particularly important during transitions, when the foundational rules of the game are in flux. Without institutional safeguards to regularize behavior, actors must find other bases on which to structure their interaction. The informal normative structures inherited from the period of struggle against the old regime can then play a crucial role in shaping how formal institutional rules develop (Grzymala-Busse, 2010).

There is significant evidence that nonviolent resistance has this normative effect. For example, Omar Garcia-Ponce and Leonard Wantchekon (2017) find that people in African countries that achieved independence after primarily nonviolent urban protests are much less likely to express support for the use of violence in politics and are much more likely to engage in protests, strikes, or other forms of collective action.

The Power Mechanism

The third mechanism is the diffusion of *power*.[3] Nonviolent resistance diffuses a set of tools to its participants that enable them to have a greater impact on politics. Because nonviolent resistance has much lower barriers to entry than either violent rebellion or elite politics (Chenoweth & Stephan, 2011), the population of these participants is quite large and includes many different segments of society.

The first of these tools is a greater sense of both individual and collective efficacy (Drury, Cocking, Beale, Hanson, & Rapley, 2005), that is to say, a sense both that the individual can have a meaningful impact on political outcomes and that people collectively can change politics. Such an enhanced sense of efficacy tends to translate to greater support for democracy and to greater political participation (Lee, 2006). Overthrowing a nondemocratic regime is an outcome that even activists typically see as almost impossible ex ante. When it occurs, it spreads a sense of the fragility of established power structures and the vulnerability of established elite positions to threats from below. Participation in nonviolent resistance is often contingent on an initial "cognitive liberation" in which previously unthinkable action becomes conceivable (McAdam, 1982). Once this cognitive liberation has occurred, it can continue through the period of transition.

The second tool is more practical. Nonviolent resistance movements typically leave in their wake a network of diverse groups with experience and skills in political action. These groups are then well positioned to serve as the core of both a nascent civil society and opposition during the transition and in the following regime. Why is this the case? Because nonviolent resistance movements rarely rely on a hierarchical, top-down structure.[4] Indeed, hierarchical structures are often uniquely ineffective in nonviolent resistance because governments can easily repress them, shutting down dissent by cutting off the head of the organization (Bob & Nepstad, 2007). Nonviolent resistance movements typically involve a complex set of actors from numerous social settings who coordinate their actions by coming to consensus.[5]

When the movement is over and the transition has begun, there are typically many centers of political action with the skills and resources to deploy the powerful tools of nonviolent resistance when necessary. These may include traditional civil society organizations such as human rights nongovernmental organizations, but also more quotidian organizations such as labor unions or religious groups. Indeed, having power diffused not just to resistance groups but to groups with a mandate to continue advocating for policy change during the transition and in the new system often has a particularly potent democratizing effect (Butcher, Gray, & Mitchell, 2018).

The diffusion of a sense of cognitive efficacy and practical skills to engage in resistance can be beneficial to democratic deepening during a transition. Democratic deficits in initial transitional arrangements are likely to be resisted by groups whose demands are not fully met, requiring additional compromises and expansion of democratic arrangements (Lauth, 2000). This diffusion of cognitive and practical power also means that any moves to revert to an authoritarian regime are likely to face significant checks. No actor, political or social, is likely to have the ability to assert their own singular authority when such a complex decentralized web of power actors is in place to prevent them.

For example, in 2014 a primarily nonviolent movement successfully ousted the authoritarian president of Burkina Faso, Blaise Compaoré. Years of low-profile organizing led to a sudden six days of revolution, defying expectations and skillfully initiating the power mechanism's cognitive and practical effects. One key Burkinabe activist group, Le Balai Citoyen (the Citizen's Broom), so took these lessons to heart that they traveled to other quasi-democratic countries in Africa spreading the knowledge of how they were able to achieve Compaoré's ouster.[6] With Compaoré gone, Burkina Faso began a transition with the goal of holding free and fair elections in 2015.

However, before the elections could be held, Burkina Faso's presidential guard, known as the RSP, attempted to stage a coup. The transitional government's moves to reduce the RSP's traditional power and privilege, as well as potential threats of prosecution for crimes under the Compaoré regime, motivated the RSP to seek its own power. The popular reaction by Le Balai Citoyen and other activist groups was immediate, forceful, and widespread. The RSP was able to repress some opposition in the capital city of Ouagadougou, with soldiers opening fire on public protests, but outside of the capital the protests immediately showed that the coup lacked popular support and that the authority of the coup plotters was limited to a very small area of the country. Pressure from the continued rejection of the coup by the people, as well as international condemnation, finally led the regular army to condemn the coup as well. The army's top leadership had initially sat on the sidelines, but finally announced that they would send troops to the capital to end the coup.

Nor was stopping the coup the end of the diffusion of power to ordinary people from the experience of the 2014 revolution. A "readiness of key activist networks and ordinary citizens to mobilize again when necessary" (Harsch, 2017, p. 211) has become central to Burkinabe politics, with prominent movements advocating for land rights and transparency and against corruption. Many of the protests have been effective, leading to major policy changes and greater openness to public input from Burkina Faso's new president (Harsch, 2018).

Nonviolent resistance tends to set transitions in a more democratic direction relative to other forces for initiating transition. These three mechanisms—the elevation of individuals with democratic preferences to positions of leadership, the establishment of norms of limited, nonviolent contention, and the diffusion of power—help carry this direction through the transition.

The Challenges of Civil Resistance Transitions

This articulation of mechanisms brings us back to the book's original puzzle: If nonviolent resistance can initiate such powerful democratizing forces, why does it so often fail to result in democracy? The answer is that none of these mechanisms occurs by necessity; each can break down based on choices made by actors during the transition. And if the mechanisms break down, the democratization process does not occur.

These breakdowns are not simply random deviations from an expected path; they tend to occur in consistent ways, even across wildly different transitions. This means that we can study the breakdown process directly and compare similar breakdowns in terms of a common set of *challenges* that countries face during their transitions. I group the potential breakdown processes in terms of two key challenges.

The first challenge is *transitional mobilization*. By this I mean maintaining a level of civic engagement, public pressure, and protest during the transition that is like the level of engagement during the period of struggle against the old regime. If rapid demobilization follows the beginning of the transition, then the balance of force shifts back to the old regime, and we are back in a traditional, elite-led transition to democracy. The process of expanding the winning coalition fails to occur, and each of the three mechanisms for translating the public's greater position of power and influence into a more inclusive polity is undermined.

First, a lack of mobilization undermines the installation of new leaders from the nonviolent resistance movement. In many cases during transitions these figures are still seen as outsiders by elites. If these leaders are to be placed in positions of influence it will typically be because those in power fear the consequences if they ignore popular demands. For instance, when Tunisian president Ben Ali fell from power in 2011, the initial transitional government was dominated by figures from the Ben Ali regime, particularly Prime Minister Mohamed Ghannouchi. Their plan for a quick presidential election (with the clear goal of retaining Ghannouchi in power) was derailed by protests from Tunisia's civil society, which demanded a transition led in significant degree by people from outside the Ben Ali regime. These protests successfully led to Ghannouchi's resignation and the creation of the Ben Achour Commission, a body of representatives from civil society and opposition parties (Stepan, 2012) that shepherded Tunisia's transition in a more democratic direction.

Continued mobilization is also crucial for the transmission of democratic norms. As outlined earlier, norms of peaceful dispute resolution are maintained through practice. If nonviolent resistance is simply a one-time occurrence, a flash in the pan that is not carried forward with continued practice, then these norms are unlikely to be transmitted through the transition into the subsequent regime.

Finally, mobilization is crucial for the operation of the power mechanism. The diffusion of power through nonviolent resistance, as identified by Gene Sharp (1973, 2005) and others,[7] is not an abstract quality transmitted to individuals through their participation in strikes and protests. It is constituted by the continued exercise of resistance. If this exercise does not occur, then the diffusion of power does not occur.

Demobilization may occur for any number of reasons. The existence (real or perceived) of legitimate channels for expressing grievances may encourage those previously hitting the streets to instead simply wait at home for their chance to hit the ballot box (Kingstone, Young, & Aubrey, 2013; Muller & Seligson, 1987). Alternatively, diverse coalitions that came together to oust the old regime may divide over differing visions of the new regime, reducing the available resources for public mobilization (Beissinger, 2013). Moderate opposition forces may even support repression against elements that seek to continue mobilization, as occurred in several important cases of CRTs, such as Chile's (Hipsher, 1998).

The second challenge is reducing *maximalism*.[8] By this I mean shifting political and social mobilization away from revolutionary goals and tactics and into new institutionalized political channels. The experience of a successful civil resistance campaign can be highly empowering for the leaders of social and political forces able to mobilize the mass numbers necessary to achieve success (Sharp, 1973). This is a crucial aspect of the *power* mechanism that I discussed earlier. However, by its nature civil resistance involves disruptively going outside of the bounds of institutional politics. Such disruption can be extremely powerful in ending oppression. However, on a more basic level it can be used as a potent tool to shift the balance of power. In the weakly institutionalized setting of a transition from authoritarian rule, the forces that came together to oust the previous regime, or other social or political forces inspired by their example, may rely upon this particularly powerful tool to further their own narrowly defined interests. In many cases this leads to a radicalization of politics, a constant move to the streets when electoral outcomes or government policies fail to satisfy the demands of particular forces. This move to fight fire with fire in turn undermines the very possibility of regular democratic politics and can shift public opinion away from support for democracy and toward authoritarian nostalgia (Ketchley & El-Rayyes, 2019).

This is a challenge for the relationship between members of the civil resistance movement and the old regime and where there are conflicts among the forces that came together to oust it. While outside observers often portray these civil society forces in rosy terms during the campaign against the old regime, they typically consist of groups with conflicting visions of the future and little tying them together but anti-incumbency (Beissinger, 2013; Pishchikova & Youngs, 2016; Tucker, 2007). As Adam Przeworski (1991, pp. 66–67) says:

> Conflicts inherent in transitions to democracy often occur on two fronts: between the opponents and defenders of the authoritarian regime about democracy and among the proto-democratic actors against one another for the best chance under democracy. . . . Societies are divided in many ways, and the very essence of democracy is the competition among political forces with conflicting interests. This situation creates a dilemma: to bring about democracy, anti-authoritarian forces must unite against authoritarianism, but to be victorious under democracy, they must compete with each other.

Maximalism takes different forms depending on the society's preexisting social and political cleavages. In societies deeply divided along ethnic or religious lines, these points of identity cleavage often become the touchstones for competing civil resistance campaigns, as in Kenya following the fight for restoration of multiparty democracy in the 1990s.[9] Alternatively, parties led by charismatic individuals may become the centers of this maximalist mobilization, as in Bangladesh following the ouster of President Hussain Muhammad Ershad (Schaffer, 2002). And in some cases both political parties and identity-based groups may serve as the basis for this type of mobilization, as in Madagascar in the early 2000s (Marcus, 2004).

Maximalism works through but simultaneously undermines all three of the mechanisms whereby nonviolent resistance positively affects democratization. First, it elevates a different kind of leader than the democratizing Mandelas and Wałęsas to positions of power. If struggle becomes focused on deploying the tools of nonviolent resistance for narrow partisan goals, then leaders who can mobilize people along these lines are likely to be elevated.

Second, it changes the set of norms that the period of struggle against the old regime transmits to the constitution of the subsequent regime. The norm of peaceful dispute resolution and unity in the face of an overwhelming opponent is replaced by a norm of ratcheting up tension over even minor disputes and refusing to accept losses. The rhetoric is still often focused on the ideals of nonviolent resistance, but its practical content is very different.

Third, the maximalism challenge works even more strongly through the power-diffusing mechanism of nonviolent resistance. Because nonviolent resistance diffuses a sense of power and efficacy more widely throughout the polity, more actors can use these tools of social action to seek to disrupt arrangements that they do not find to their advantage.

The specific contours of contention vary depending on actors' capacity to impose costs. When the balance of forces is even, irregular alternations in power will be frequent as factions take advantage of short-term advantages of position. This has been the case in Thailand, where from 2006 to 2014 the primarily urban Yellow and primarily rural Red factions engaged in several back-and-forth resistance campaigns, often succeeding in achieving power but never moving from temporary achievement to a consolidation of power and institutionalization of alternation in power (Jarernpanit, 2019; Naruemon, 2016).

In cases where one group possesses significantly more mobilization capacity than another, yet maximalism remains high, alternations in power are less likely. However, because the institutional mechanisms for loyal opposition are either nonexistent or lack legitimacy and influence, politics remains fractious, with the dominant group relying on more directly coercive mechanisms to suppress dissent. Simultaneously the weaker group attempts to undermine the dominant group's position through constant moves to disrupt mobilization. This dynamic characterized the relationship between the government of Mohamed Morsi in Egypt and the liberal opposition from 2012 to 2013, ultimately motivating the liberal opposition to seek the support of the military in ousting Morsi in the 2013 coup (Abdalla, 2016; Roll, 2016).

In contrast, in transitions characterized by low maximalism political players limit the forms of political action to less disruptive tactics and primarily pursue their goals through the development of new institutional avenues. Protest is a tool for preventing backsliding, not a constant resort for a narrow political agenda.

In short, the two challenges of civil resistance transitions arise from the simultaneously empowering and disruptive character of civil resistance. The empowering characteristic of civil resistance must be maintained through strong mobilization, and the disruptive characteristic—which can undermine democracy as well as dictatorships—must be attenuated by reducing maximalism. When countries successfully navigate these challenges of transition, democracy is the likely result.

The Ends of Civil Resistance Transitions

The implications of this theory for the regimes likely to occur after civil resistance transitions go beyond a one-dimension prediction about the levels of democracy. In the introduction I mentioned the four endpoints that I argue generally obtain: a new authoritarianism, an elite semi-democracy, a fractious semi-democracy, and a democracy. These four endpoints flow directly from the four possible outcomes of mobilization and maximalism. Table 1.1 presents these four predicted endpoints categorized by their relationship to mobilization and maximalism.

This typology, which is similar to many others in the democratization literature (Collier and Levitsky, 1997; Diamond, 1999), is useful because of their relationship to the challenges I have described. It allows for a parsimonious theoretical view of the links between transitional challenges and long-term political equilibria. Articulating this typology of regimes also allows for qualitative testing of my theory in the subsequent chapters. I focus my descriptions on the more novel categories of elite semi-democracy and fractious semi-democracy as the general categories of democracy and authoritarianism are better understood.

It is important to note that all four of these categories are regimes, not transitional stages. The core characteristic of a regime is that it is a regular set of norms and institutions around which actors center their expectations (Geddes, Wright, & Frantz, 2014). Democracy and dictatorship are not the only stable form of political regime. Political systems that are often treated as transitional between these states can themselves be long-term sustainable equilibria (Beresford, Berry, & Mann, 2018; Carothers, 2002).

Elite semi-democracy is the result of a civil resistance transition in which transitional mobilization is low and maximalism, if it occurs, occurs solely within the ranks of the elite. In an elite semi-democracy the slogans of the nonviolent revolution are adopted and the forms of democracy are generally put in place.

Table 1.1 Regime Types after Civil Resistance Transitions

	Low Mobilization	High Mobilization
Low Maximalism	Elite semi-democracy	Democracy
High Maximalism	Autocracy	Fractious semi-democracy

Elections occur and in most cases are likely to impact the distribution of power. Elites fear to go too far beyond the bounds of democratic practice lest they incur the ire of the people who revolted against the old regime.

However, while there are certain guardrails that prevent the wholesale rapid devolution of democracy, these guardrails do little to ensure that de jure forms of democracy are honored de facto, or that progress is made toward ensuring the country's democratic quality improves, or that the will of the people is faithfully represented.

Why does this occur? A lack of mobilization cuts off the *power mechanism*, meaning that the elites who come into power during the transition do not believe that the public will hold them accountable for their actions. Any accountability mechanisms will either be within the elite or from international sources. In the first case, any constraining effect of accountability can be managed by using state power to distribute private goods among the elite and maintain a comfortable balance of power and resources.

Because the lack of mobilization undermines the *leaders mechanism*, power structures are suffused with elites from the old regime who lack strong democratic preference and have often had decades of practice in ruling their nation top-down for their private benefit. Those who attempt to resist the co-optation of democracy are generally few, lack resources, and find themselves unable to call upon popular resistance to restore momentum toward the bright democratic future envisioned during the nonviolent revolution.

International sources of accountability, while inconvenient, can be assuaged with the general forms of democracy, while the overall practice of democracy, so much more difficult to reliably observe, can be manipulated to serve elites' private interests. The impact of international forces may be as a guardrail to prevent a wholesale return to a nondemocratic system but is unlikely to be effective in comprehensively pushing such countries to major implementation of higher democratic standards absent some major change in mobilization by the people of the country themselves.

Without a domestic mobilization shock, an elite semi-democracy can remain indefinitely as an equilibrium state. Domestic norm entrepreneurs find themselves leaders with few or no followers; the elite maintains comfortable control over the nation; and the international community can do little to directly hold them accountable.

Elite semi-democratic regimes are likely to destabilize into another regime type under two conditions. First, a major move for power by one elite faction may spark popular resistance. An ambitious leader may push against the guardrails, leading to popular pushback that destabilizes the elite bargain and may initiate a new transition. Alternatively, a continued lack of mobilization over time may lead to a progressive erosion of democracy as elites gradually push politics further and further away from the democratic ideal. At a certain point this pushing reaches such an extent that it is no longer meaningful to even describe the political system as semi-democratic and instead we have a nondemocratic regime.

The picture is radically different in fractious semi-democracies, which have high mobilization in the wake of the civil resistance campaign. People truly take to heart the destabilizing message of civil resistance: change is possible with even a relatively small degree of mobilization if they employ the tools of resistance skillfully. Yet absent a centralizing nondemocratic opponent, factions channel this resistance into their own narrow interests.

The attachment to the power of noninstitutionalized resistance results in a move to employ these tools almost constantly. When elections occur they are mainly exercises in which all sides seek to ensure that they alone benefit from the electoral contest. Each actor knows that the other is prepared to employ whatever tools are necessary to gain power and undermine the other. Whenever one side does achieve some degree of power, they attempt to manipulate the rules of the game to ensure that this power continues indefinitely. Perceiving this, the other side accuses them of attempting to establish a dictatorship and uses their behavior as justification for continued maximalist resistance.

As long as support for the warring factions remains high and maximalist attitudes are widespread throughout the population, then fractious semi-democracy can also be an indefinite equilibrium. However, second- and third-order effects of this mode of political action are likely to ultimately destabilize it. The economic and social instability caused by a failure to establish regularized democratic politics is likely to be extremely costly for the average citizen. Jobs will be scarce, economic development problematic, and the constant back and forth of maximalist contention wearying and ultimately angering. Popular opinion may shift away from the actors fighting things out in the political arena toward more stable alternatives.

It is uncertain which direction the appeal of these alternatives is likely to push the regime. Frustration over political dysfunction may lead ordinary people to mobilize for greater democratic protections and respect for government institutions. Yet it seems more likely, based on historical experience, that the appeal will more generally be for an authoritarian alternative. People will crave a strong leader who can eliminate these dysfunctional politicians and return the country to stability and productivity. If such a leader can be found, there may be a serious authoritarian reversal (Linz, 1978).

Although I spend less time discussing democracy and authoritarianism as endpoints, a few relevant words about the path to a return to autocracy bear mentioning. High maximalism typically requires high mobilization, but this is not necessarily the case. Individual leaders may pursue maximalist agendas without large numbers of followers. In this case a return to authoritarianism seems almost inevitable. A situation wherein small groups of elites seek to disrupt the political system by pursuing maximalist goals and tactics, yet they lack the mobilizational capacity to truly threaten the system, can lead to some of the worst outcomes. Old regime elites or others with power will have strong incentives to use antidemocratic tools to eliminate the nuisance of maximalist challenges, and there will be little mobilization to keep them accountable and prevent them from doing so.

Up to this point I have presented the basic definitions of my concepts, my empirical puzzle, and my argument for its solution. In the following section I take on some of the alternative explanations for democratization that I am responding to.

Do Choices Really Matter? Addressing Structural Explanations

My explanation for democratization in nonviolent revolutions focuses on the patterns of behavior during transitions. It stands in stark contrast to structural explanations for democratization such as modernization theory. These argue that a set of preexisting political or economic factors in the domestic or international environment can fully or at least satisfactorily explain democratization outcomes (Barro, 1999; Lipset, 1959). In these approaches the actions that make up a democratic transition, including the mechanism that initiated the transition, such as nonviolent resistance, are epiphenomenal to deeper structural factors.

Few scholars argue for a "strong" structural explanation that would claim that exogenous structural factors are fully deterministic of decision-makers' actions.[10] Most structural explanations are "weak." Individual actions may matter, but they do not matter in a way that is analytically meaningful. While a weak structural explanation would acknowledge that there is no direct line from structural factors to final outcomes, the argument would be that the deviations from the structural story are minor and random, and so not a meaningful object of scholarly examination. I raise both theoretical and empirical objections to structural explanations of democratization, beginning with a theoretical critique of structural explanations generally and then moving on to a more empirical critique of a few specific structural explanations.

There are critically important philosophical debates on the role of structure and agency in human action in general and politics specifically.[11] Addressing these debates directly is beyond the scope of this book. Thus, instead of an extended philosophical discussion, I ground my theoretical argument against structural arguments on a much simpler concept: contingency. During civil resistance transitions there is contingency in how particular actors make the choices that lead to patterns of mobilization and maximalism. The choices are not sui generis, but neither are their specific causes easily attributable to structural factors. Rather they are based on a multitude of personal factors that, from the perspective of an outside observer, we may safely treat as random.

I, along with much of the literature, assume that political actors seek to maximize their utility, typically by seeking to maximize their personal power and time in office (Bueno De Mesquita, 2005; Riker, 1962). This assumption means that in many circumstances we can reduce behavior to its exogenous constraints since all actors will behave similarly given a similar situation. Yet during a transition, the fundamental uncertainty in the rules of the game and its set of players undermines those players' ability to make these rational calculations. From the position of an outside observer without intimate knowledge of leaders' thought processes, their actions can appear almost random.

This randomness is likely to be even greater in the context of a nonviolent revolution than in other transitions because these transitions usually involve massive change in the number of players. In top-down liberalizations, the initial opening is typically made by a small group of players who are familiar with the current set of institutions. For instance, Spain's democratic transition in the 1970s, the archetypal example of a democratic transition initiated by top-down liberalization, was largely a matter of deals worked out between a small group of elites, with perhaps no more than 10 individuals playing truly key roles (Jimenez-Diaz & Delgado-Fernandez, 2016, p. 3).

In civil resistance transitions the numbers are typically much greater. As Elizabeth Wood (2000) has pointed out, transitions from below involve shattering the close-knit interior set of elites. A group of counterelites who do not know how to play by the rules are suddenly involved in the political game, and everyone must rethink their behavior. For instance, in the Hungarian roundtable talks, which culminated that country's nonviolent revolution and led to its democratic transition, there were dozens of people seated around the table. They ranged from longtime elites to union leaders and students, some of whom had little or no exposure to politics before their involvement in upending the Hungarian communist regime.[12]

Civil resistance transitions are likely to involve many more players than appear in violent revolutions. Civil wars doubtless involve a complex set of actors. Yet victorious rebel groups are typically those who have overcome this fragmentation through enduring alliances or a single, strong hierarchical structure (Akcinaroglu, 2012; Cunningham, 2006; Cunningham, 2013; Findley and Rudloff, 2012). In contrast, few nonviolent resistance movements, even successful ones, have had single central hierarchies. They are dominated by complex fronts of different kinds of actors typically brought together in a "negative coalition" defined almost solely by its opposition to the regime in power (Beissinger, 2013).

Behavioral economics and psychology have shown us that human beings are poor strategists when it comes to games with too many players, unfamiliar players, and complex or unpredictable rules (Camerer, 2003; Cheung & Friedman, 1997). Indeed, as the number of players in a game increases, chaotic nonequilibrium choices become ubiquitous (Sanders, Farmer, & Galla, 2018). Players make choices based on instinct and cognitive heuristics that are often inappropriate to the situation at hand.

Thus the patterns of strategic decision-making and political practice during transitions do not arise directly from their structural preconditions, particularly in civil resistance transitions. This implies a few things. First, models predicting transitional outcomes that rely purely on structural factors are likely to have poor predictive power.[13] Second, this poor performance is likely to be exacerbated for civil resistance transitions. Third, while patterns of behavior during transitions are not random they can be treated as relatively randomly assigned because of the high level of uncertainty and contingency that goes into their assignment.

O'Donnell and Schmitter (1986) make similar arguments about transitions in general. They emphasize the importance of contingency and discuss how leaders' individual virtu in transitional moments can crucially shape outcomes. Some have misinterpreted their book as actually laying out a strict structure of how transitions develop (Carothers, 2002). In fact, they argue the opposite (O'Donnell, 2002). Transitions are "multilayered chess" in which few people understand the rules and some players can choose to throw away the board and stop play if the game isn't going the way they prefer (O'Donnell & Schmitter, 1986, pp. 66–67).

This does not imply that structural factors do not matter. Contingent choices are made in a structural context. Yet the random variation that arises from personal contingency gives us analytic space to separate choices during transitions from their structural preconditions. Two elites facing the same set of economic conditions, the same international environment, and the same political cleavages will respond to those constraints in different ways, and those differing responses will then have differing effects.

Yet admitting that there is analytical space between structural explanations and political outcomes for the influence of transitional challenges like mobilization and maximalism does not imply that these patterns will help us understand the phenomenon in question. This is primarily an empirical question. I take it up in the subsequent statistical and qualitative chapters, using a standard toolkit to address issues of omitted variable bias and relative quality of model fit on the statistical side, and performing qualitative counterfactual analysis and carefully examining causal mechanisms on the qualitative side. However, a few words on specific alternative explanations that speak directly to my theoretical dynamics are warranted here.

The democratization literature is well developed, with compelling evidence presented for the effects of many diverse factors on democratic transitions. I will not attempt to comprehensively review this extensive literature, as this work has already been done exceedingly well elsewhere, and I have briefly mentioned some of its more important dimensions in the introduction.[14] Instead, in this section I will briefly sketch some of the most prominent explanations for democratization that could plausibly interact with my theory.

Two plausible alternative explanations are socioeconomic modernization and international influence. Modernization theory at its core argues that high levels of economic development and the attendant social changes that such development entails tend to lead to the breakdown of authoritarian regimes and successful democratic transition and consolidation. While it has recently enjoyed a resurgence (Boix & Stokes, 2003; Che, Lu, Tao, & Wang, 2013), this finding remains controversial. Przeworski and his coauthors (2000) argue that development has no impact on democratic transitions, but only influences democratic consolidation. And even this finding may be subject to revision after the recent democratic backsliding in relatively wealthy countries such as Turkey, Hungary, and Poland. Yet the consistency of the relationship between development and democracy (despite recent exceptions) means that it is crucial to account for these explanations. I do so by incorporating high-quality measures of modernization into my empirical analysis in subsequent chapters.

What of the more recent and robust set of arguments relating democratization to factors in the international environment? This argument—that international influence is the critical factor in explaining democratization—takes several forms. The power position of a democratic hegemon is one major international influence (Fordham & Asal, 2007; Gunitsky, 2014); linkage to the West is another (Levitsky & Way, 2010); and connection to international organizations is a third (Pevehouse, 2002, 2005). Daniel Ritter (2015) has linked close connection to a liberal patron specifically to the outcomes of nonviolent revolutions. Yet perhaps the most common and influential version of this argument is that democracy tends to diffuse from democratic neighbors.[15] What is the underlying story for why this relationship obtains, and what can that tell us about the plausibility of structural explanations of democratization?

Kristian Skrede Gleditsch and Michael Ward (2006) argue that democratic neighbors increase the likelihood of a democratic transition because democratization is a struggle over power. Networks of power and influence transcend national borders. Elites and institutions in democracies will provide support to pro-democratic opposition movements in nondemocratic countries in their regions. This support will then be sufficient to tip the balance of power such that democratic transitions will be initiated and democratic regimes will come to power. Other diffusion models rely on similar mechanisms, for instance assuming that actors within regimes receive some kind of benefits when their regime closely matches that of their neighbors (Brinks & Coppedge, 2006).[16]

Many scholars have statistically demonstrated this broad relationship. Yet, as the authors typically admit, they cannot actually test the mechanisms through which they claim their relationship obtains (Brinks & Coppedge, 2006, p. 467). The diffusion model as articulated by Gleditsch and Ward assumes, first, that democratic governments will seek to encourage similar democratic changes in their neighbors; second, that pro-democratic partners within their neighbors exist to receive their assistance; third, that such efforts to encourage democratic changes will successfully increase the political capacity of these nascent democratizers; fourth, that the increase in capacity will be sufficient to motivate pro-democratizers to in some way challenge the status quo; fifth, that this challenge will be successful in bringing the pro-democratizers to power; sixth, that once in power the pro-democratizers will seek to put in place a democratic regime; seventh, that they will succeed in doing so.

To accept diffusion's direct impact on democratization we must assume that all these steps flow naturally from a country having many democratic neighbors. Yet, as is clear once the steps are presented, not one of them can be so assumed. Take, for example, the idea that democracies seek to encourage democratic change in their neighbors. The history of US foreign policy toward Latin America and the Caribbean quickly shows that such democratic support has been at best part of a much wider range of strategies toward governments in these regions. The United States, despite highly valuing democracy domestically, has energetically supported nondemocratic regimes in many of its neighbors when such support was perceived to be in the US national interest. Even when ostensibly seeking to encourage democracy, its support has often been directed not toward a full-fledged democratization but toward a more limited form of democracy still dominated by a small elite (Robinson, 1996). Similar critiques could be leveled at all the other assumed steps in the naturally flowing story of democratic diffusion.

The response of weak structural arguments similar to this one is that these theories are probabilistic, and the fact that a statistically significant relationship obtains between the percentage of democratic neighbors and a country's level of democracy means that we can unproblematically treat each of these steps as at least probabilistically being pushed in a particular direction. This is true, but it raises another question: How adequate is our model's levels of explanatory power? For most structural models of democratization, as described earlier, this level of explanation tends to be quite low, as measured by standard statistics such as the r^2.[17] This is a powerful indication that there is a lot going on in each of these probabilistic steps that remains to be examined, opening up significant room for research that systematically examines the patterns of behavior that take place in the space between structural forces and political outcomes. In each of the steps between independent structural variable and dependent variable there is unexplained variation, points at which, for the natural flow to occur, particular actors must make particular choices that are by no means fully determined or even meaningfully determined by the observable structural factors.

This is not to argue that structural factors are unimportant or that analyses based on structural factors are incorrect. Indeed by focusing on structural factors, the democratization literature has given us a wealth of knowledge about which remote factors may influence democratic progress. However, by looking at the spaces between structure and outcome we can meaningfully add to our understanding of the rare but important phenomenon of democratic transitions.

If structural factors neither fully explain transitional outcomes nor fully account for the impact of strategic factors, as I have argued here, then the space is open to theorize and test which strategic factors will matter in specific transitional contexts. Arguing against purely structural explanations does not in itself provide evidence for my preferred strategic explanation of democracy in civil resistance transitions being facilitated by high mobilization and low maximalism. But showing the flaws in more purely structural explanations opens crucial space to make the examination of strategic factors such as mobilization and maximalism meaningful. Without such a theoretically and empirically rooted critique of structural explanations, the theory and empirics of this book would be on shaky ground, subject to the critique that they do little more than capture the aftereffects of deeper underlying forces. My critique here seeks to defend the empirical testing from this objection. If measures of mobilization and maximalism indeed have a statistically significant relationship with democracy after civil resistance transitions, and explain more of the variation in democratization than purely structural models, we may say that their impact is not purely epiphenomenal.

Summary

This chapter has laid out the unique character of civil resistance transitions based on how nonviolent resistance changes the power positions of political actors at the beginning of the transition, and the set of mechanisms during the transition through which this changed power position translates to democratization: the elevation of leaders, transformation of norms, and diffusion of power. These mechanisms do not arise of necessity either from structural factors or from the influence of nonviolent resistance. Hence they can be undermined or not occur at all.

Two key patterns of behavior that can undermine these mechanisms are captured in the challenges of maintaining high mobilization and reducing maximalism. The first challenge primarily works by undermining the power mechanism. The second primarily works by undermining the norms mechanism. Both, in different ways, also undermine the leader mechanism.

Figure 1.1 summarizes how the various elements in my theory fit together. Each nondemocratic country has a certain baseline likelihood of democracy based on structural conditions, but this possibility has very wide error bars, particularly wide because at this point in the story the country may or may not even experience a transition. At each stage forward from the structural context actual events set a new baseline possibility of democracy, while the range of possibilities around that baseline shrinks. For example, the specific case depicted in the figure symbolizes a civil resistance transition, in which the transition *mode* (civil resistance) increases the baseline likelihood of democracy relative to pretransition conditions. However, the range of possible outcomes around this baseline likelihood is still large. What narrows it down to the final outcome are the transitional challenges in the next stage. The background structural conditions certainly determine the wide bounds within which the transitional challenges operate. But they leave significant room for variation if we do not directly examine variation in transitional challenges.

Whether or not this model of civil resistance transitions is accurate and whether the specific challenges described in this chapter indeed affect democratic prospects in the way that I have described here is an empirical question.

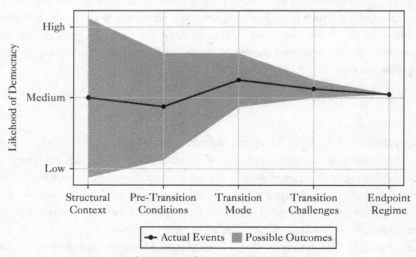

FIGURE 1.1 Summarizing the Theory of Transitional Challenges

Thus the subsequent chapters move into the empirical testing of the theory. The first step in answering this question is statistical, testing whether in the global population of transitions CRTs are indeed more democratically inclined than other transitions, and whether patterns of mobilization and maximalism can explain variation in democratization among the population of CRTs.

2

The Challenges at Work

TESTING THE CIVIL RESISTANCE TRANSITIONS DATA

IN THE PREVIOUS chapter I argued that we should expect high levels of mobilization and low levels of maximalism to push civil resistance transitions toward greater democracy. These two patterns of behavior carry the democratizing advantage of nonviolent resistance through the transitional period, when the character of the coming regime is still in question. In this chapter I move on to demonstrate empirically that this is a robust and meaningful way of understanding CRTs.

The discussion in the previous chapter laid out some of the tasks necessary to satisfactorily demonstrate that this relationship is meaningful. I must show that mobilization and maximalism can be measured and that when measured they can be shown to have a statistically significant relationship with democratization in the expected directions (positive for mobilization and negative for maximalism). Yet before that, it is necessary to show that civil resistance transitions indeed have the democratizing character that I described, making it useful for the study of democratization to consider them independently of other kinds of transitions.

In addition, in order to address the objections of the strong and weak structural arguments, I must show that the effects of mobilization and maximalism are substantive and independent enough to distinguish my model's predictions from the predictions of a purely structural model. The inclusion of these variables should improve the predictive power of the model relative to the structural model. Only if all these statistical thresholds can be met can we say that my approach offers something meaningful for the study of democratization generally and the specific question of CRTs.

Thus, in this chapter I take on three tasks. The first is the task of measurement, clearly and carefully operationalizing the abstract concepts from Chapter 1. The second is testing whether civil resistance transitions are more democratizing than other transitions. As I outlined in both the introduction and Chapter 1, this finding has been widely replicated in the literature. My tests here extend this earlier work in three ways. First, I incorporate a definition of transition, particularly transitional endpoints, that is more theoretically developed than that employed by previous scholars. Second, I compare model fit measures between structural models and models including the civil resistance variable, providing an additional test of the explanatory impact of civil resistance. Third, I compare all forms of transition, not only change in the aftermath of violent or nonviolent resistance, as in Chenoweth and Stephan (2011), or transitions to democracy alone, as in Bayer, Bethke, and Lambach (2016) and Bethke and Pinckney (2019). Performing this test is central to demonstrating that civil resistance transitions are a distinct population that deserve their own unique examination.

The third task is then selecting the population of civil resistance transitions and testing the impact of mobilization and maximalism in these transitions. The tests provide strong evidence for my theory. High mobilization and low maximalism during a transition strongly predict democratization at the transition's end. Their impact is substantive and significantly improves model fit over a model limited to structural factors.

Operationalizing Concepts

The theory that I laid out in Chapter 1 concerns periods of *transition*, that is, the period between the breakdown of one political regime and the establishment of another. I am distinguishing transitions from one another based on two key characteristics: how they begin (whether they are initiated by civil resistance) and their interior political dynamics (their levels of mobilization and maximalism). Empirically testing this theory thus involves using the entire transition as my primary unit of analysis.

Combining existing well-respected data sources on political transitions (Chenoweth & Shay, 2019; Geddes, Wright, & Frantz, 2014) leads to a population of 315 political transitions initiated between 1945 and 2011.[1] Of these, 78 meet the criteria for civil resistance transitions as I defined that category in the introduction: civil resistance played a crucial role in initiating the transition, such that absent civil resistance a transition would not have occurred or the shape of the transition would have been unrecognizable compared to what actually occurred.

These 78 cases, spread across 64 countries, come from every region of the world and have diverse backgrounds and precipitating conditions. This is not a European story, a Latin American story, or an African story, but a global story. Figure 2.1 shows all the countries with at least one CRT.[2]

The next important question is identifying these transitions' boundaries. When do transitions begin and end? The beginning of a transition is straightforward to

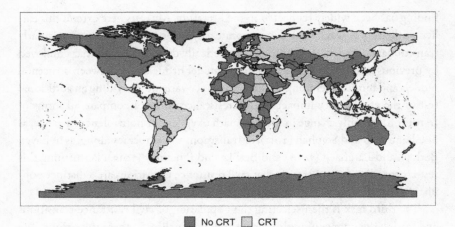

No CRT   CRT

FIGURE 2.1 Countries with Civil Resistance Transitions, 1945 to 2011

identify. I do so primarily by relying on the preexisting definition from Barbara Geddes and her coauthors (2014, pp. 317–18). Transitions occur when a regime, that is, the system of rules and rule-makers currently in place for determining the authoritative allocation of values, ceases to function. Rules are destabilized and uncertain for a time before restabilizing, typically in a different form or at least with different players at the helm.

It is not as straightforward to identify transitions' ends. Regime breakdown is typically a dramatic event and easily distinguishable because it moves politics from regularity into irregularity. During this period of irregularity there are many different candidate events for the establishment of a new regime. Yet time quickly shows that many of these events herald only temporary realignments of power, not the creation of a stable set of norms and institutions. How can we resolve this challenge?

The bluntest approach is to assume that transitions cannot go on forever, and so if we pick an arbitrary point relatively distant in time from the transition's initiation we have a reliable proxy for conditions at the transition's end. However, there are strong theoretical reasons to suspect this approach. There are vast differences in time between empirical markers of transitional endpoints across cases. For example, while in Brazil a constitution was ratified and promulgated in 1988, only three years after their transition in 1985, in Nepal a constitution was not ratified and promulgated until 2015, almost 10 years after the Second People's Movement overthrew the Nepali monarchy and initiated the transition.

However, it could be the case that such distinctions are not substantive when considering the aggregate level of democracy in a country and so would not

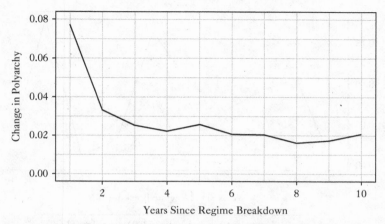

FIGURE 2.2 Average Annual Change in Democracy after Regime Breakdown

significantly impact the results of the kind of analysis I perform in this chapter. One way to tell if this is the case is to look at the variation in the change in democracy in countries at fixed points in time after their transitions. Do we see a global trend of a certain temporal point at which variation begins to decline to a level where it is no longer meaningful?

Figure 2.2 shows the average absolute change in one measure of democracy— the polyarchy score from the Varieties of Democracy project (Coppedge et al., 2018)—of countries over time after regime breakdown initiates a transition. As the line in the figure shows, there is a sharp decline in the average amount of change over the first two years following the beginning of a transition. After that point the mean change in polyarchy on an annual basis stabilizes at an average of around 0.02.

Based on this graph, the most meaningful point in time to choose as a transition's end might be two years after the transition. However, while to do so might be accurate in the aggregate, it poorly captures a great deal of variation in transitions that occurred over longer periods. To illustrate, Figure 2.3 shows the change in polyarchy scores for three different countries over a 10-year period following the beginning of a transition. As the widely divergent lines show, there is no clear cutoff point where variation in polyarchy scores levels out, indicating an end to transition and institutional stabilization. Picking an arbitrary point will not be a reliable means of measuring the end of transitions.

Democratization scholars have suggested several empirical markers that could be used to mark a transition's end (Gasiorowski & Power, 1998; Huntington, 1993; O'Donnell, 1996; Schedler, 1998; Valenzuela, 1990). These tend to be defined as either the point at which the democratization process is complete or when

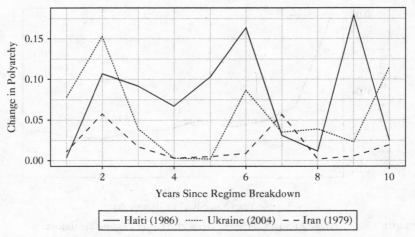

FIGURE 2.3 Absolute Change in Democracy in Iran, Ukraine, and Haiti after Civil Resistance

democratic consolidation has occurred. One of the most influential of these come from Juan Linz and Alfred Stepan (1996, p. 1), who define democratization as complete when the first election for the executive occurs that is relatively free and fair.[3] They subsequently argue that the process of democratic consolidation is complete when democracy has become "the only game in town" behaviorally, attitudinally, and constitutionally (p. 5).

The first of these definitions can easily be empirically applied across a global sample of cases. Any number of different data sources collect information on the occurrence of elections and offer informed opinions on their relative freedom and fairness.[4] However, this measure fails to capture that these formal institutional measures of democratization have different significance for the underlying question of the establishment of a regime. These measures are also democratization-specific and offer little insight into the mirror question of how to measure the end of a transition that leads to a nondemocratic regime.

The measure of the "only game in town" better captures the end of a transition, though this standard might be a bit too high to truly be reliable. If a regime is the set of rules and rule-makers that are reliably expected by other actors to define how values are authoritatively allocated, then one can consider a regime to be in place when its "game," while perhaps not the "only" one major actors consider, is at least the predominant game that most actors reliably expect to follow most of the time. This definition would apply, of course, no matter which game actors are playing: the game of full-fledged democratic politics, authoritarian politics, or some quasi-democratic hybrid of the two. The key is that the rules of the game have stabilized into a reliable pattern.

This is the most empirically meaningful way to examine the question of transition outcomes. We are not strictly interested in the regime type at a fixed moment in time, but instead in the characteristics of the political game that reliably continue. Given this, it makes the most sense to measure the end of the transition as the point at which we observe fluctuation in regular measures of the characteristics of the political system declining and remaining below some predefined threshold. In doing so we are measuring the characteristics of the system when they have empirically begun to reproduce themselves reliably into the future.

I do not assume that these institutions continue indefinitely. My sole assumption is that by measuring the dependent variable this way I am capturing an equilibrium point in the political game. New stimuli may disturb this equilibrium, but that is a question for other research.[5] My concern is with the endpoints of civil resistance transitions. I incorporate enough stability in my operationalization of the subsequent regime to make the distinction between transition and regime meaningful, but I am agnostic about the subsequent regime's long-term stability.

Since the characteristic of the political regime that I am examining is democracy, it makes the most sense to measure the end of the transition at the point at which the regime's level of democracy ceases to dramatically fluctuate.[6] This is what I do in all my subsequent tests.

There have been several efforts to create cross-national measures of both democracy and its various institutional components, such as free and fair elections.[7] Yet these measures often rely on meaningfully different conceptions of democracy and can lead to very different results (Högström, 2013). Thus it is important to briefly discuss how and why I operationalize democracy. As I described in the previous chapter, on a theoretical level I rely on both a threshold institutional notion of democracy based on the work of Schumpeter (1942), Przeworski (2000), and others that focuses on free and fair elections, and an ideal-type notion of democracy based on the work of Dahl (1973). A regime is democratic in a binary sense if it crosses Schumpeter's threshold. It is democratic in a continuous sense to the degree that it approximates Dahl's ideal of a political system perfectly and equally responsive to its citizens.

My binary measure of democracy is more straightforward to observe and identify: if a country has elections that are widely regarded as free and fair, then it passes this test of minimal democracy.[8] For my continuous measure of democracy, I use the polyarchy score from the Varieties of Democracy (V-Dem) project (Coppedge et al., 2018). This measure is directly inspired by Dahl's conception of democracy, and thus is the closest theoretical fit to the ideal type that I seek to capture. V-Dem has several strengths over other common data sources on democracy as well. It builds its scores on the insights of multiple country experts and gives confidence intervals for all its scores. It also provides a wealth of information on how individual institutional measures are aggregated into its top-line indexes of democracy, allowing those using it to carefully examine and verify its assumptions.

The next step is to operationalize my independent and control variables. Operationalizing mobilization and maximalism is difficult because both capture latent characteristics of a political system. Mobilization, for instance, can take any number of different forms. We can observe empirical indications of these different forms but not the underlying dimension of mobilization. The same is true of maximalism. These are not defined by any single action. Instead they are dimensions of the entire system that many different empirical indicators can give us information about but never perfectly capture.

Because of this, when operationalizing mobilization and maximalism, rather than rely on a single empirical indicator I use primary factor analysis to capture the underlying dimension of both these phenomena. Factor analysis uses the patterns of covariance between different empirical indicators to describe the underlying dimensionalities that they share. What kinds of indicators do we need to construct these factors? To answer this question I delve in more detail into what patterns of behavior constitute transitional mobilization and maximalism.

The first to consider is mobilization. How can we tell if a populace has remained mobilized during the transition and is putting pressure for continued reform on the elites?

The most basic and straightforward indicator here is the actual level of political activity. How great is political participation in the transition? Participation can be roughly divided into two basic forms: institutional and noninstitutional. The first refers to how widespread and comprehensive is participation in the institutions being set up during the transitional process. Electoral turnout would be one key measure here. Measures of public engagement and consultation in matters of policy, how much interest the public takes in these matters, would be another. Noninstitutional refers to methods of political participation that are outside of institutional channels but still seek to achieve goals such as public protests and demonstrations or strikes. These are the tactics of nonviolent resistance applied not just during the struggle against the old regime but as part of a larger effort to keep the new regime accountable.

A high level of mobilization during the transition will be characterized by high levels of both these categories of participation. Mobilized and engaged citizens will turn out to vote and access official channels in large numbers but will also engage in action outside of these avenues. This is particularly true during transitions because by definition these institutional channels remain novel and untested and noninstitutional methods are likely to be the most widely understood and powerful.

There are many ways to operationalize these two forms of participation. The literature on political participation on advanced democracies has developed very detailed and comprehensive means of measuring participation (Verba, Nie, & Kim, 1987). Ideally an operationalization of mobilization could rely on these types of measures, looking at the prevalence of common categories such as voting, contacting an elected official, or participating in a protest. However, consistent cross-national survey data is limited in this regard and does not cover most of the countries during transitions. Given this, we must rely on more general observational data.

However, scholars of democratization have produced many different data resources that allow us to reliably measure these forms of participation. For example, many data projects have sought to capture counts of protests, strikes, and other forms of noninstitutional participation. Other data sets rely on expert knowledge to measure degrees of public engagement and civil society activism. I use two variables from V-Dem and one measure from the Phoenix Historical Event Data produced by the Cline Center at the University of Illinois to construct my mobilization factor (Althaus, Bajjalieh, Carter, Peyton, & Shalmon, 2017).

The first indicator measures the degree of popular involvement in civil society activity.[9] The second indicator measures the degree of public deliberation, that is to say, how involved ordinary people are in discussing and evaluating matters of public policy.[10] These measures capture the actions of the masses of ordinary people, not elites' decisions. They also speak to the more positive aspects of nonviolent resistance that Sharp (1973) argues for. High scores on these measures give evidence that following a successful nonviolent resistance campaign ordinary people have taken to heart the lessons of the efficacy of nonviolence and become involved in shaping the transition's direction, encouraging greater accountability from leaders.[11]

The third indicator, from the Phoenix data, captures more traditionally considered nonviolent resistance. It is a sum of the number of protest events in a country in a year, according to the CAMEO ontology (Schrodt, Gerner, Yilmaz, & Hermreck, 2005), with adjustments for temporal and geographic reporting bias.[12] This is a broad set of events that includes subcategories such as "rally or demonstrate" and "conduct strike or boycott."

When run through principal factor analysis these three measures combine to create a single factor above the common standard of an eigenvalue greater than 1, strongly suggesting that their covariance can be best explained in terms of a single underlying dimension.[13]

Observing the maximalism challenge involves two key elements: the stated goals of political actors and the tactics they use to pursue those goals. The stated goals questions are these: Do certain groups make claims related to fully transforming the political system? Do they follow an absolutist discourse in which they alone represent the national interest and their opponents are not just rivals but enemies of the people?

There are many examples of this type of discourse during CRTs. For instance, in Egypt the Tamarod movement, which sought to remove President Mohamed Morsi from office, painted Morsi not simply as an opponent but as a figure whose continued presence in power was a fundamental threat to Egypt. This was shown powerfully in the lead-up to Morsi's removal but also afterward, when, under the control of General Abdel Fattah el-Sisi, Tamarod enthusiastically endorsed the slaughter of Morsi supporters in the massacre at the Rabaa al-Adawiya mosque.[14]

There are various means of measuring such claims. Collecting the public statements of leaders, party manifestos, and other textual artifacts of the political process can provide a wealth of information on the messages that parties communicate. Scholars can then apply textual analysis to measure the intention and sentiment of the documents and estimate attitudes toward the political system.[15] However, the work required to collect such information cross-nationally is prohibitive, and interpreting the contextual signals from such documents consistently is difficult to reliably achieve.[16]

In lieu of developing a comprehensive analysis of cross-national political communication we may look to certain consistent signs to determine whether maximalism is becoming prevalent in the system. Of these, I argue that the most consistent and reliable is a refusal to accept electoral results. If elections occur and the outcome is unfavorable for a party, in an institutionalized political system the parties accept the results and begin mobilizing to achieve a better outcome in the next election. If instead parties immediately seek to call into question the results of the election and rhetorically mobilize their supporters to overturn it through extra-institutional action, this is a key indicator that maximalism is under way. To make such a claim, particularly in the context of a popularly initiated civil resistance transition, is to invoke the rhetoric of the movement to achieve a particularistic aim. It is to call back previous resistance and equate the uncertainty of transition with the control and oppression of the old regime. Therefore it undermines the ability of a democratic politics with a mix of cleavage and consensus from consolidating.[17]

It is important to note as well that this mode of political discourse and action, while supportive of democracy, is by no means identical to democracy. So, while one might rightly observe that it is difficult to imagine a sustainable democratic politics suffused with maximalist discourse, this is demonstrating my argument by showing the strength of this factor in supporting democracy, not simply reducing to a tautology that democracy is difficult to imagine without democracy.

The articulation of maximalist, antisystemic goals is insufficient to indicate maximalism. At the very least it is a faulty indicator. Political discourse in many countries, including highly developed democracies, relies on such language. The American antiabortion movement, for instance, is full of the language of genocide, and those who allow abortion to continue are frequently painted as almost demonic figures, worse than Nazis in the scale of their atrocities. Yet if pressed, most political leaders from this movement or others in developed democracies who employ similar types of rhetoric will argue that they themselves do not truly believe the things they say. Or at least they express horror when their accusations of genocide are taken literally by their followers. For a truly reliable view of maximalism, we must go beyond rhetoric and consider political actors' behavior.

What actions fit this mold? How can we know that political actors really believe what they say? There are a few important indicators. First, the level of political violence is an important and reliable indicator of at least some degree of maximalism. If political actors, particularly large actors central to the political system, use violence to achieve maximalist goals, then we may safely assume that they are willing to put their money where their mouth is and both impose and suffer high costs to achieve them.

Yet violence is not the only or even the primary area in which we should look for concrete actions that match this picture of maximalism. The key way that maximalism relates to the initiation of a transition through civil resistance is that the experience of civil resistance, particularly large, successful civil resistance, puts the knowledge and tools of *nonviolent* resistance in the hands of actors throughout the political system. It reveals the fragility of political orders.

This is, for the most part, a positive development. The success of nonviolent resistance makes ordinary people and civil society groups aware that they need not interact with those in power with fear and trembling. They know that, when organized, even without weapons ordinary people can achieve major concessions and undermine the integrity of oppressive systems. This is a powerful accountability mechanism. Yet the larger revealed fragility of the political system can encourage nonviolent mobilization that destabilizes the establishment of emerging norms and practices.

This somewhat negative view of nonviolent resistance fits poorly with the very positive view of popular mobilization prominent in the academic and popular literature on nonviolent action. For good reason, scholars of nonviolent action have been hesitant to describe their tools as anything but positive empowerment for those suffering under oppression or violence. But by no means do all those who wield the nonviolent sword have goals that are civic and democratizing.

There are numerous examples of movements of a primarily nonviolent character whose goals are deeply antidemocratic and destructive. At the very least such
movements may be particularistic and pursue the benefit of their own leaders at
the expense of the larger public interest.

For instance, the so-called Yellow Shirt movement in Thailand has, since
2005, pursued multiple, primarily nonviolent campaigns for power, first against
Prime Minister Thaksin Shinawatra and later against various iterations of his
movement. These movements have relied on tools easily recognizable to scholars and practitioners of nonviolent action, locatable in Gene Sharp's (1973)
magisterial listing of 198 tactics of nonviolent action. They have occupied
buildings, staged marches, and organized strikes to great effect. Since 2006 the
Yellow Shirts have ousted three governments and become a major force in Thai
politics. Yet it is difficult to argue that their largely nonviolent repertoire has
been a positive force in Thailand. Their constant move to the streets to oust
rivals from the Red Shirt movement has been deeply destructive to the Thai
economy, and ultimately to the Thai political system. The constant back and
forth of nonviolent action from 2006 to 2014 ultimately resulted in a lack of
popular faith in democracy that supported a successful military coup in 2014
that has moved Thailand from an increasingly robust democracy to a military
dictatorship.[18]

Not just violence but also forms of nonviolent action, when pursued for maximalist politics, are deeply problematic and destabilizing to democratic transitions. One kind of nonviolent action that is a strong indicator of maximalism is
electoral boycotts. An electoral boycott is certainly a form of nonviolent action
and justified in certain circumstances, yet in the main it is a form of action that
indicates an unwillingness to play by democratic rules. Boycotting an election
that one anticipates not being able to win shows a lack of faith in the democratic
process and indicates that nonviolent action is being directed not toward improving democracy but rather toward undermining it for particularistic ends. No electoral system is perfect; even in highly developed nations such as the United States
the rules of the electoral game are often stacked in favor of one party or another.
In some cases the stacking of the deck may be so extreme that there is simply
no credible way that an opposition party interested in promoting democracy
can in good conscience give even the slightest legitimacy to the process. Yet if
such extreme circumstances do not appear to hold and yet widespread electoral
boycotts occur, this says less about the nature of the system and more about the
nature of the actors. These actors are afraid of electoral results and seek to avoid
humiliation and play for power not on the field of democratic institutions but
rather in the streets, where their inferior numbers may nonetheless be employed
with greater strategic effect than at the ballot box.

Fortunately, several data sources exist that meld these twin concerns of rhetoric and action. The Varieties of Democracy data set (Coppedge et al., 2018), for instance, measures the degree to which antisystem movements are present in the political system. This blends the idea that such rhetoric is employed in political discourse with the idea that it is carried out on the streets.

The maximalism factor is constituted using some variables from V-Dem as well as one from the Polity IV data set, one of the most long-standing and well-respected datasets on democratic institutions (Marshall, Gurr, & Jaggers, 2016). Three measures relate to elections. The first measures the degree to which political actors engage in electoral boycotts.[19] The second measures the degree to which electoral results are accepted.[20] The third measures the degree to which antisystem movements are present in the political system, defined as "any movement—peaceful or armed—that is based in the country (not abroad) and is organized in opposition to the current political system" (Coppedge et al., 2017, p. 247).[21] Such as movement has original values that range from "practically non-existent" to "a very high level of anti-system movement activity, posing a real and present threat to the regime" (p. 247).

I also include a measure from Polity IV based on their "regulation of participation," or *parreg,* variable. One level of this variable captures whether politics is "sectarian," that is, according to the Polity IV codebook, a political system wherein "political demands are characterized by incompatible interests and intransigent posturing among multiple identity groups and oscillate more or less regularly between intense factionalism and government favoritism" (Marshall, Gurr, & Jaggers, 2016, p. 26). This description closely approximates a system characterized by maximalism, so I created a binary transformation of the *parreg* variable capturing whether a country was sectarian in a year. As with the mobilization factor, principal factor analysis of these indicators generated only a single factor with an eigenvalue greater than 1, indicating that a single underlying dimension explains their covariation.

Finally, due to the structural arguments discussed in the previous chapter, it is insufficient to only put these behavioral patterns into a regression model and see whether their relationship with the polyarchy score is significant. I must show that these behavioral patterns are a meaningful addition to the preexisting structural model of democratization. Therefore it is important to include structural variables not only to control for them but to show the explanatory impact of these variables over and above the explanatory power of a structural model.

The first key aspect of the structural model is modernization. I follow Jan Teorell's (2010) lead in building a single factor that captures the underlying dimension of modernization through several empirical indicators.[22] I also account for two important international influences on democratization: regional diffusion and linkage with the West. My specific measures for these influences are the percentage of democracies in a country's region, the annual flow of exports and imports between the country and the West, and a country's degree of connectedness to Western-dominated international nongovernmental organizations (INGOs).[23]

Finally, I control for the level of democracy in the regime that preceded the transition. This is important to control for because, as with almost any political phenomenon, the best predictor of the future value is almost always the past value. Past democratic experience has been shown to be a significant predictor of the likelihood of democratization in other research (Teorell, 2010). I use the average polyarchy score over the five years preceding the transition as my primary operationalization of the past level of democracy.

Methodologists caution against "garbage can" or "kitchen sink" regression models in which every potential confounder is "thrown in" to see what happens (Achen, 2002, 2005; Clarke, 2005). Yet in a complex phenomenon like democratization it is critical to capture as much of the variation as possible. The variables selected here capture the most distinctive and influential structural explanations of democratization, and so in my primary tests they are the only control variables included. However, to show that my results are not spurious to some influential omitted variable, I also run many additional models with additional control variables. Table 2.1 includes the full list of potential confounding variables.[24]

Establishing causality in any observational statistical study is difficult. Absent experimental conditions, any finding may be suspect. Even meeting all the traditional measures of statistical significance, effect size, and model fit is subject to concerns of data validity and massaged results. The single reported highly significant statistical result means little if it is merely the visible tip of an iceberg of negative findings. This is the phenomenon of p-hacking, something increasingly recognized as a problem in many different scientific fields (Head, Holman, Lanfear, Kahn, & Jennions, 2015; Ioannidis, 2005). Observational studies are particularly vulnerable to p-hacking since the population one examines, the parameters for defining independent and dependent variables, and the set of potential confounders included in the model are all dependent on the researcher's choices (Bruns & Ioannidis, 2016).

I address the problem of p-hacking by using several different statistical models to establish the plausibility of my approach and transparently presenting the results of all these varied tests, either in this chapter or in the appendix. With each positive result it becomes less and less plausible to argue that my findings are the result of p-hacking or statistical artifacts from the data. I am also transparent about statistical tests that do not generate positive results, providing the skeptical reader with the full spectrum of results run from many different kinds of models

Table 2.1 Control Variable Operationalization and Sources

Primary Controls

Variable	Operationalization	Data Sources
Modernization	GDP per capita, infant mortality, urbanization, education	V-Dem
Democratic Neighbors	Percentage of democracies in country's region	Haber and Menaldo (2011)
Western Linkage	Imports and exports to Western countries divided by GDP, INGO network centrality	IMF DoT data, Paxton et al. (2015) INCS scores
Previous Democracy	Polyarchy score average from five years before transition	V-Dem

Secondary Controls

Geographic Area	Land area in square kilometers (logged)	Haber and Menaldo (2011)
Inequality	Gini coefficient	World Income Inequality Database
Muslim Population	Percentage of Muslims	Maoz and Henderson (2013)
Oil and Gas Dependence	Annual oil and gas revenue	Haber and Menaldo (2011)
British Colonialism	Binary measure of past British colonialism	ICOW Colonial History data set

and with different tweaks on the operationalization of my study population and model variables.

The first type of model I use is OLS linear regression. These models measure the effects of maximalism and mobilization during a CRT on the level of democracy at the conclusion of the transition. I run OLS models with a variety of different controls and the different operationalizations of my variables discussed in this chapter. The second set of tests are logistic regression models. These models use the Geddes data set's definition of democracy and measure whether a country was democratic the year after its transition period ended.[25] These two sets of tests are the core of my analysis as they most directly test the core theoretical setup of my question: What is the shape of the regime that comes into power following a CRT?[26]

I also perform tests using propensity score matching, reporting the average treatment effect on the treated in my tests of the impact of civil resistance on posttransition democracy. For my tests of the patterns of transitional behavior I use Bia and Mattei's (2008) extension of dose-response function estimation using a generalized propensity score as developed by Hirano and Imbens (2004) since my independent variables are continuous.[27]

For many of my variables missing data is a major issue. Many of these transitions have occurred in developing countries where data for several of my variables is infrequently collected. This means that, for models that include the full suite of control variables, the number of observations that can be employed drops precipitously, potentially biasing the coefficients. To address this problem, I use the Amelia II multiple imputation algorithm developed by James Honaker and his coauthors (2011). Amelia II uses the data present in an incomplete time-series cross-sectional data set and creates multiple "complete" data sets with all the missing data filled in.[28] I then perform tests on each of the imputed data sets and average the coefficients, standard errors, and p-values across tests. Amelia II is an increasingly common tool employed by social scientists to address missing data problems (Hill, 2010; Houle, 2009; Ross, 2006).

In the next section I describe the data using descriptive statistics for my main independent, dependent, and control variables before reporting the results of my statistical testing.

Describing the Data and Testing the Effects of Civil Resistance

Table 2.2 contains summary statistics on all the variables used in the subsequent analysis, including values in the original data set and the average values from the imputed data sets after the Amelia procedure.[29] As I described earlier, this population of CRTs begins in 1945, at the end of World War II. The first case in the data is the overthrow of Jorge Ubico in Guatemala, and the last cases are the Arab Spring revolutions in Egypt, Tunisia, and Yemen in 2011. There is a high degree of temporal and geographic dispersion across cases, with examples of anticolonial struggles, campaigns against military juntas, single-party regimes, and personalistic tinpot dictators.

As a shrewd scholar of democratization would expect, the cases cluster temporally and geographically. Most cases in the 1950s and 1960s are decolonization struggles in Africa. In the 1980s there is a wave of movements in Latin America, and in 1989 the breakdown of the communist bloc in Eastern Europe and the Soviet Union make up the single largest wave of cases. There is a second African wave in the 1990s, then the handful of "Color Revolutions" in the early 2000s, and finally the Arab Spring in 2011.

Table 2.2 Summary Statistics

Variable	N	Mean	Std. Dev.	Min.	Max.
Polyarchy Score	314	0.3476	0.227	0.0235	0.9017
Democratic Regime	289	0.4187	0.4942	0	1
Civil Resistance Transition	315	0.2444	0.4304	0	1
Mobilization	315	0.1158	0.7215	−1.938	1.7762
Maximalism	315	0.0724	0.8262	−1.6252	3.8012
Modernization	315	−0.278	0.8773	−2.4596	1.8841
Democratic Neighbors	315	0.2066	0.1987	0	1
INCS Score	315	0.2174	0.199	−0.1172	0.8461
Trade Linkage	315	0.0194	0.1284	−0.8855	1.7337
Old Regime Polyarchy	315	0.2241	0.1281	−0.0127	0.6816
Area (logged)	315	12.2894	1.6671	5.6971	16.6546
Muslim Population	314	0.3077	0.3835	0	1
Gini Coefficient	294	0.4349	0.2276	0	1
Oil Revenue (logged)	266	1.2776	2.1636	0	9.621
British Colonialism	315	0.2444	0.4304	0	1
Prior Military Regime	315	0.1778	0.3829	0	1

As with the phenomenon of large civil resistance campaigns more broadly, there is a marked increase in cases over time. The increase peaks in the 1990s and declines thereafter. As Erica Chenoweth (2015) has shown, while the frequency of nonviolent resistance campaigns has continued to increase in the first two decades of the 21st century, their success rates have declined from previous peaks. I would argue that it is therefore unsurprising that we should find a declining number of regime changes following civil resistance campaigns after the year 2000.

By definition, as I stated earlier, all these cases took place in nondemocracies. Therefore the peak level of polyarchy prior to the transition is necessarily circumscribed. Taking this into account, the mean level of polyarchy is 0.23, and the median slightly smaller. In other words, the regimes in which civil resistance campaigns are succeeding in sparking regime change are highly undemocratic.

CRTs have a strong positive effect on a country's level of democracy. In the year following the end of a CRT the average level of polyarchy jumps to 0.55, a significant increase considering the variable's range. However, this is a mean level short of a well-functioning democracy, or even a democracy at all. There is also significant variation in these scores, with the standard deviation roughly 0.22.

Table 2.3 Cross-Tabulation of Transitional Endpoint Polyarchy in CRTs and
Non-CRTs

	N	Mean	Std. Dev.	Min.	Max.
Non-CRTs	244	0.2821	0.1866	0.0235	0.8836
CRTs	78	0.5493	0.2225	0.1179	0.9017

Democratization after civil resistance is clearly a phenomenon with significant variation.

A simple cross-tabulation of mean polyarchy scores at transitional endpoints (displayed in Table 2.3) shows a strong positive effect on the level of polyarchy from a transition being initiated by nonviolent resistance. In all the incidents of authoritarian regime failure recorded by Geddes and her coauthors (2014) that are not CRTs, the average level of polyarchy at the end of the regime transition is around 0.29, well in the undemocratic range, validating the finding that most authoritarian regime breakdowns result in a new nondemocratic regime, not in democracy.

Figure 2.4 breaks down these averages to show the range of outcomes of CRTs and non-CRTs. Over 50% of non-CRTs end with very autocratic regimes in place, while fewer than 20% end in even a minimal democracy.[30] In contrast, over 60% of CRTs end up as at least slightly democratic, and only 13% end as very autocratic.

The two types of transitions have some important contextual differences. CRTs have a slightly higher level of modernization and more democratic neighbors. Their level of connection to the West is not significantly different, nor is their past level of democracy. In fact CRTs tend to occur in slightly less democratic contexts. Thus their more democratic outcomes do not appear to be a result of their simply arising in more democratic and open contexts.

What does the relationship between civil resistance and democratization look like in a statistical model appropriately controlling for these differences in context? First, I test the effect of a transition being initiated by civil resistance on the polyarchy score in the year after the end of the transition. Table 2.4 reports the results of this test in Model 1. The indicator of a civil resistance transition is highly significant, with an effect size of roughly 0.18, large considering that the polyarchy score only ranges from 0 to 1.[31] For comparison, the effect of civil resistance is roughly equivalent to having a country increase the proportion of its democratic neighbors by 82%. Including the CRT measure also increases the model's r^2 by 19% over the structural model, indicating increased explanatory

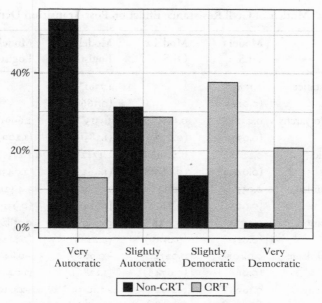

40%

20%

0%

| Very Autocratic | Slightly Autocratic | Slightly Democratic | Very Democratic |

■ Non-CRT ▨ CRT

FIGURE 2.4 Distribution of End-of-Transition Polyarchy Scores in CRTs and Non-CRTs

power and supporting my contention that civil resistance is not simply a direct consequence of structural factors.[32]

Indeed for the most part the structural factors have inconsistent effects across models. Only the measure of democratic neighbors is consistently significant. The INCS measure, the modernization factor, and the previous level of polyarchy all keep the same sign but lose significance when moving from one model to another. The trade linkage measure is the most inconsistent, never reaching significance and switching signs between the linear models and the logistic models.

The graph on the left side of Figure 2.5 plots the marginal effect of civil resistance transitions on the level of democracy with all the control variables held at their means. CRTs also have a strong effect on countries crossing the democratic threshold. Model 3 in Table 2.4 is a logistic regression model of whether a country was democratic in the year after the end of its transition. Initiating a transition through civil resistance significantly increased the odds of this being the case relative to other kinds of transitions and controlling for the major explanations of democratization. The graph on the right side of Figure 2.5 plots the effects of civil resistance transitions on the likelihood of passing the democratic threshold, as before with all control variables held at their means.

Table 2.4 Models of Civil Resistance Effect on Post-Transition Democracy

	Model 1 OLS	Model 2 OLS	Model 3 Logistic	Model 4 Logistic
Civil Resistance	0.1785***		1.7381***	
Transition	(0.0225)		(0.3666)	
Previous Polyarchy	0.4323***	0.3835***	3.3315**	2.6991*
Level	(0.07)	(0.077)	(1.2831)	(1.209)
Democratic	0.2208***	0.2291***	2.1742*	2.2355*
Neighbors	(0.0494)	(0.0542)	(1.0627)	(1.0431)
Western Linkage	0.057	0.1781**	2.7092**	3.4426***
(INGOs)	(0.0574)	(0.0622)	(1.0163)	(0.9319)
Modernization	0.0784***	0.0948***	0.2159	0.3582
	(0.0132)	(0.0149)	(0.2245)	(0.2128)
Western Linkage	0.0408	0.0272	−0.9087	−0.8485
(Trade)	(0.0684)	(0.0746)	(1.2286)	(1.0458)
Constant	0.1698***	0.2012***	−2.4739***	−2.0398***
	(0.0251)	(0.0281)	(0.4842)	(0.4499)
N	315	315	289	289
R2/AUC	0.5603	0.4684	0.8259	0.7831

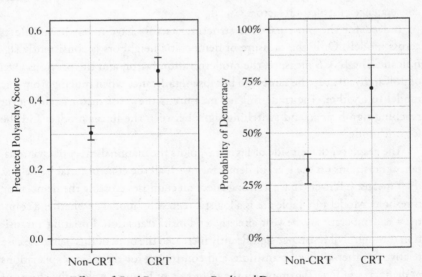

FIGURE 2.5 Effects of Civil Resistance on Predicted Democracy

I use propensity score matching to control for the potential that the higher rates of democracy in CRTs are being explained by a greater propensity for democracy in the population of CRTs. Matching procedures attempt to capture the impact of a factor (typically referred to as the "treatment") by compiling a sample where treated and control groups are as comparable as possible. After assembling the balanced samples, the researcher can then simply measure the difference between the average values of the treated and untreated groups, commonly referred to as the average treatment effect on the treated (ATT). I matched transitions using the same set of control variables included in my earlier models: modernization, trade linkage, INGO network centrality, the percentage of democratic neighbors, and the lagged polyarchy score. I use Diamond and Sekhon's (2013) genetic matching algorithm to produce the matched samples.[33] Far from eliminating the effects of civil resistance on posttransition democracy, the matching procedure suggests that the standard OLS models are understating the effect of civil resistance on posttransition democracy. The ATT of the CRT variable averages roughly 0.2 across the five Amelia imputations, slightly larger than the estimated effect in the OLS models, with the lowest value of a 95% confidence interval well above zero.

This section's findings are unsurprising, considering the large number of studies that have previously found a positive and significant relationship between nonviolent resistance and democratization. Yet they further bolster our confidence in the importance of nonviolent resistance in leading to democratization by increasing the methodological rigor applied to testing the connection between nonviolent resistance and democratization. They also highlight that distinguishing transitions based on the presence or absence of nonviolent resistance is a meaningful way of disaggregating democratic transitions, and they speak to the importance of focusing on nonviolent resistance to understand democratization.

Yet they also further highlight the importance of this book's central puzzle. If indeed nonviolent resistance has such a strong democratizing effect, why does this effect sometimes not obtain? How can we systematically understand when CRTs will end in democracy and when they will not? To answer that I turn to testing the core argument of this book: the positive effects of transitional mobilization and the negative effects of transitional maximalism.

Testing the Challenges of Civil Resistance Transitions

I expect that higher levels of mobilization and lower levels of maximalism will have two main effects. First, they will move countries closer to the democratic ideal. The patterns of behavior in response to each challenge will push a country's political system closer to or farther away from a system that is equally responsive to all its citizens. In some cases this means that countries will approach close to Dahl's democratic ideal. In others it means that formerly autocratic countries will move into slightly more representative or partially democratic orders. Yet on average the shifts will be more toward democracy.

Second, a related but distinct effect will be a greater likelihood of moving across Schumpeter's democratic threshold, moving from a nondemocratic to a democratic regime. For some countries this implies only a minor shift, say, in moving from unfair to fair elections. For others it implies large changes in institutions, moving from highly authoritarian systems to at least minimally democratic ones.

Model 9 in Table 2.5 presents the primary test of these relationships. As the model shows, higher scores on the mobilization factor and lower scores on the radicalization factor are highly significant predictors of increased levels of democracy. In addition, including these factors significantly increases model fit, meaning the model is more accurately capturing the real patterns in the data. This is evidenced by the significantly increased r^2 in Model 9—which

Table 2.5 Main Tests of Transitional Challenges on EOT Democracy

	Model 9 OLS	Model 10 OLS	Model 11 Logistic	Model 12 Logistic
Maximalism	−0.0683**		−1.0661*	
	(0.021)		(0.5322)	
Mobilization	0.1795***		3.2192**	
	(0.0285)		(1.0114)	
Modernization	0.0743**	0.1355***	−1.0259	0.0343
	(0.0237)	(0.028)	(0.6743)	(0.4595)
Democratic Neighbors	0.243**	0.1518	2.9506	1.5749
	(0.0803)	(0.1058)	(2.9161)	(2.5307)
INCS Score	−0.0072	0.0659	2.5357	2.9687
	(0.0749)	(0.0937)	(2.1188)	(1.7223)
Trade Linkage	0.1167	0.3549	−3.2521	1.0316
	(0.193)	(0.2478)	(5.4041)	(4.6625)
Previous Polyarchy Level	−0.1689	0.0612	−1.4826	1.9466
	(0.121)	(0.1487)	(3.6928)	(2.7549)
Constant	0.382***	0.4323***	−0.9334	−0.4148
	(0.0413)	(0.0533)	(1.2572)	(0.9587)
N	78	78	78	78
r2/AUC	0.6898	0.4642	0.8875	0.7198

* $p < 0.05$, ** $p < 0.01$, *** $p < 0.001$

includes the mobilization and maximalism variables—over Model 10, which does not.

In the logistic regression model (Model 11) maximalism and mobilization are the only statistically significant predictors of democracy at transition's end. This speaks to the unpredictability of civil resistance transitions, as discussed in the previous chapter. When so many new actors have entered the political arena, as is typical in CRTs, the impact of structural factors is less direct and their predictive capacity decreases.

What is the real impact of these transitional challenges? Figure 2.6 shows the predicted effects of moving from one end of the mobilization and maximalism factors to the other with all other variables held at their means. Moving from one extreme of the variable to the other predicts sizable differences in polyarchy at the end of transition. In both cases, this is roughly a difference in polyarchy score of 0.4. Considering the polyarchy score only ranges from 0 to 1 this difference is important. To give a sense of how important, this is roughly the difference in the level of democracy in 2016 between Pakistan and Iceland.

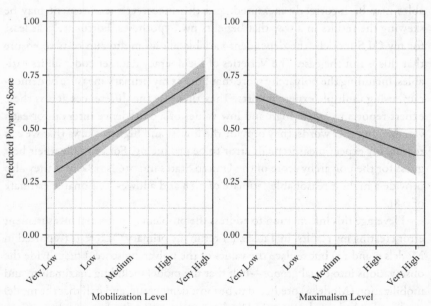

FIGURE 2.6 Predicted Levels of Democracy across Mobilization and Maximalism Scores

Ensuring Robust Results

How confident can we be in these results? Because my arguments related to mobilization and maximalism are new, I submit them to closer scrutiny than the tests of the impact of nonviolent resistance alone. In this section I address the potential statistical problems, while in the subsequent case study chapters I examine whether this statistical relationship holds true when one looks at the dynamics of specific cases.

The first potential statistical problem is multicollinearity. Mobilization and maximalism may simply covary closely with one of the structural factors also present in the model. I examined two standard measures to see whether this could be a problem: the variance inflation factor (VIF) and the condition number. VIFs for all the variables are well below the standard rule of thumb of a VIF of 10 for problematic multicollinearity. As with the VIF, the condition numbers are also well below standard rules of thumb for problematic multicollinearity.[34]

When multicollinearity is present to a significant degree in a data set, the effect is an increase in standard error size, making it more difficult to reject the null hypothesis for any one variable. Hence multicollinearity is much more likely to generate false negatives than false positives. The fact that both the mobilization and maximalism variables and several of the structural variables are significant suggests multicollinearity is not affecting the results.

Another potential problem is measurement error. One or more of the variables may be incorrectly measured, and this incorrect measurement may be skewing the results in a way that benefits my hypotheses. Fortunately, at least for my OLS models, the dependent variable allows me to run tests to ensure that this is not the case. The Varieties of Democracy data set codes all its variables, including the polyarchy score that I use as my primary measure of democracy, using multiple expert reports. They then use the differences across these expert reports to create high and low values of a confidence interval for each variable. In other words, they provide the lowest and highest skews that we can reasonably expect measurement error to be producing. For example, their best guess for the polyarchy score of the United States in 2016 is 0.84. But they also provide a highest reasonable estimate of 0.88 and a lowest reasonable estimate of 0.81.

I leverage this information to address the problem of potential measurement error creating my results. In Table 2.6 I rerun my primary OLS tests (reported in Models 9 and 10) but replace the values of the polyarchy score. I first divide the observations into equal groups—half that the model including maximalism and mobilization (Model 9) predicted to be most democratic, and half that the model predicted to be least democratic. For the group predicted to be most democratic,

Table 2.6 Hard Test Models

	Model 13 OLS	Model 14 OLS
Maximalism	−0.0516**	
	(0.0191)	
Mobilization	0.1549***	
	(0.0265)	
Modernization	0.0678**	0.1182***
	(0.0216)	(0.0243)
Democratic Neighbors	0.2011**	0.1277
	(0.0723)	(0.0912)
INCS Score	−0.0449	0.0142
	(0.0659)	(0.0799)
Trade Linkage	0.0399	0.2717
	(0.1777)	(0.2135)
Previous Polyarchy Level	−0.1403	0.0564
	(0.1086)	(0.1308)
Constant	0.4169***	0.4566***
	(0.0376)	(0.0463)
N	78	78
r2	0.647	0.4393

$*p < 0.05, **p < 0.01, ***p < 0.001$

I replace the polyarchy score with the lowest possible estimate from V-Dem. For the group predicted to be least democratic, I replace the polyarchy score with the highest possible estimate from V-Dem. I then run the model again with these new estimates of the polyarchy score as my dependent variable.

The effect of this change is to make the bounds of measurement error work as hard against me as reasonable. I am, in effect, assuming that for all 78 CRTs the experts at V-Dem coded the polyarchy score in a way that skewed toward my hypothesis, and correcting for that skew by making it as hard as possible for my hypothesized relationships to still hold true.

Even having imposed this heavy penalty, the relationship between my mobilization and maximalism and the level of polyarchy at the conclusion of the transition remains robust. Both mobilization and maximalism are still highly significant and with coefficients of the expected signs. Mobilization has a positive effect on end-of-transition (EOT) democracy and maximalism has a negative effect. They both also still add to the r^2 of the structural model.

For the logistic regression models I am unable to use the Geddes data—my source in my primary tests—in the same way because it does not provide higher and lower standards for crossing the democratic threshold. Instead I estimate how many cases the Geddes data would have to be incorrectly coding as democracies for my results to lose significance.

To do this, I compared the Geddes data with the EOT polyarchy scores for the 78 CRTs. The Geddes data codes 61 of the 78 CRTs as ending in democracy. Some of these 61 cases have very high polyarchy scores, as one would expect, but many have quite low scores. It is reasonable to assume that those cases that are most likely to be coded in error are cases in which the Geddes data and the polyarchy score disagree. In other words, if the Geddes data codes a country as a democracy but the country's polyarchy score is extremely low, we should treat those cases with more suspicion. If both data sources agree that a country was democratic, we may be more confident that it was indeed a democracy.

Informed by this assumption, I tested the sensitivity of maximalism and mobilization's effect on the likelihood of crossing the democratic threshold by rerunning the logistic regression model with the mobilization and maximalism factors (Model 11) several additional times. Each time, I changed the country coded as democratic by the Geddes data with the lowest polyarchy score as nondemocratic. Figure 2.7 shows the results for both the mobilization and maximalism factors. The figure's x axis is the number of countries artificially switched from democratic to nondemocratic. The y axis is the p-value of either the mobilization or maximalism variable in a model with these artificial switches. The horizontal line is the standard $p < 0.05$ boundary for statistical significance.

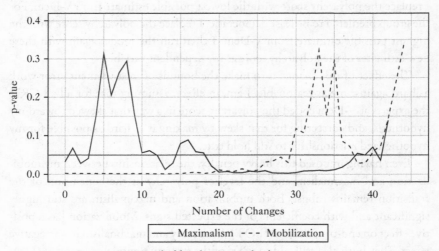

FIGURE 2.7 Democracy Threshold Robustness Check

The mobilization variable is extremely robust, remaining above conventional standards of statistical significance until 29 changes. In other words, the Geddes data would have to be incorrectly coding 30 nondemocracies as democracies for the mobilization variable to lose statistical significance. Fifty percent of the countries the Geddes data codes as democratic would have to be nondemocratic for the mobilization variable to not significantly predict EOT democracy. The maximalism variable is less robust. A single incorrect coding causes it to lose statistical significance, although it regains significance at higher numbers of changes. After 40 changes, neither variable ever regains statistical significance.

Based on these two tests, we may confidently reject the notion that measurement error explains the relationship between the transitional challenges and democracy at the end of the transition. For both the polyarchy score and the binary Geddes measure, the amount of error would have to be well outside the realm of reasonable plausibility to undermine the significance of my results.

Another potential problem with these results could be that the cases with high levels of mobilization and low levels of maximalism are systematically different from other cases in ways that we cannot directly observe or that aren't accounted for by including control variables in a model. To address this problem, as with the tests of the impact of nonviolent resistance relative to other modes of transition, I relied on matching procedures to balance my sample between cases that fit my hypotheses well and those that do not.[35]

The predictions of matched models are very close to those generated by the main linear regression models. Indeed the analysis after matching suggests that the linear models are understating the positive effects of mobilization and negative effects of maximalism. The linear model predicted differences of around 0.4 in the polyarchy score when moving from one end of the mobilization or maximalism variables to the other. The matched model predicts a difference of around 0.5 for the mobilization variable and nearly 0.6 for the maximalism variable.

The findings could be statistical artifacts of my modeling choices, such as the use of multiple imputation to deal with missing data or the control variables I included. However, this objection is not borne out in the data. The results are almost identical when run on unimputed data, though there is some slight variation due to the number of observations dropped due to missingness. The coefficients for mobilization and maximalism also remain significant and of a similar size when included in a model containing all the potential confounders described earlier, as well as a version of this model run through a stepwise deletion process, and other robustness checks as well.[36]

Having met these stringent tests, we may confidently say that mobilization and maximalism during civil resistance transitions have strong, significant, and consistent relationships with posttransition democracy.

Summary

In this chapter I have quantitatively tested both the core contention that civil resistance pushes transitions toward democracy and the impact of mobilization and maximalism on the levels of democracy at the conclusion of the transition, as well as the likelihood of crossing the democratic threshold. The data strongly support CRT's positive effect on democratization. Civil resistance at a transition's initiation strongly pushes the transition toward democracy, controlling for plausible alternative explanations. This validates the current literature on civil resistance and democratization, providing one of the most rigorous tests of this relationship currently performed. Civil resistance initiating a transition increases a country's polyarchy score at the end of the transition by 0.17, or 17% of the range of the polyarchy score.

What does this difference amount to? Are regimes separated by 0.17 on the polyarchy score really that different? One way of answering this question is to look at real regimes that have this difference. Among democracies in 2018, this difference is roughly equivalent to the difference between Sweden (0.903) and Senegal (0.833). Among nondemocracies, it is roughly the difference in polyarchy score between Syria (0.152) and Zimbabwe (0.329). The effect is not the difference between the highest and lowest extremes of democracy and dictatorship. Nevertheless a quick look at the differences in the politics between the countries just mentioned will immediately confirm its substantive importance.

In 2018 the Syrian government, "one of the world's most repressive regimes" (Freedom House, 2019b), was engaged in systematic violence against its own people, including the use of barrel bombs and targeting of humanitarian aid. Legal political opposition was nonexistent. In Zimbabwe, by contrast, 2018 saw a presidential election in which the opposition was largely able to campaign freely and received nearly 50% of the vote (Magaisa, 2019). The country was still heavily authoritarian, and the regime used the instruments of the state to repress opposition and maintain its position of power (Beardsworth, Cheeseman, & Tinhu, 2019), but the level of protection for basic civil and political freedoms was far from the devastating violence of Syria. Clearly regimes this far apart are meaningfully different.

Civil resistance is not the only factor that significantly affects a country's level of posttransition democracy. The country's level of modernization, democratic history, and neighborhood are all robust predictors of its future level of democracy. Measures of Western linkage are less robust, significantly predicting democracy in some models but not in others. Yet while some of these structural factors matter, their predictive accuracy and model fit is substantively improved by adding civil resistance to the picture.

Within civil resistance transitions there is strong evidence to support the impact of both of my theorized patterns of behavior. High levels of public mobilization and low levels of maximalism during the transition exert a strong and consistent effect on the level of democracy at the end of the transition, and a slightly less robust but still substantive impact on the likelihood of crossing the democratic threshold.

This relationship maintains significance when run through many different tests to ensure its robustness, in particular when run through tests that address the potential for measurement error and when addressing underlying differences in these cases with the dose-response model.

What is the substantive importance of these patterns of behavior? Nonviolent resistance increases the predicted polyarchy score by roughly 0.17 over a transition with no nonviolent resistance. Reducing transitional mobilization and increasing maximalism in a CRT by 1 standard deviation each reduces the predicted polyarchy score by 0.19. In other words, even relatively low levels of variation in these transitional challenges can completely wipe out the democratizing advantage of civil resistance. The democratic trajectory of civil resistance transitions depends critically on successful navigation through these challenges.

Or does it? So far I have shown only that there is a robust statistical correlation between the successful resolution of these challenges and more democracy. It remains to be seen whether this statistical correlation matches the processes we observe in specific countries. It may be that mobilization and maximalism do not function at all in the way I have described, or that what I have measured here is a proxy for some other empirical process. In the following chapters I turn from statistical analysis to the careful examination of particular cases.

Introduction to Case Study Chapters

The Case Selection Process

The three chapters that follow present case studies of political dynamics in transitions following civil resistance movements. The goal of these chapters is not to perform a strict comparison to tease out causal impact but rather to examine the dynamics of the two transitional challenges of mobilization and maximalism in three specific environments. Having shown that a quantitative correlation exists between these challenges and posttransition democracy, do we observe that relationship in actual cases? What are the observable impacts of each challenge in specific historical cases? In other words, through the case studies I am seeking not to establish a causal effect but to examine a set of causal mechanisms (Gerring, 2004).

I selected the cases following a nested analysis research design (Lieberman, 2005). Quantitative and qualitative analysis have different strengths, and attempting to apply a single logic of inference to both is not appropriate (McKeown, 2004). Instead of treating qualitative analysis as statistics with an insufficient number of cases, or quantitative analysis as comparative case study research with insufficient time to examine each case in depth, scholars should draw on what each of these approaches can offer to the other (Munck & Snyder, 2007). As Sidney Tarrow (2004, p. 180) suggests, researchers should seek to leverage the strength of both forms of analysis in order to "triangulate" real causal relationships from different analytical perspectives. Nested analysis is one way of achieving this triangulation.[1]

In a nested analysis the research process follows these steps. First, generate a theoretically informed model of the relationship that you wish to explain. Second, perform a statistical analysis to examine the robustness of that theoretical model. If the model proves to be robust, then select cases that are well-predicted by the model for intensive case study analysis ("model-testing small-*n* analysis"). The purpose of this analysis is to show that "the start, end, and *intermediate* steps of the model . . . explain the behavior of real world actors" (Lieberman, 2005, p. 442). If the case studies generally confirm the model's proposed causal mechanisms, then you may conclude their analysis and make a convincing argument that their hypotheses have been supported. If either the statistical or the case study analysis fails to produce robust results, return to an earlier step in the process and continue to do so recursively until either finding satisfactory results or determining that your initial theoretical insight was flawed.

In addition to the criterion that cases in model-testing small-n analysis be well-predicted by the model, scholars should select cases that show a wide degree of variation in the model's independent variables. This shows that the model's mechanisms operate in many different contexts (Lieberman, 2005, p. 444). For this analysis, this criterion meant selecting cases wherein mobilization and maximalism varied.

In addition to predicting general levels of democracy, my theory offers specific predictions about the regimes that follow the different constellations of values on my independent variables: "fractious semi-democracy" through high mobilization and high maximalism and "elite semi-democracy" through low mobilization and low maximalism. I was unable to statistically test whether this implication of my theory was correct because both these categories should end up with similar polyarchy scores. The case studies allow me to examine this implication now. If the cases exhibit the characteristics of these regime subtypes, that is good evidence not just for the link between high mobilization, low maximalism, and democracy overall but for the specific transitional pathways leading from these challenges to specific forms of politics.

I also selected cases that varied widely in structural factors that are not built into my model but would plausibly bound the external validity of my theory. So, for instance, I selected cases that came from different regions of the world, occurred in different time periods, and had radically different prior regime types.

Several potential cases in the 78 CRTs from the previous chapter fit these criteria. After identifying cases that were well-predicted by the theory, I then narrowed down the number of possible cases based on the feasibility of conducting in-depth fieldwork, as well as the length of time that had elapsed since the transition in question. I was interested in cases that had occurred in the recent past to maximize the number of firsthand participants in the transition that I would be able to interview.

I selected three recent cases to illustrate three out of the four endpoints described in Chapter 1: the Second People's Movement in Nepal in 2006 as an example of the path to fractious semi-democracy, the Movement for Multiparty Democracy in Zambia as an example of the path to elite semi-democracy, and the Diretas Ja movement against military rule in Brazil as an example of the path to democracy.

I had both practical and theoretical reasons for omitting a case study on the path from nonviolent resistance to full-fledged authoritarian resurgence.. Practically speaking, my qualitative research process—which I describe in detail in the following pages—involved in-depth interviews with activists and key decision-makers in the nonviolent resistance movement and subsequent transition. Since I was looking at cases of transition in the recent past (and thus an authoritarian regime that had resulted from such a transition was likely to still be in place), I was concerned about my ability to ensure my safety and that of my potential interviewees in a more repressive autocracy.[2] From a theoretical perspective, as the summary statistics in Chapter 2 show, relatively few civil resistance transitions end in highly repressive autocracies. Almost all the nondemocratic cases end as some form of hybrid regime. Thus to gain analytical leverage into the cases that explain why nonviolent resistance sometimes does not lead to democracy it made the most sense to focus on hybrid regimes.

These case studies are not intended to establish a causal relationship through a formal "most different case selection" research design since such an analysis would require similar values on the dependent variable and on a single independent variable (Mill, 1967; Przeworski & Tuene, 1970). The external validity of my argument comes from the statistical analysis performed in Chapter 2. Instead the logic of choosing cases that differ from one another so radically is to demonstrate that the model's internal validity is not limited to an easily identifiable subcategory of cases.

The Qualitative Research Process

The first step in each case study was an exhaustive examination of the existing secondary literature on the cases, as well as any available primary sources. In the case of Brazil this examination provided much of the necessary content for examining the core question of whether mobilization and maximalism indeed had their expected impact. Much has been written about the Brazilian transition, and while few have directly examined the questions of this book, many of the insights from the existing literature were invaluable in tracing the impacts of these challenges through the transition process.

For Nepal, and particularly for Zambia, the secondary literature was much sparser. Because of this sparseness, I built on my knowledge of the cases from the secondary literature with fieldwork in each country to serve as the core of my analysis. For the fieldwork I interviewed key decision-makers during both the civil resistance movement that sparked the transition and the transition itself. I also interviewed journalists, academics, and other close observers of the events surrounding the transition. I conducted a total of 128 interviews over roughly three months of fieldwork.

In the total population of interviewees I sought to cross all of the relevant political and social cleavages so as to triangulate as complete a picture of the dynamics of the transition as possible (Berry, 2002; Leech, 2002). For instance, in Nepal I conducted interviews with leaders from all the major parties: the Nepali Congress, the Communist Party of Nepal (United Marxist-Leninist; CPN-UML), the Communist Party of Nepal (Maoist Center; CPN-MC), parties representing the Madhesi community from southern Nepal, and members of the monarchical government under former King Gyanendra. I identified potential interviewees through an in-depth reading of the secondary literature on the case prior to beginning fieldwork, consultation with leading experts on the country's history and politics, and partnerships with local NGOs that shared names and contact information with me.[3]

The interviews were semistructured and roughly an hour long.[4] The bulk of the interview consisted largely of "grand tour" questions (Leech, 2002, p. 667), in which I invited the interviewee to give me an overview of what they considered to be the important events of the movement leading up to the transition and the transition itself. I would typically follow up a grand tour question with a set of informal prompts, picking up on significant aspects of their answer to the grand tour question and asking them to elaborate.[5] I kept my own direction of the interview to a minimum, allowing the interviewee to offer any comments they thought relevant and appropriate.[6] After obtaining informed consent, I recorded all the interviews to have a detailed record of interviewees' comments, as well as to encourage a more conversational style (Aberbach & Rockman, 2002). I then either transcribed or created detailed notes on the recording from which to draw my quotations and general inferences.

Relying on retrospective reporting of significant political events comes with major empirical challenges, particularly when the events in question are many years (or even decades) in the past. Political and social elites may intentionally seek to mislead the researcher or may simply recall events differently from how they actually occurred (Morris, 2009). Standard works on interview methodology with political elites recommend in particular being careful of elites' tendency to overstate the importance of their own personal contribution to major political outcomes (Ball, 1994; Berry, 2002).

In the chapters that follow I employed multiple strategies to address the problem of retrospective bias. First, as mentioned, I obtained interviews from as many different political perspectives as possible in order to triangulate a narrative of events separated from any one political perspective. Second, before the interview I carefully studied publicly available information (or information from prior interviews) on my interview subjects' personal histories and involvement in the major events of the transition (Mikecz, 2012). This knowledge of the general sequence of events and of the interviewee's personal contribution helped to build trust and rapport and to reduce the incentive for interviewees to tell a deceptive narrative of past events. Of course, this external information also provided a crucial check on any specific sequence of events described by any one interviewee. These strategies should ameliorate the challenges of relying too heavily on any one elite's perspective to shape the narratives in the subsequent chapters. However, they cannot fully eliminate the challenges of either retrospective bias or attempts by particular elites to reshape the historical narrative. Thus, in the following chapters whenever a specific empirical point relies solely on the report of a single or small group of elites I am careful to note this limitation.

In all three cases the events in question remain politically relevant and often controversial, particularly in Nepal, where contemporary politics is deeply shaped by the transitional patterns of behavior I am describing. Thus I chose to keep the information presented in the interviews de-linked from the interviewees' identities. While I present a list of the names and positions of the interviewees in the appendix (Tables A.16–A.18), I do not connect this list in any way with specific claims and quotes made in the case studies.

The chapters are arranged in terms of their significance for the theory rather than chronology. I start with the two cases illustrating the two most common negative outcomes for civil resistance transitions: fractious semi-democracy (in Nepal) and elite semi-democracy (in Zambia). Presenting these two cases first helps highlight the contrast with the successful democratic transition in Brazil.

For all three cases the first step in my argument is to show that the cases in fact fit the basic values on the variables that I have assigned to them. I then relate historical context, laying out the antecedents to the transitions I am examining. I follow this with a detailed account of the events of the transition, tracing the steps whereby these countries arrived at their respective regime endpoints. I conclude each chapter with analysis, evaluating the impact of my proposed pathway argument and considering alternative explanations.

3

"The Elephant's Tail"

NEPAL'S TRANSITION TO FRACTIOUS SEMI-DEMOCRACY

THIS CHAPTER OUTLINES Nepal's transition, beginning with the successful civil resistance campaign of 2006 against the regime of King Gyanendra Shah. I examined the transition in Nepal to test my proposed path from high mobilization and high maximalism during a civil resistance transition to a fractious semi-democratic regime in which resistance pressures new leaders to implement a full democracy, yet instead of moving to normal democratic politics, new forces use civil resistance for their own narrow ends. There is widespread defection from the rules of the game, leading to a failure of democratic institutionalization.

As I argued in Chapter 1, fractious semi-democracy is a regime, not merely a transitional stage. It can become a long-term equilibrium, particularly if no single political force is strong enough to establish control over the system. However, it is a suboptimal equilibrium for the public. Back-and-forth battles for control typically lead to a failure in service delivery, economic development, and other outcome legitimacy aspects of governance. This suboptimality makes it unstable. If service and economic growth cannot be delivered, widespread public disillusion with democracy can empower nondemocratic challengers.

How well does Nepal fit this picture? Few would dispute that Nepal's politics since 2006 have been fractious. Nepal's parties have fought vigorously for control of the center, with agreements made and broken in rapid succession and alliances shifting rapidly based on short-term incentives. Since 2006 there have been 11 different administrations (as of this writing in late 2019), none of which has lasted more than two years. Since in the same time period there have only been three elections—in 2008, 2013, and 2017—the primary method of turnover has not been electoral. Instead parties have relied on a combination of internal political

defection and external disruptive tactics such as general strikes and road block-
ades to create pressure to achieve their objectives and destabilize their opponents.

Nepal is also firmly semi-democratic. This is prominently displayed in scholarly indexes on democracy. V-Dem has rated Nepal from 0.3 to 0.6 on the polyarchy score since 2006, with similar middle-range rankings coming from the Polity
data set (Marshall, Gurr, & Jaggers, 2016) and the Unified Democracy Scores
(UDS; Pemstein, Meserve, & Melton, 2010). Figure 3.1 displays these scores.[1]

Nepalese[2] elites interviewed for this chapter typically responded to questions
about Nepal's level of democracy by arguing that the official forms of politics,
particularly the constitution, reflected democratic norms, but that these norms
were only "cosmetic" or "formal" and that the substantive functioning of politics
fell well below democracy. As one put it:

> In terms of process we are completely democratic, but democracy is also [a
> matter of] culture. And in terms of culture . . . there is a sense of suprem-
> acy. Some sections of the people think that they are supreme. They are
> supreme because they have been ruling, and others are ruled. That psy-
> chology is hampering [democracy].[3]

Thus the outcome seems to match the picture of fractious semi-democracy well.

What about the roles of high mobilization and high maximalism? Here too
Nepal's transition largely confirms my theory, but with some important caveats.

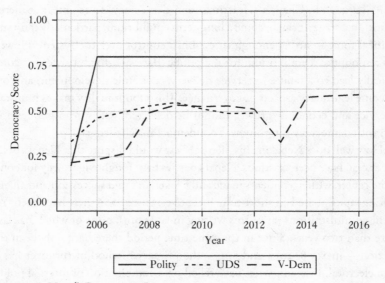

FIGURE 3.1 Nepal's Democracy Scores

While mobilization was high, as predicted, the character and shape of this mobilization was influential. It was in large part captured by political parties, while independent civil society groups largely demobilized. The case thus confirms mobilization's importance but suggests that to maintain its democratizing pressure it must be pursued with some autonomy from direct political competition. If mobilization is simply deployed by elites rather than initiated by autonomous civic forces, then it is unlikely to have a strong democratizing effect.

There was significant maximalism throughout the transition, and this maximalism had deleterious effects on democratic progress. There were frequent attempts by political parties and social groups to employ all-or-nothing extra-institutional tactics to disrupt the progress of the transition for short-term particularistic advantage. This had major deleterious effects on the democratic transition. As one party leader put it:

> After the major problem is solved then all of us try to get one up on each other. When there's a huge crisis we get together . . . but after that we wanted to get one . . . one above the other, you know. So in Nepali we say *haati chhiro puchchar adrakiyo*. That means "Elephant has got through, but his tail is stuck." This is the problem with the Nepalese politicians.[4]

The specific patterns of mobilization and maximalism were by no means predetermined by Nepal's political or social structure. Instead contingent decisions by political actors and the combined choices of ordinary people led to high levels of popular mobilization directed through maximalist channels. These high levels of mobilization and maximalism in turn played a critical role in shaping Nepal's transition. Thus, while the case suggests several important caveats and other factors that interact with the role of mobilization and maximalism, I consider it generally to well support the book's theory of civil resistance transitions.

In the remainder of this chapter I give an overview of the major events of Nepal's transition since 2006. I then discuss and dismiss alternative explanations for Nepal's current situation and conclude by reiterating the contribution of my theory.

Background of the 2006 Transition

Certain historical context is central to understanding Nepal's 2006 transition. The very name of the movement that initiated the transition, the Jana Andolan II or Second People's Movement, indicates the movement's history. The 2006 Second People's Movement was a direct descendant of Nepal's First People's Movement in 1990, itself a direct descendant of an even earlier popular mobilization for democratic rights in the 1940s and early 1950s.[5]

Nepal's modern politics, commonly marked as beginning with the end of the oligarchic Rana regime in 1951, was characterized by a series of back-and-forth struggles between Nepal's traditional monarchy and a series of emergent political forces: initially the Nepali Congress Party, then the communist movement, and finally Maoist revolutionaries. Brief democratic breakthroughs in the 1950s and 1990s were rapidly undermined by the resurgent power of a monarchy unwilling to limit itself to ceremonial functions.[6]

The second democratic breakthrough, in 1990, critically shaped the events of 2006. The Nepali Congress, Nepal's traditional democratic party, had attempted violent uprisings against the monarchy several times in the 1970s and 1980s but had failed to undermine the monarchy. In 1990 they attempted a different strategic path, joining forces with Nepal's communists in a nonviolent resistance movement (Baral, 1994; Hachchethu, 1992). This movement successfully pressured King Birendra Shah to end the system of direct monarchical rule, known as the Panchayat system, and allow a new constitution to reduce his role to that of a ceremonial monarch.

Opinions on the new regime initiated in 1990 vary within Nepal's elites. Many of them, particularly members of the Nepali Congress party, are quite positive about this period. While inequality and other social and economic problems remained, they argue that the country was on a positive, pro-democratic path, and, had it been given sufficient time, would have fully democratized.[7] Critics, particularly those from the far left, argue that the regime was fundamentally flawed. Maintaining the monarch in a central position and constitutionally enshrining Nepal's identity as a unitary Hindu state meant that the government could never be fully democratic but would always be shot through with degrees of feudalism.[8] Economic, regional, and ethnic inequality remained major issues that democracy left unresolved, and corruption at the center was pervasive (Roka, 2004).[9]

Nepal is an ethnically diverse country. The 2011 government census reported 125 different caste and ethnic identity groups (Central Bureau of Statistics, 2014).[10] At the most aggregated level, most elites I spoke to divide Nepal into three major identity groups: hill-based Brahmin-Chhetris, Madhesis, and Indigenous groups (also referred to as Adivasi or Janajati groups), each of which accounts for roughly a third of Nepal's population.[11] Of these three groups, the Brahmin-Chhetri have dominated Nepal's politics and society for almost all its history. This has been the case both for periods of domination by the monarchy and during periods of ostensible democracy. The Panchayat system of 1960–90 was dominated by Chhetris, while the 1990 democratic system was dominated by Brahmins.

Until 2006, Brahmin-Chhetri dominance took place against the backdrop of an ostensible single Nepali identity. First the monarch and then the democratic system strongly argued that Nepal was as much a single ethnic unit as a political unit and discouraged or persecuted the use of languages and customs other than those of the Brahmin-Chhetri elite (K. Jha, 2017). For example, one interviewee described a sequence of confrontations in the 1990s between the king and Madhesi members of the Nepali Parliament who sought to wear their traditional dress and speak in Hindi during parliamentary sessions.[12]

In part it was this domination by the Brahmin-Chhetri elite that inspired certain factions of Nepal's far left,[13] led by the ideologues Mohan Vaidya, Baburam Bhattarai, and Pushpa Kamal Dahal (or Prachanda, as he later became known), to issue a list of 40 demands to the Nepalese government in February 1996 (Adhikari, 2014; Lecomte-Tilouine, 2004).[14] The demands were far more than even a sympathetic government would have granted, so the leftists soon left Kathmandu to begin a Maoist-style insurrection against the government, initiating Nepal's 10-year civil war.[15]

Throughout five years of war Nepal remained a robust, though flawed democracy. However, in 2001 and early 2002 a series of events led to the unraveling of Nepal's democratic system and the establishment of a quasi- and then full-fledged dictatorship under the king. The process began with the assassination under mysterious circumstances of King Birendra, along with much of the royal family, in 2001.[16] One of the few surviving royals, the king's brother Gyanendra, ascended to the throne promising to take a harder line against the Maoists and expressing skepticism over his brother's openness to democratic reform. In 2002 the democratically elected Parliament was dissolved, and the king began appointing prime ministers.[17] He rapidly increased the intensity of the conflict against the Maoists, leading to a spike in casualties as the two sides clashed with increasing violence. The quasi-democratic elements of the monarchical regime ended in February 2005 when the king dismissed the final prime minister and began ruling by decree, arguing that such direct rule was necessary to bring an end to the conflict with the Maoists.

The king's coup in 2005 echoed the actions of his father, King Mahendra, in 1960. However, as many interviewees observed, the situation was no longer amenable to such interference.[18] The king's move was deeply unpopular and served as a major mobilizational moment. The political parties, particularly the Nepali Congress, had been leading protests and other civil resistance actions against the monarchy for some time. Yet their campaign had remained small, dominated almost entirely by longtime party cadres. The public at large was deeply skeptical of the parties' leadership, many viewing them as corrupt and ineffective. However, when the king assumed direct power in 2005, no longer even maintaining an appearance of democratic rule, opposition spread rapidly throughout society. In particular, a widely respected community of civil society and human rights activists began to condemn the king's move and act against it.[19] One former activist reported:

> Before the parliament was dissolved . . . people were agitating on the call
> of the political parties. But it wasn't going anywhere. And people like
> me, to be very honest with you, were disenchanted with those parties
> so much . . . so why should I bother? But when the king dissolved the
> Parliament, took over the reins of government, and installed a cabinet,
> started appointing cabinet members, the prime minister at will, at his dis-
> cretion . . . our liberal minds wouldn't accept that. And that's when we
> came to the street in support of the political parties.[20]

One of the largest civil society groups to mobilize against the king was the Citizens' Movement for Democracy and Peace (CMDP). Led by a former civil servant named Devendra Raj Panday and human rights activist Krishna Pahadi, the CMDP began organizing civil disobedience actions against the king's curfews and other restrictions on civil liberties. Even their initial events were met with a massive mobilization response, as ordinary Nepalese citizens joined forces with these activists. The activists lent their support to the struggling political parties, inviting party leaders to attend their events and hear what the people had to say.

A second critical impact of the king's coup in 2005 was to firmly push together the mainstream parties and the Maoist rebels. The major parties, joined under the mantle of the Seven-Party Alliance (SPA), wanted the Maoists' support in Nepal's rural districts to bring pressure against the king. The Maoists, on the other hand, had reached a clear point of military stalemate with the Royal Nepalese Army (RNA): the RNA was unable to dislodge the Maoists from their rural strong-holds, but the Maoists lacked the manpower and equipment to directly engage the RNA. One interviewee reported:

> By 2005 [the Maoists] had control over more than ninety percent of the
> countryside, [but]they did not manage to establish control over a single
> district headquarters. . . . They knew they had to make a political trans-
> formation. They couldn't unilaterally take over the state. They had to ally
> with a section of the political class.[21]

Because of this realization, for several years Maoist leaders had opened negotia-tions, both with the palace and with the political parties, to seek some form of set-tlement. The king's coup eliminated the possibility of a Maoist accommodation with the palace and instead drove the Maoists and the SPA into each other's arms.

The Maoists and the SPA reached an agreement in November 2005, the so-called Twelve Point Agreement, signed in Delhi. Under the agreement, both sides acknowledged the monarchy as the primary obstacle to Nepal's political development and agreed to work together to eliminate it. The Maoists agreed to give up arms and accept the principle of multiparty democracy. The SPA, which had previously been fighting simply for the restoration of the democratically elected Parliament and wanted to maintain the constitutional monarchy, agreed to a Maoist core demand for a constituent assembly to rewrite Nepal's constitution, making the country a republic.[22]

With the Maoists, the political parties, and civil society all in alignment against the king, Gyanendra found himself with few allies. Mobilization swelled through late 2005 and early 2006, peaking in April 2006, when a general strike called by the SPA achieved a success greater than even the most optimistic leaders had anticipated. Millions of residents of Kathmandu created a miles-long procession on the city's ring road, shutting down the city, while massive protests across all of Nepal's social groups took place in urban centers across the country (Upreti, 2008). In more rural areas Maoist cadres blockaded roads and shut down district administration centers.[23] The coordination of tactics across the strengths of these different groups was crucial in shutting down the monarchy's capacity to govern (Subedi & Bhattarai, 2017).

Attempted violent repression of the initial protests by the military (on the grounds that the Maoists were orchestrating the demonstrations) failed to suppress the movement, instead leading to a massive increase in participation. When family members of the security forces participating in the demonstrations called on the army to stop firing on the protesters (Upreti, 2008), the RNA informed the king that they would no longer follow orders to suppress the movement (Dixit, 2006, p. 120). Fearing an imminent popular assault on the palace, Gyanendra agreed to give over power to the former Parliament and left the palace on April 24, 2006.

From People's Movement to Fractious Semi-Democracy

In this section I trace 10 years of the development of Nepal's current regime, beginning with the king's removal from power in 2006 and concluding in late 2016 with the struggle over amending the new constitution. I structure my narrative roughly chronologically but focus on my two key challenges of mobilization and maximalism.

Contestation between major political forces was intense from the transition's beginning. Indeed the major parties participating in the Jana Andolan disagreed over whether the king's restoration of the old Parliament was in fact the victory they had been hoping for. The Maoists, for instance, wanted a more immediate push for a constituent assembly rather than the restoration of one of the institutions they had waged their initial struggle against (P. Jha, 2014).

Several of my interviewees critiqued the ad hoc or even antidemocratic nature of the new regime under Prime Minister G. P. Koirala.[24] The Parliament Koirala headed had been elected in 1999 with a five-year mandate, long expired by April 2006. Its leading members were the same Kathmandu elites who had been deeply criticized for corruption and lack of effective service delivery in the 1990s. Could putting this same group of people in power truly be the outcome of such a massive popular uprising?

The long-term goals of the movement itself had been somewhat unclear. Ordinary people wanted the restoration of freedom and peace with the Maoists. This simple two-point agenda was the common rallying cry.[25] However, the movement represented different things to the different groups. Elites interpreted the movement as legitimating their own goal of restructuring the Nepalese state. Maoist leaders saw the Jana Andolan as a legitimation of their long-term goals of a communist people's democracy.[26] Leaders of Madhesi and other minority groups saw the mandate of the movement as ending discrimination against their people and the political dominance of hill-based Brahmin-Chhetris.[27] And the old-time democrats of the Nepali Congress saw it as legitimating their own vision of representative multiparty democracy, with themselves in a privileged position.[28]

These divergent visions were bound to conflict. Yet the modality of the conflict was by no means predetermined. Instead early crucial actions initiated a repeating pattern of radicalized, winner-take-all contestation based on short-term expediency rather than long-term national interest. Several interviewees cited the restoration of the Parliament, and particularly the introduction of Maoists as parliamentarians despite their never having been elected, as a prominent example.[29] Developing rule of law or even consistent rules of the game was downplayed in favor of a focus on accommodating the interests of the de facto politically powerful.

Mobilization by civil society also began to suffer early in the transition.[30] Initially the leaders of the CMDP, one of the most powerful forces behind the Jana Andolan, had intended to keep their movement in existence, arguing that it was necessary to hold the political parties accountable. Yet declining numbers, fractures over policy disagreements, and departures from the movement to join parties led to the decline of CMDP's independent voice. One interviewee recalled:

We had said, "Our citizens' movement for democracy will remain active, our movement will go on until the constitution is framed." And when that happened our colleagues, political parties, civil society, NGOs, deserted us . . . and then they tried to delegitimize us and slowly the whole entire civil society forces became more or less status quo oriented: "We've got our democracy back, what more do you want?" You know, the Maoists are now back, the peace process is now going on, they will surrender their arms, and that's it. And that they were satisfied. But then our wings were clipped . . . [and] enough pressure was not put on the constituent assembly.[31]

One demand of the movement had been accountability of the king and others who had been complicit in the abuses during the period of direct monarchical rule, particularly violence toward the peaceful protesters of the Jana Andolan II. There were moves early in the transition to address this problem, and a commission was formed under the guidance of a respected elder judge, Krishna Jung Rayamajhi. The commission made several recommendations for prosecution of figures from the old government who were particularly complicit in human rights abuses. However, the interim government refused to take up the recommendations of the Rayamajhi Commission, and to date no government has publicized the commission's recommendations.

Since the recommendations have not been made public, most of my interviewees could only speculate about the reasons why the commission's report was so completely disregarded. However, most of them suspected that the report implicated figures who remained integral to Nepal's politics, particularly the Maoists.[32] Nearly all the major figures of Nepal's democratic movement, including the prime minister and head of the Nepali Congress, Sher Bahadur Deuba, had served in the increasingly authoritarian regime of King Gyanendra. Had prosecutions begun, the Nepalese elite were concerned about where they might end.[33]

In addition to the Rayamajhi Commission, whose work was actually completed, the parties had made several commitments in their various agreements to investigate the abuses of the past. The last point of the 2005 12-point agreement was a commitment by the SPA and the Maoists to investigate any "inappropriate conduct . . . among the parties in the past" and "take action over the guilty one" (Nepal Ministry of Peace and Reconciliation, 2005, p. 5). More specifically, the later Comprehensive Peace Agreement between the Maoists and the government of Nepal committed the country's political parties to establish a truth and reconciliation commission and a commission to investigate disappearances. Yet multiple governments delayed the creation of both throughout the transition, and today, despite the fact that the commissions have finally been created, they have remained understaffed and in large part have failed to hold conflict parties accountable (Jeffery, 2017).

Civil society figures I interviewed condemned this failure of accountability and environment of impunity.[34] Criticism in Nepal's media has also been extensive.[35] Yet no nonpartisan mobilization against the continued role of old regime figures or for prosecutions of severe human rights abuses of sufficient size and scope to change the incentives against impunity has been forthcoming.[36]

The landmark achievement of the first year of the transition was undoubtedly the Comprehensive Peace Agreement signed by Interim Prime Minister Koirala and the Maoist leader Pushpa Kamal Dahal. This agreement formally ended Nepal's civil war and incorporated the Maoists into the interim Parliament. It also marked the achievement of the second of the Jana Andolan's key goals: a formal end to Nepal's 10-year civil war.

The agreement is lofty in its rhetoric and aspirations. Beyond its direct provisions for ending violence, it also obligates its parties, among many other things, to restructure the state to end caste, ethnic, language, cultural, religious, and regional discrimination (Article 3.5), implement "scientific" land reform (Article 3.7), and make Nepal "advanced and economically prosperous in a just manner within a short span of time" (Article 3.12).

The agreement's lofty goals may have doomed it from the start, but regardless of whether one makes such a deterministic claim, that the agreement was almost immediately broken is without doubt. In particular, while their People's Liberation Army moved into the cantonments, the Maoists moved quickly to establish an alternative, quasi-military wing through its youth organization, the Young Communist League (YCL), which "received extensive training in unarmed combat. . . . Cadres openly carr[ied] knives, sticks, iron bars and other improvised weapons" (Skar, 2008, p. 6). The YCL quickly became the enforcers of Maoist control in their traditional rural strongholds, engaging in typical "rebel governance" (Mampilly, 2012) activities of controlling road traffic and punishing criminals (Ogura, 2008, p. 35), as well as intimidating the Maoists' political opponents (Adhikari, 2012).

The growth of the YCL reinforced the conception for the mainstream parties that the Maoists' move to accept multiparty politics was purely tactical and that, if given the chance, they would attempt to capture the state and use the organs of state power to establish a single-party dictatorship. These fears grew after the first constituent assembly elections were held and the Maoists emerged as the largest party, which I discuss in more detail later.

So, from its beginning the Nepalese transition was characterized by a number of practices that would stymie the country's democratic development: a demobilized civil society, despite its important role in the 2006 Jana Andolan; a lack of trust in and confrontational, winner-take-all politics among the political parties; and impunity for those from the king's dictatorship (and the Maoist rebellion) who were accused of severe human rights abuses.

Into this context came a second earthquake in Nepalese politics: the Madhesi movement of 2007.[37] Madhesi activists, long a peripheral force in Nepalese politics, had played a prominent role in the 2006 people's movement. As many of my Madhesi interviewees reported, the goals of ending discrimination against and disempowerment of Madhesis were by no means separate or distinct from the 2006 movement. Indeed it was the hope of a "New Nepal" free of regional discrimination that had been a central force in mobilizing Madhesis to participate.[38]

The view was not accidental. As a mobilizing tactic, the 10-year Maoist rebellion had long since abandoned a purely abstract Marxist vision of class struggle and instead argued that in the Nepalese context a people's republic would require empowerment of oppressed ethnic and caste groups, including the Madhesis. Many prominent Madhesi political figures, including future Madhesi movement leader Upendra Yadav, joined the Maoist rebellion for these reasons. When the Maoists joined forces with the political parties in the 2006 movement, Madhesis considered it natural that their own demands for greater empowerment, particularly federalism, would be met (K. Jha, 2017).

However, major political parties, particularly the Nepali Congress, resisted any moves toward federalism. Thus, in the interim constitution federalism made no appearance whatsoever, and the electoral system failed to meet Madhesi demands for greater representation (K. Jha, 2017). When the government released the interim constitution, making the abandonment of federalism clear, widespread protests broke out across the Tarai of southern Nepal.

Madhesi activists and politicians point to this movement as a direct and logical consequence of the 2006 movement.[39] The second Jana Andolan focused on achieving democracy that for the first time would truly represent the interests of all Nepalese, not just the *pahadi* elites.[40] The ouster of the king—perhaps the ultimate symbol of hill high-caste domination—was only a step along the road, not the ultimate goal. Thus the interim constitution, from their perspective, was a step backward, a setback for the goals of the movement that had brought millions of Nepalese citizens to the streets.

Mobilization of the movement was rapidly accelerated by a heavy-handed response to the initial protests by the government and *pahadi* residents of the Tarai. In particular, on January 16, 2007, the Madhesi social and political pressure group Madhesi Jana Adhikar Forum (MJF) organized an event in which Madhesi leaders burned copies of the interim constitution. When the leaders were arrested, widespread protests broke out across the region (K. Jha, 2017). During these protests, some MJF supporters clashed with Maoist cadres in the town of Lahan, and a young Madhesi activist named Ramesh Kumar Mahato was killed, sparking popular resentment across the Tarai. Mobilization in the Madhesi movement exploded.

The Madhesi movement, like the 2006 movement itself, is a powerful example of the influence of ordinary people trumping the intentions of elites. The
2007 uprising was not planned. Madhesi leaders such as Yadav and the MJF were
caught by surprise when the sudden wave of popular support for the cause of
federalism and Madhesi empowerment swept across their region (K. Jha, 2017,
p. 42). Protests and strikes were widespread, and, perhaps most important for the
role of the Madhesis in the remainder of the transition, the Madhesi movement
succeeded in shutting down the supply routes from India to Kathmandu.

The geography of Nepal, a landlocked country with the world's highest
mountain range on its northern border, gives Madhesh this natural advantage
over the rest of the country. Nepalese society is almost entirely dependent on
critical imports from India, particularly for fuel but also for basic foodstuffs.[41]
And every single one of the routes for these critical imports to reach the power
center of Nepal in the Kathmandu Valley runs through Madhesh. When mobilized, the Madhesis have the capacity to starve the Nepalese elite into submission.

This vulnerability has created no little resentment against the Madhesis from
those same Kathmandu elites. Few incidents during the transition evoked more
heated emotion from my interviewees than the Madhesi (and later Indian) block-
ades of the road and rail lines from India to the hilly and mountainous regions
of Nepal. One interviewee in particular spoke alternately wistfully and defiantly
about plans for a coming Chinese rail line to Kathmandu, Pokhara, and Lumpini
that would allow Nepal to import basic commodities from China and bypass
India and Madhesh entirely.[42]

Despite its negative emotional resonance the tactic was effective. The Nepalese
government engaged in a gradual set of concessions, with Interim Prime Minister
Koirala promising federalism in a speech at the end of January, the interim
Parliament amending the interim constitution to promise federalism in April,
and a series of agreements later in the year between *pahadi* elites and Madhesi
leaders cementing these moves.

The Madhesi movement catapulted a new set of elites into public prominence, such as MJF's leader Yadav. When Nepal finally held its twice-delayed
elections for the constituent assembly, tasked with writing a new constitution,
Madhesi parties had an unexpectedly strong showing, capturing 45 out of a total
of 601 seats.

While Madhesi gains were a major surprise in the election, the biggest shock
was the overwhelming victory of the Maoists. Nepali Congress and CPN-UML
figures had comfortably assumed they would resume their pretransition position
as the first and second parties in Nepalese politics, with the Maoists a comfortable distance behind. In contrast, CPN-MC had a commanding electoral victory
across the country, capturing 220 out of the 601 seats and becoming the largest

party in the interim legislature—larger than the Nepali Congress and the CPN-UML combined.

To what can we attribute the Maoists' surprising victory? Scholars and my interviewees had different interpretations of this electoral outcome. Maoists viewed the election of 2008 as a vindication of their long struggle in the jungle and the streets in 2006. They argued that the people had clearly shown their preference for the Maoist agenda of federalism, greater ethnic representation, and dismantling the traditional structures of Nepalese politics, with the ultimate goal—sometimes stated, sometimes left unstated—of a one-party communist state. Members of other political parties and independent civil society observers pointed to widespread voter intimidation and fraud in many parts of the country.[43] While the People's Liberation Army ostensibly remained in its cantonments, not threatening its former supporters or victims, the YCL was out in full force.

Other parties also engaged in election-related violence, with the heaviest clashes taking place between Nepali Congress and CPN-UML cadres in the Dhading district west of Kathmandu. The general pattern was one of tit-for-tat violence, with no individual party solely responsible.[44] In addition, many more radical Madhesi groups rejected the election outright and attempted to depress voter turnout and delegitimize the electoral process through both violent and nonviolent intimidation. Some groups attempted to enforce *bandhs* (general strikes) in various Tarai districts, while others detonated small improvised explosive devices (Cooper, 2008).

The truth behind the Maoists' victory is likely somewhere in the middle, between genuine support for them and intimidation by the growing force of the YCL. International election observers judged the election free and fair, and while some instances of intimidation did occur, they were not crucial to the outcome.[45] Many of my interviewees argued that most Nepalese voters were interested not so much in the particular platform the Maoists espoused but simply in the possibility for change.[46] The country wanted to see fresh faces in Kathmandu, and CPN-MC seemed to be the easiest way to get them.

Whatever the reasons, the Maoists' victory in 2008, followed soon thereafter by the accession of the Maoist leader and former guerrilla near-legend Prachanda to the prime ministership of Nepal, shocked Nepalese politics. It heightened the fear and uncertainty on the part of the traditional democratic parties that the Maoists would take advantage of their electoral success to seize the state and ultimately unravel the democratic system.

Before moving on to the (first) Prachanda government, though, it bears mentioning that the election of the constituent assembly was, on its own, a historic achievement and in many ways marked the final culmination not just of the 2006 movement but of Nepal's long democratic tradition since the early 20th century.

The demand for a constituent assembly to write a people's constitution for Nepal had been first articulated by the Nepali Congress in its armed uprising against the Rana regime in the 1940s. King Tribhuvan had promised to meet the demand, but the promise remained unfulfilled when his son Mahendra ended Nepal's first democratic regime and instituted the Panchayat system.[47] The 1990 movement against the monarchy had made great strides but had given up the idea of a constituent assembly in exchange for concessions from the monarchy, establishing the constitutional monarchical system of the 1990s. The Maoist rebellion had made the demand for a constituent assembly a central plank of their long armed struggle. Now, finally, the Nepalese people would have their own elected representatives determining their future institutions.

The first action by the constituent assembly was equally historic, as they voted almost unanimously to formally abolish Nepal's monarchy, which had technically only been suspended since King Gyanendra bowed to the Second People's Movement two years before, and make Nepal a republic. They also voted to eliminate Hinduism as the state religion and instead make Nepal formally a secular state.

These are historic achievements, representing fundamental change of a type and degree rarely seen even in the course of democratic transitions. Many questioned them at the time, and many do still today. Public polling in the months leading up to the 2008 election found that 49% of Nepal's population still supported at least some role for the monarchy, and even more (59%) supported the idea of a Hindu state (Sharma & Sen, 2008, p. v). The vote to eliminate the monarchy was wreathed in controversy and intrigue, as a vote meant to take place immediately upon the opening of the first session was delayed and delayed until late in the evening. Several interviewees sympathetic to the monarchy pointed to these dynamics as evidence of underhandedness on the part of leaders attempting to push through major changes they knew were not the will of the Nepalese people.[48]

With the monarchy abolished and Hinduism no longer in its pride of place as the official state religion, the constituent assembly set about its work of writing a new constitution, while the former rebels of the CPN-MC for the first time moved into the formal government offices in Singha Durbar in downtown Kathmandu. The fears of many of Nepal's conservative elites had come to pass.

A number of moves by Prachanda over the next year did nothing to assuage those fears. Interviewees pointed to several incidents, beginning with attempts to remove the South Indian Hindu priests at Pashupatinath Temple, the center of Nepalese Hinduism. Several actions following this, including the systematic installation of Maoist cadres in the civil service and other government positions, solidified the impression in the minds of the other parties that Prachanda was attempting to build an unassailable position from which CPN-MC could never be dislodged (Adhikari, 2012).

The final straw in this series of actions came in 2009, when Prachanda attempted to dismiss the chief of army staff General Rookmangud Katawal. Maoist interviewees painted this move in nonthreatening terms, arguing that it would have been taken by any leader in Prachanda's situation, facing a figure like Katawal, a longtime royalist. As one prominent Maoist figure said:

> The action against [General Katawal] was nothing but rational and logical and appropriate. The army chief was disobeying orders, humiliating the prime minister and the defense minister. . . . Any government would take action against such an army chief.[49]

Under a well-known pseudonym Katawal had written a number of public op-eds during the civil war calling for "enlightened despotism," and though he swore allegiance to Nepal's new democratic regime after being elevated to chief of army staff by Prime Minister Koirala in the months following the Second People's Movement, his core sympathies were widely believed to be with the palace. He had played a key role in the RNA entering the war against the Maoists, during which time soldiers under his command had been accused of severe human rights abuses. He also faced inquiries over potential abuses by troops under his command during the Second People's Movement in 2006.

Most prominent in Prachanda's desire to remove Katawal, however, was that the general had become a highly prominent critic of the Maoist government. When forced to follow orders from his Maoist arch-enemies, Katawal had resisted, fighting back against, among other things, the integration of Maoist cadres into the army, the retirement of several army generals, and a freeze on recruiting new non-Maoist soldiers (Adhikari, 2014). Prachanda attempted to get Katawal to step down in May 2009 by offering him an ambassadorship. When Katawal refused, the prime minister fired him.

For Nepal's non-Maoist political establishment, as well as the army itself, this was unacceptable. The Nepalese Army was widely seen as the one functioning institution unable to be co-opted by the Maoists. With Katawal out, Nepal's political parties feared that a full-scale Maoist takeover of the state would soon follow. One figure closely associated with the army and the Nepali Congress described the situation this way:

> This was an aggressive action taken to undermine and totally topple the army. . . . The chief was not happy with the Maoists and all the things that were going on, so yes, at times he was a little abrupt with them, so what. . . .

The Maoists were a bunch of terrorists! Declared terrorists! And there was
a series of events, this was not a single thing. . . . You could see them trying
to take over everywhere.[50]

Katawal refused to step down, and, in a continuation of the pattern of follow-
ing short-term incentives rather than the formal rule of law, Nepal's president,
Ram Baran Yadav, a member of the Congress party and a strong opponent of the
Maoists, successfully kept him in place. The abrogation of the prime minister's
authority was too much for Prachanda to take and he resigned shortly afterward.[51]
Intense jockeying for power followed, ultimately resulting in the establishment of
a new government under Prime Minister Madhav Kumar Nepal, a member of
CPN-UML.

The Maoists, excluded from government despite their continued position
as by far the largest party in Parliament, refused to go quietly, and in May 2010
attempted a full-scale nonviolent defection. Bringing tens of thousands of supporters from around the country to Kathmandu they attempted to replicate the
conditions of the 2006 movement and force the Nepal government to fall. This
time, however, the Maoists lacked alliances in civil society and the political parties, and their attempted civil resistance takeover failed to take hold. With dwin-
dling numbers of supporters enforcing their general strike in Kathmandu and no
prospect of success, the Maoists ended the strike.

Intense competition continued, though, ultimately leading a few months later
to Prime Minister Nepal stepping down in an attempt to break the deadlock.
Nepal's gesture, however, failed to achieve its desired effect. Instead, for the next
several months the nation functioned without a prime minister as the various
parties voted repeatedly, with no candidate able to achieve an electoral majority.
Finally, after seven months of voting, the Maoists agreed to back the CPN-UML
candidate, Jhala Nath Khanal, and a new government was formed. The Khanal
government was followed quickly thereafter by another governing crisis and the
establishment of a government under the Maoist leader Baburam Bhattarai.

During Bhattarai's tenure Nepal reached another critical turning point in the
transition. The constituent assembly elected in 2008 to write the new constitution had originally been given a one-year mandate. As unwillingness to reach
compromises and focus on the power struggles in Singha Durbar made the actual
work of writing a constitution more and more difficult, the assembly had voted
to grant itself several extensions. However, in 2013 the Supreme Court ruled that
the assembly no longer had the right to continue to extend its mandate.

This put Nepal's politicians in the position of once again making a short-term
compromise outside the framework of the institutional rule of law. The eventual
compromise position was that Prime Minister Bhattarai would step down and

hand over power to a technocratic government headed by the chief justice of the Supreme Court, Khil Raj Regmi. Regmi would have a very brief mandate, just long enough to plan and execute elections for a new constituent assembly.

Democratic flaws aside, the Regmi regime did succeed in organizing elections in a relatively brief time. And just as the Maoist victory in 2008 had been a shocking outcome for Nepal's elites, the outcome of the 2013 election was similarly shocking. The new, progressive forces of CPN-MC and the Madhesi parties faced electoral annihilation. From being the largest party in the constituent assembly by a wide margin CPN-MC fell to a distant third behind the two traditional political parties, the Nepali Congress and CPN-UML, its number of MPs dropping from 237 to 80. Madhesi parties were almost wiped out, with only a scattering of figures remaining in the second constituent assembly.[52]

What explains this change in electoral outcome? Interviewees were divided. Some simply attributed it to a revelation of the population's natural preferences when better voter rolls were in place and voter intimidation by the Maoists and their YCL had been largely eliminated.[53] Others argued that, as in 2008, the Nepalese public simply wanted change. They were angry over the Maoists' failure to deliver a new constitution in line with their promises in the jungle and in the lead-up to the 2008 election, and so honored their rivals in the Congress and CPN-UML. Others point to more sinister conspiracies, often with a common Indian flavor.[54] The Maoists also suffered from internal divisions over the proper approach to the elections, with some factions pushing for a full-scale boycott (Gellner, 2014).

Whatever the reason, Nepal's traditional elites were now firmly in charge of the government once again, an outcome that alarmed not just supporters of the Maoists but the spectrum of Nepalese progressive forces, those who still saw the 2006 movement as one not just for restoring the elite-dominated democracy of the 1990s but for fundamentally restructuring the Nepalese state.

The process of constitution writing and competition over control of the central government remained contentious during the second constituent assembly. In particular, a number of identity-based movements waged intense resistance struggles to ensure that the rights they had hoped to obtain from the Maoist-led first constituent assembly were maintained in this second, more conservative assembly.

One prominent example of this was the struggle in 2015 by several Dalit organizations to ensure the protection of Dalit rights in the new constitution. The movement was sparked by rumors coming from Dalit members of the assembly that guarantees of proportional representation in elections and affirmative action for Dalits in public service promised during the first constituent assembly were on the verge of being rescinded in the new constitution. One interviewee involved in the movement reported:

We came to know that some of our main agendas were no longer incorporated [in the new constitution] . . . because the ruling party was quite regressive. So then senior members from the Dalit community started having discussion among themselves . . . the first time you can see all the Dalit civil society community coming together, even some sister wings of political parties and Dalit politicians from political parties coming together.[55]

The Dalit movement engaged a major push of coordinated street activism and advocacy within the constituent assembly to get protections for Dalits reinstated in the constitution. Their activism was successful, and many of the guarantees were reinstated (Bishwakarma, 2019; *Kathmandu Post*, 2015).

The contentious process of constitution writing might have followed the same outcome as in the first constituent assembly, when infighting and political jockeying prevented the establishment of any final document, except that in April 2015 a major exogenous shock struck the country in the form of a massive earthquake, with an epicenter close to the heavily populated Kathmandu Valley. Thousands were killed and hundreds of thousands more made homeless. The quake had two major effects on Nepal's political development. First, it resulted in a massive outpouring of international aid for disaster relief. Aid had been a major industry in Nepal since the beginning of the transition in 2006. As one interviewee observed, "For many years the biggest industry in Nepal has been the peace industry."[56] Yet the scale of aid ramped up significantly following the earthquake. These inputs of aid further demobilized Nepalese civil society from political activism, as NGOs shifted focus to earthquake-related service delivery and relief.

Second, the earthquake proved to be a potent motivator for Nepal's elites to finally come together and agree on a constitution. In the months following the earthquake Nepal's parties departed from their typical pattern of winner-take-all politics to finally pass (with 90% support) and promulgate Nepal's new constitution, its first to be written by an assembly elected by the people.

Nepal's constitution is a progressive document, with lofty goals and protections for many fundamental rights. Yet, following the pattern of Nepal's prior agreements, the rhetoric agreed to by the parties has often failed to be realized in practice. When asked about the quality of Nepal's democracy, this was a point emphasized by almost every interviewee from every sector. The guarantees of the constitution, the institutions called for by the constitution, are *highly* democratic, far more democratic than any other legal framework in South Asia. Yet on almost no count are they fully implemented.

Beyond the problems of implementation, certain groups were deeply angered by the constitutional arrangement itself. In particular, Madhesi, Janajati, and

Tharu groups condemned the constitution as continuing the dominance of Brahmin and Chhetri *pahadis* (K. Jha, 2017, p. 47). The proposed borders of Nepal's new federal states, along with constituency boundaries, diluted Madhesi control by adding some hilly area districts into one of the proposed Tarai-based states and removing some others.

The Madhesis and their allies responded by launching a new movement and once again employing their most powerful tool: a blockade of the main road and rail lines from India to the Kathmandu Valley and other hilly regions. In this they were heavily assisted by the Indian government (though India disputes this; Gurung, 2017). As in 2007 the blockade proved potent in achieving its desired outcome, and the Nepalese government agreed to amend the new constitution to change the state boundaries and accommodate Madhesi demands.

Upon promulgation of the constitution the constituent assembly redefined itself as a legislative parliament and extended its mandate until national elections could be held in 2017. They also planned to hold local and provincial elections in the same time period, a triple electoral process that would ostensibly mark the end to Nepal's lengthy transition. This timeline was complicated by the Madhesi agitation of 2015 and early 2016, which put the federal boundaries in question.

However, despite the Madhesi agitation, the triple election process was successfully held throughout 2017 and early 2018, with local elections held in May, June, and September 2017, elections to provincial parliaments and the lower house of the federal Parliament held in November and December 2017, and indirect elections for the upper house of the federal Parliament in February 2018. The major outcome of the elections was an overwhelming victory for leftist forces, as Nepal's two major leftist parties, the CPN-UML and the CPN-MC agreed to merge to form a single united front: the Communist Party of Nepal. The combined Communist Party captured nearly two-thirds of the seats in Parliament.

A focus on maximized competition and a lack of faith in institutions remained evident in the 2017 elections, despite their relative success and lack of electoral violence. In particular, the three major parties refused to delineate a method for provincial assemblies to indirectly elect the national assembly, instead using the lack of institutional arrangements as an opportunity to jockey for short-term power (Strasheim, 2018). The elections of 2017 are undoubtedly a major step forward in Nepal's transition process. Yet it remains to be seen whether a departure from transition in any practical, institutional sense will move Nepal away from its position as a fractious semi-democracy.

Reasons for skepticism lie in several areas, but primarily in the structure of Nepalese political competition, a structure that seems unlikely to change with the simple move toward a more normal electoral system. Every one of Nepal's political parties is structured hierarchically, with key decisions on platform and personnel made almost exclusively by a small circle of senior leaders (Gyanwali, 2016). Loyalty from lower-level cadres is maintained primarily by the promise of future patronage and career advancement.

This lack of internal party democracy has undermined the establishment of ideological-based distinction and party competition based on service delivery. Instead competition tends to be based on absolute numbers of people who can be drawn into the individual party's patronage network. Since control of the center is the ultimate means of expanding one's patronage network, political logic is focused almost exclusively on being part of the ruling coalition rather than achieving one's own ideological goals.

This dynamic in turn makes political alliances unstable and undermines trust between the parties. In contrast to ideological commitments, whose implementation is at least to some degree zero sum, the benefits of patronage are fungible between different alliance partners. Alliance partners are interchangeable in the distribution of patronage, and negotiation becomes simply a matter of marginal degree. Knowing that they are interchangeable, and seeing the pattern of shifting alliances and betrayal of prior agreements, parties have reasons to be skeptical of one another's guarantees. Yet this lack of trust in guarantees continues to exacerbate the maximized conflict over control of the center and de-emphasize competition over positive service delivery and implementation of an ideological platform.

Greater implementation of the new constitution, particularly through lower-level elections, could have an important impact on these dynamics. A new cadre of young, local leaders could shake up the top-down, patronage-based structure of Nepal's political parties and bring to the fore new blood who would be incentivized to seek public support based on a political platform or delivery of government services. Yet it is certainly possible that even in these circumstances the patterns of politics engrained by Nepal's parties to date will continue to shape and shove new leaders into its mold. The future is open-ended, but it seems highly likely that Nepal's status as a fractious semi-democracy will continue.

Analysis

What explains this trajectory? Why has Nepal been able to make such tremendous progress toward social and political transformation and yet failed to move to a more consolidated democratic system? In this section I lay out the specific argument connecting my theoretical model to the Nepali case. While the fit is imperfect, as is to be expected when applying ideal types to empirical cases, my theoretical picture predicts the Nepalese transition quite closely.

First, it is undoubtedly true that mobilization remained high throughout Nepal's democratic transition and continued to powerfully shape the transition process. The most visible example of this is the Madhesi movement. Yet a fine-grained look at the Nepalese transition reveals hundreds of causes inspiring mobilization during the transition. My interviewees gave witness to this, describing the frequent instances of popular mobilization, from street demonstrations to general strikes, that have characterized Nepal's transition. Other scholars' work confirms this dynamic. For example, the UN Department of Safety and Security recorded 4,451 general strikes in Nepal from 2008 through 2013. The overwhelming majority of these were conducted by political parties and other groups pushing particular political agendas, not trade unions or other traditional labor groups (Shrestha & Chaudhary, 2013).

Did mobilization shape outcomes? Again, the answer is very clear. As Anand Aditya (2016, p. 79) observes, the first lesson of the transition was that "protest and pressure work." Throughout the transition, when political forces hit the streets they often achieved their goals and redirected the endpoints of the transition process. This is most clearly seen in the example of the Madhesi mobilization, but various other mobilizations, such as the Dalit movement in 2015, were very successful in pressuring elites into concessions. While some observers argued that social movements other than the Madhesis had little impact—"On a scale of 1 to 10 their impact is maybe a 1"[57]—this attitude was in the distinct minority.

Was mobilization a check on democratic backsliding? Some indirect evidence of this effect was offered by several of my interviewees. While many expressed fear (or hope!) of a move toward a more authoritarian system, all expressed a firm belief that such a reversion would be impossible because of the degree of political activation of ordinary people since the revolution. One interviewee said, "If the people remain awake and alert, no one can harm our democracy."[58] Elites were closely attentive to the signals emerging from the streets and recalibrated their positions based on this mobilization.

However, there was one major factor undermining the democratizing effect of mobilization: little of it was independently connected to ordinary citizens outside of political formations. Political parties, or civil society groups closely linked to them, manipulated much of the mobilization for their own narrow ends. They adopted the mantle of democracy in most cases to bring people to the streets but largely used the mobilization to advance their own particularistic agenda.

What of the challenge of maximalism? The empirical dynamics are certainly there. Some of the most disruptive civil resistance tactics have been used repeatedly by particular factions in order to pursue a revolutionary agenda, and the use of such tactics and rhetoric has been a normal, even routine form of contention during the transition. As one interviewee described it:

The situation was so bad, like strikes and *bandhs,* shut-downs almost every day. This situation made public life miserable and the state . . . I wouldn't say the state had failed, but we were almost close to being a failed state, because the state mechanisms were not properly functioning and there was so much interference from all sides.[59]

Maximalist themes also ran through the political parties' attitudes toward elections. The results of both the 2008 and 2013 constituent assembly elections were contested as unfair at the time, and some of those on various sides of the Nepalese political spectrum still consider them unfair.[60] The 2010 attempt by the Maoists to bring down the CPN-UML–led government was one of the starkest examples of maximalism at work, combining radical street action with the revolutionary goal of toppling the existing system and fully derailing the transition.[61]

The rhetoric used by the various factions to describe one another is also maximalist. On the progressive side, the Nepali Congress and similar political groups are described as secret agents for the restoration of the monarchy and a return to full-scale domination of national politics by a small caste-based elite. On the more conservative side, Nepali Congress and CPN-UML interviewees described the Maoists as only temporarily accepting the norms of multiparty democracy and hiding their real preferences for a single-party dictatorship.

Maximalist mobilizations have played key roles in preventing Nepal's constituent assemblies from writing constitutions. Had it not been for the intervention of the 2015 earthquake, it seems quite likely that even the 2015 constitution would not have been passed. Even in interviews after the ratification of the constitution, several Madhesi respondents described the constitution as fundamentally based on the interests of traditional elites and motivated by ethnic prejudice. One Madhesi political leader related:

This constitution is totally based on racism. . . . These Congress and UML people do not want Madhesis to get their rights, or indigenous people to get their rights, or Dalit people to get their rights. . . . They've [even] started saying that the country doesn't need secularism, or federalism, that the country was better off [before the revolution].[62]

Meanwhile, Congress and CPN-UML respondents often described the Maoists, despite their move into the mainstream of politics, as fundamentally seeking to destroy the democratic political system, and the Madhesis as a force for the dissolution of the country.

Maximalism's effects on derailing democratic progress are strongly evident in Nepal. The important question, then, is whether this pattern represents meaningful agency. Does maximalism affect democratization in its own right, or is it reducible to the deterministic workings of the underlying structure of Nepalese politics?

The question is of course difficult to suss out empirically, for many of the reasons eloquently described in the seminal discussions of structure and agency in political action.[63] Structure certainly plays an important role. It is difficult to imagine, for example, the maximalism over ethnic federalism without the long-standing ethnic division between Madhesi and *pahadi* and the history of exclusion of Madhesis by the *pahadi* class. The presence of two powerful neighbors, one of whom is seen as particularly manipulative of Nepalese politics, is another crucial structural factor that shaped these dynamics. The distinction between *rastrabadh*—nationalists—and *lampasarbadh*, those who are willing to give in to Indian interests, is an easy frame to draw on to delegitimize one's opponents, pointing to them as a threat to Nepal's sovereignty and territorial integrity.[64] Without a history of domination by a powerful neighbor, this frame would be unavailable to Nepal's elites.

Yet other structural factors would strongly lead us to not expect such a distinct pattern of maximalist politics. In particular, since 1990 Nepal has had at least nominally democratic political institutions that could easily serve as avenues for nonmaximalist contention. The functioning of these institutions was significantly disrupted by the civil war and the royal seizure of power, but once the 2006 movement removed the king from power they were restored to prominence.[65]

Social and political structure is undoubtedly the raw material of maximalist political contention. These structures provide the frames into which maximalist discourse can be fit and the motivation for maximalist action. Yet on their own these structures are simply latent possibilities of action. It takes contingent choices to turn these latent structures into real patterns of behavior. And these contingent choices do not arise automatically. Rather they are based on factors specific to the situation. Several critical juncture points in the transition could have shifted in very different directions had contingent, individual-level decisions been different (Acharya, 2009).

For instance, one major event that undermined trust between the political parties and continued to shift Nepal toward maximalist politics was the attempted dismissal of General Rookmangud Katawal in 2009. The underlying dynamics of structural-historical factors such as caste division and the historical legacy of the monarchy were certainly at play in the event. Yet the event itself was sparked by decisions made by General Katawal to criticize the Prachanda government, choices very much driven by his own personal history. It is easy to imagine a counterfactual scenario in which a different chief of army staff with a less emotionally salient personal connection to the monarchy kept his reservations about the Maoist government to himself and was not dismissed. Without this dismissal, Prachanda would not have resigned shortly thereafter, and Nepal's first constituent assembly might even have succeeded in writing the constitution.

My argument is not that this single event fully explains Nepal's transition, or even its pattern of maximalist politics. Instead the attempted dismissal of General Katawal illustrates the implausibility of the structural story and emphasizes the importance of contingent choices. This series of events was one of many blunders invoked by my interviewees, situations in which choices that do not appear ex post to be rational when looking at a fuller picture of the structural environment had critical effects. Time and again interviewees pointed to choices that hung in the balance only to be resolved at a suboptimal level for all concerned. Elites miscalculated the dynamics of a situation and made strong, ultimately failed plays for power. Ordinary people rewarded or punished elites for actions in ways that retrospectively do not flow from the prior conditions. These dynamics are the norm, not the exception, in the story of Nepal's transition. So it is difficult to argue that the pattern of maximalism that has disrupted Nepal's democratic transition is necessarily or even sufficiently explained by a prior set of structural conditions. As one interviewee said:

> There is no logical next big step. Let's be very clear about that.... You have elections in the US in November, one of the parties will win, then there will be a transition team, then on January 20 the president takes over. That's logical, it's a set thing. We don't have that, okay? What will happen next will happen through [a] series of political or historical accidents. We don't know, by definition, what an accident will be like.[66]

Perhaps the most damaging consequence of Nepal's maximalist politics is how it has undermined faith in the functioning of democracy. Early in the transition, support for democratic principles was extremely high across almost all segments of society (Sharma & Sen, 2006, p. 39). However, when maximized politics first prevented the formulation of a constitution and later undermined effective government development and service delivery, faith in democracy declined.[67]

This decline in faith in democracy is not limited to the poorly educated or informed. Several of my interviewees from the highest elite levels of Nepalese politics and civil society expressed nostalgia for an authoritarian past in which a single leader could do away with the disturbances entailed by maximized politics. Some argued that the only way to fix the current dynamics of Nepalese politics would be to do away with democracy and impose order with a period of military rule or a return to monarchy. As one put it:

Democracy cannot give justice in Nepal. . . . . That's why I've told many people just for ten years, or maybe twenty (we have to have a timeline), ten years, twenty years we have to have an autocratic system. [Because] from 1990 until now every day and every year is crisis and crisis, struggle and struggle.[68]

Such a return to autocracy was almost universally depicted by my interviewees as extremely unlikely. They argued that the freedom of expression and association brought about by the 1990 and 2006 movements had moved society too far toward democracy for significant backsliding, and that any serious move to reverse the past two decades of democratic progress would result in significant public backlash.[69] However, if Nepal's political class continues to fail to institutionalize democratic politics and service delivery remains extremely poor, then the likelihood of major democratic backsliding seems at the very least plausible.[70]

Nepal's politics, for instance, currently resemble the situation in Thailand from the mid-2000s until the 2014 military coup. Constant struggle by diametrically opposed factions in that case eventually led to the end of Thailand's most recent democratic experiment. Interviewees connected with the Nepalese military discounted the possibility of a military takeover, emphasizing the professionalization of the officer corps.[71] However, similar dynamics in Bangladesh, a country whose military is similar to Nepal's in many respects, puts this in question (Milam, 2007).

There are several potential alternative explanations for the trajectory of Nepal's transition, from the literature specifically on Nepal and the broader democratization literature. Do any of these provide a better explanation of the transition than the one I have outlined?

The first explanation relates to Nepal's neighbors, particularly India. Indian underhanded behavior is a favorite explanation for almost any event in Nepal indefinitely into the past until today. Different accounts offer different rationales for India's interference, but a focus on Indian involvement is important in almost any description of the trajectory of Nepal's transition. One interviewee went so far as to describe the primary division in Nepal's politics as between nationalists and those who are willing to give in to Indian interests.[72]

Indian perfidy is particularly prominent in discussions of the Madhesi movement. The Madhesis are often painted as tools of Indian foreign policy to divide Nepal and provide India with a frontier region under easily controlled leaders. The close linguistic, ethnic, and familial ties between the populations of the neighboring Indian states and the Madhesis make such connections easy to draw. One interviewee explained:

India thought that this is a good opportunity to establish their perma-
nent influence in Nepal through the Madhesi parties. So they demanded
that there should be one Madhesh from east to west. . . . They thought
these Madhesis would support them because many of the Madhesis are
newcomers in Nepal. They were from Bihar or Uttar Pradesh. . . . We wel-
comed them all, [but] they wanted to misuse that. . . . These people are
guided by the Indian establishment, and they want to fell the constitution,
[because] India thinks that we should only make the constitution under
their guidance.[73]

That India has played an important role in the transition is undeniable.
Indian mediation played an important part in bringing together the Maoists and
the seven-party alliance before the 2006 Second People's Movement.[74] The 12-
point agreement between the two was signed in Delhi, under the watchful eye
of the Indian government. The Indian ambassador in Nepal has also played an
important role at key moments of crisis, throwing his weight behind one faction
or another in order to achieve particular outcomes.

A weak version of the argument that Indian influence explains Nepal's transition certainly has some merit. In specific instances, when tracing the political
process, one often finds Indian actors in the middle. However, several key pieces
of evidence undermine the stronger argument for an overwhelming causal role
for Indian foreign policy. The first is the character of popular mobilization in the
Jana Andolan II and then in the Madhesi movement and subsequent mobilizations. While India played a role in bringing the political elites together in the 12-
point agreement, in the 2006 movement these elites initially played a marginal
role. Due to a widespread loss of legitimacy, few people were willing to mobilize on
the streets in support of the political parties. Instead it was independent civil society leaders who organized the first large-scale protests against the monarchy. The
political parties and Maoist revolutionaries were later folded into the movement,
but they were not the instigating actors nor the majority of those who participated.
Even assuming all those who agreed to the 12-point agreement were acting as tools
of Indian foreign policy (itself a challenging argument), the movement itself cannot be explained solely or even primarily through their actions. It was a massive
popular upswell driven by civil society and popular attitudes more broadly.

Some interviewees alleged that the mobilization itself was simply the result of
Indian money—that protesters on the streets were paid by India.[75] While I cannot rule out this accusation, several data points make it extremely unlikely. The
first is the sheer size of the 2006 movement. Estimates vary, but even conserva-
tively the participation was at least in the millions, with demonstrations in almost
every municipality in the country. In Kathmandu alone, according to multiple

interviewees from different political and civil society groups, during the height of the Jana Andolan II the march along Kathmandu's ring road filled the entire circumference of the road, which would put the number of participants at minimum in the hundreds of thousands. While it is impossible to rule out that some participants in these demonstrations received financial compensation, it stretches plausibility to assume a significant portion did so.

The second piece of evidence is the testimony of an overwhelming percentage of interviewees. During my fieldwork I had access to many of the most central leaders in the 2006 movement. They all told a consistent story about the progression of the movement's mobilization, with differences that would be expected based on their different positions at the time. As with the number of participants, I am unable to determine with complete confidence the veracity of individual statements made to me; however, the existence of a consistent conspiracy begins to stretch plausibility as the number of those speaking against it increases.

It is difficult to argue that India played a sufficient role in the 2006 Jana Andolan. Absent popular mobilization by fiercely independent civil society leaders such as Devendra Raj Panday and the CMDP it is difficult if not impossible to imagine the 2006 movement following the trajectory that it did. Was Indian intervention necessary? Here the causal question is more complex. Certainly the 12-point agreement was an important moment enabling the movement and helping to spark mobilization, since people went into the streets not just for democracy but also for peace, and the 12-point agreement made it clear that peace would be achieved only if the king was out of the picture. Yet even here India's position is unclear. The agreement was signed in India, but it was preceded by various negotiations that were not orchestrated by India. Counterfactually it is not difficult to see a situation in which an agreement between the parties could have been reached without Indian intervention. Thus, whether India's involvement was necessary for the success of the 2006 movement is also questionable.

So much for India's grand role behind the 2006 movement. What of the major events in the succeeding 10 years of transition? Did India derail Nepal's transition for its own nefarious intentions?

Perhaps the strongest piece of evidence against a central Indian role is the absence of a consistent story among Nepal's elites as to what exactly the Indian disruption was. Many if not all were clear that India's foreign policy harmed the transition, yet their view of that harm varied significantly depending on their political position. Those further on the left, particularly Maoists, argued that India's interference was essentially on behalf of the Hindu right, to ensure that Nepal remained a Hindu state. Those further on the right pointed to India's connection with the Maoists and argued that India fundamentally sought to destabilize Nepal, to prevent Nepal from standing on its own two feet.

Consistent historical instances in which Indian interference derailed the transition process are also difficult to find. My interviewees listed very few, and none consistently across different political positions. The one exception to this rule was regarding the 2015 border blockade. Apart from some Madhesi activists, all my interviewees condemned this instance as a clear attack by India on the successful completion of the constitution, and prime evidence of India's destabilizing hand.

Yet was this in fact the case? The blockade certainly imposed heavy costs on the Nepalese economy and forced Nepal's parties to negotiate with the Madhesis over provincial boundaries. Yet it does not appear to have had any particularly differentiating impact on Nepal's transition. Indeed, as evidenced by the 2007 Madhesi movement, it seems doubtful that Indian interference was even necessary for a major costly blockade to be imposed. Had the promulgation of the constitution gone forward without amendment, Madhesi mobilization alone could very plausibly have led to similar concessions. Furthermore, while this remains a point of intense contestation, it is not a unique point in Nepalese politics. Rather it follows a pattern of practice common beyond the 2015 blockade and the Madhesi issue more generally. Even in the most heavy-handed of India's alleged actions during the Nepalese transition, it is difficult to discern a determinative Indian influence on the political trajectory.

To reiterate, this in no way implies that India has played no role in the transition. The Indian embassy has doubtless been actively involved in Nepalese politics throughout the transition period, as has been the case ever since Indian independence, but the argument that their influence has been a determinative factor in Nepal's current regime is doubtful.

I would make a similar argument about the influence of Western powers, particularly the United States. That they played, or attempted to play, a role is undeniable. However, whether their influence was either necessary or sufficient to ultimately affect the outcome of Nepal's transition is more doubtful.

The first piece of evidence in this regard is the inconsistent nature of the arguments for Western influence. Some argued it was positive, supporting and encouraging democratic development. Others argued that it was negative, encouraging a professionalization and demobilization of civil society, disconnecting politicians from their role in writing Nepal's new constitution, and forcing focus away from actual indigenous needs toward the particular program of donors. Western influence certainly played a role, but the role does not seem to have been determinative in any meaningful fashion.

What about structural determinants, such as modernization? According to the World Bank's classification, Nepal has been a low middle-income country throughout this period, with a GDP per capita of $1,684 in 2006, rising to $2,443 by 2017.[76] Some interviewees pointed to poverty as a factor shaping the transition, particularly with poverty's add-on effects on education. But can poverty really explain the outcome in Nepal?

Seymour Martin Lipset's (1959) traditional analysis of the effects of modernization on democratization, the initial insight that underlies most contemporary thinking, focused on the effects of wealth on the mindset of the poor and wealthy. In countries with high levels of poverty the poor would be attracted to radical antidemocratic ideologies against the wealthy, while the wealthy would look down on the poor with disdain and be resistant to extending the franchise to them. Does this pattern characterize Nepal's transition?

A first glance might indicate that it does. After all, Nepal's 10-year civil war was led by Maoist revolutionaries. Would this not indicate that in fact the Lipset argument about poverty is not only applicable but in fact crucial? Perhaps. But a closer look even at Nepal's Maoist revolution puts that into question. In their attempt to wage a class-based Maoist struggle the CPN-MC in fact found itself constantly thwarted, a phenomenon that forced them to change their rhetorical strategy from a focus on class, poverty, and inequality to a focus on Nepal's unique constellation of caste-based and ethnic-based discrimination. Similarly, in the transition economics has played a marginal role in the rhetoric of the more progressive parties.

Neither have the economic elites used the fear of the lower classes and the fear of redistribution as a major argument against democratization, as more recent scholarship on the role of economics in democratization has concluded (Acemoglu & Robinson, 2005; Boix, 2003). Indeed there is near consensus across all Nepal's political parties that the country should be run as a socialist democracy. The picture of the mechanisms whereby poverty affects democratization is unclear at best.

What about the traditional transitologist's picture of a democratic transition wherein elite pacts between moderates are the driving force in pushing toward democratization, and popular mobilization is a dangerous force that can put elite pacts into jeopardy (O'Donnell & Schmitter, 1986)? Here too the traditional theory is a poor fit. First, while transitology predicts a popular uprising by civil society and the masses at large in response to an initial opening on the part of the regime, in Nepal the direction is reversed. The peak mobilization of the Jana Andolan II came at the most authoritarian, most repressive moment in King Gyanendra's rule and was largely created by that repressiveness. In contrast, once the king had been removed there was a large-scale *de*-mobilization of civil society, not the pent-up upsurge that O'Donnell and Schmitter would lead us to expect. Instead mobilization shifted from a civil society uprising to a maximized winner-take-all confrontation between the parties.

And what of the beneficial character of elite pacts? Here too there is reason to be skeptical. Pact-making as a near-continuous theme throughout Nepal's transition. With the 12-point agreement before the king's fall, the series of agreements with the Madhesis in 2007, and the agreements over the constitutional amendment in 2016 and 2017, Nepal's elites are well-practiced at making pacts. Yet the pacts, far from establishing sustainable democratic politics, instead hinder that process. Pacts have enshrined the power of a small antidemocratic elite and hindered Nepal's move toward an inclusive democracy. Consequently the pact-making process has destabilized faith in democracy by groups excluded from this elite who fear the consequences (Strasheim, 2017). When pacts have been progressive, it has been because of outside pressure.

Nor is there significant evidence that pressure from "radicals" has significantly destabilized the transition or incentivized "hard-liners" to attempt to overthrow the transition and return to the status quo ante. There is pressure to return to an authoritarian system, but the source of the pressure is not primarily fear of radicalism but rather disgust with the pattern of Nepalese politics currently evidenced by the "moderates" skilled at pact-making!

Summary

Nepal's elites are almost universally proud of the 2006 movement. They list three reasons for this pride: the impressive scale of social mobilization, the relative lack of violence, and in particular the transformation of the Maoist insurgents first to a partner in nonviolent resistance and then to a mainstream political party. Yet they decry with a great deal of frustration the problems that have arisen in the years since 2006. Having accomplished the seemingly most difficult task of regime change, the final goal of a peaceful, prosperous, democratic Nepal nevertheless remains tantalizingly out of reach. To repeat the old Nepali saying from the beginning of this chapter: the elephant has gotten through the door but now his tail is stuck.

Interviewees gave many reasons given for this, from poverty to the pernicious influence of India. Yet a common thread throughout the interviews, and clearly present in the sequence of events related in this chapter, was the negative impact of a pattern of high mobilization and high maximalism. As laid out in this chapter, this pattern provides a better explanation for the Nepali transition than prominent explanations specific to the Nepal case (the influence of India) as well as major scholarly explanations such as modernization theory and transitology.

Nepal's real progress should not be understated. Thus far, while maximalist contention has disrupted a move toward consolidated democracy, there are many strong indicators of meaningful political change. For instance, the willingness of the Maoists—a formerly violent revolutionary group—to first claim and then give up state power is a critical milestone. And while many interviewees expressed concern about a return to violence or autocracy,[77] most moments of major crisis or political transformation have been primarily peaceful.

The story of the Nepali transition does offer significant insight for expansion and growth in future theory-building on transitional challenges. In particular, the evidence from Nepal problematizes the concept of mobilization. Mobilization may be high, but if it is easily captured by maximized groups, then its democratizing influence may be attenuated. Even partisan mobilization may have a good long-term effect, as it diffuses political skills across the population, but in the short term its effect is likely to be negative. To democratize, mobilization should not simply be limited to political parties or other groups with a primary goal of achieving power but should be dispersed more widely throughout society.

4

"Power Is Sweet"

ELITE SEMI-DEMOCRACY IN ZAMBIA

THIS CHAPTER IS the second of my case studies tracing whether the theoretical mechanisms linking levels of mobilization and maximalism during civil resistance transitions to posttransition democracy obtain in actual cases, and furthermore whether distinct patterns of mobilization and maximalism lead to the specific quasi-democratic regime types that I described in Chapter 1. In Chapter 3 I examined the first of these relationships in the case of Nepal: how high mobilization and high maximalism destabilized the creation of new democratic institutions and led to a fractious semi-democracy characterized by high levels of destabilizing contention. In this chapter I examine the opposite pattern of contention: whether low levels of mobilization and maximalism lead to an elite semi-democracy in which popular bottom-up pressure fails to have any significant influence on the new political regime.

The transition that I examine to trace this pathway is the 1990–91 Movement for Multiparty Democracy (MMD) in Zambia and the transition that followed its victory over the single-party autocratic regime that had dominated Zambia since independence. I find significant evidence that Zambia indeed closely followed the path from low transitional mobilization and maximalism to an elite semi-democracy. Following a large civil resistance campaign that successfully ousted the old regime, social and political mobilization declined precipitously during the transition, leading to a semi-democratic regime dominated by a small group of elites that manipulate the levers of government for their own advantage. Gero Erdmann and Neo Simutanyi (2003, pp. 65–66) write:

> The high degree of political mobilization achieved during the transition and which took many Zambians to the streets, was not maintained despite protracted hardships for the majority of the population. The government

in power therefore faced no direct threat. Even the drastic cuts in maize subsidies of 1992 . . . caused no major reaction, while a similar move only five years earlier in 1986 had triggered anti-IMF riots. . . . Before and after the controversial elections of 1996, no major demonstrations took place.

The causes for this pattern of demobilization are manifold. Many Zambian interviewees pointed to a culture of faith in the "big man," a pattern that they argued is common across many African countries.[1] Others pointed to the severe economic crisis that faced Zambia in the immediate aftermath of the 1991 election.[2] As the MMD moved away from the quasi-socialist policies of their predecessor and embraced a harsh structural adjustment program with terms dictated by the International Monetary Fund (IMF; Simutanyi, 1996), the attendant economic dislocation led ordinary Zambians away from political mobilization and forced them to focus on the increasingly difficult task of meeting their basic needs. Others were deeply critical of President Frederick Chiluba himself, arguing that from the beginning the goal of Chiluba and many in his central circle had not been greater democracy but simply occupying the seat of power.[3] Still others made an institutional argument, pointing to the level of power granted to the president by the Zambian constitution and to the ways in which Zambian institutions give the president the capacity to both repress and co-opt potential opponents.[4]

I do not attempt to distinguish between these arguments. As I explained in Chapter 1, patterns of transitional behavior can be reached through many different potential causal pathways. Any number of different historical, cultural, and institutional factors may have affected the outcomes of these strategic challenges. My key argument is that once one arrives at this pattern of behavior, the behavior itself has a long-term impact, regardless of the specific path that may have led to it. In this case, I focus on how a lack of mobilization provided space for a decline in democratic quality that prevented the MMD from fully realizing the democratic dream that inspired its first leaders.

First, a few clarifications. Is Zambia an elite semi-democracy, as I have described that regime type in Chapter 1? The country meets most of the indicators of a semi-democracy or hybrid democratic regime. Elections are held and are meaningfully contested but are often suspected of being manipulated (O'Donovan, 2004). Almost all interviewees spoke of the pervasiveness of corruption and patterns of patronage in Zambian politics.[5] The Zambian constitution, while in general laying out democratic institutions, is also almost unchanged from Zambia's days as a one-party socialist state dominated by a powerful autocratic president. Only Article 4 of the constitution, which specifically forbids the existence of more than a single party, was changed as a result of the activism of the original MMD

(Ndulo & Kent, 1996). Authoritarian legacies live on in restrictions on freedom of speech, freedom of the press, and most prominently on freedom of assembly. The Public Order Act, a colonial legacy, continues to require any group desiring to hold a public meeting to get approval from the local police up to two weeks in advance. This permission is frequently denied on explicitly partisan grounds, with opposition parties and civil society groups denied permission to meet while the ruling party is never refused permission (Freedom House, 2019).

International scholars of democracy largely agree with this analysis. Figure 4.1 shows Zambia's score on three prominent democracy indexes in the decade before and after the 1991 transition. For all three indexes, the success of the MMD prompted a jump in the level of democracy, but the jump falls short of democratic thresholds. The V-Dem polyarchy score remains roughly around 0.5, with similar rankings from the Polity data set (Marshall, Gurr, & Jaggers, 2016) and Unified Democracy Scores (Pemstein, Meserve, & Melton, 2010). This is a significant improvement from the era of the one-party state, as all the indicators show, and an achievement that should not be understated. But it falls well short of a robust, consolidated democracy.

Scholars of Zambian history and politics generally concur that the country's multiparty democratic system has largely failed to live up to the standards of democracy. Miles Larmer (2016, p. 264) refers to Zambia's political system as a "largely choiceless or disciplined democracy," and Lise Rakner (2003, p. 174), writing about the ten years of the Chiluba presidency (1991–2001), concludes,

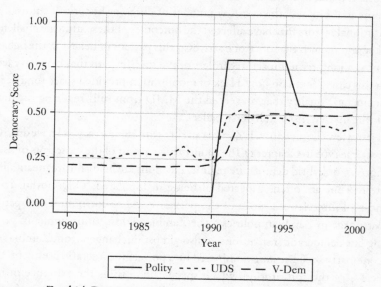

FIGURE 4.1 Zambia's Democracy Index Score

"Democratic governance in Zambia in the 1990s has remained in a 'grey zone,' a situation of partial reform." Gretchen Bauer and Scott Taylor (2011, p. 53) go much further, describing the 10 years of the Chiluba regime as a "descent into an anti-democratic kleptocracy."[6]

Zambia's political system at the end of its most recent transition also fits the "elite" variety of semi-democracy, in which politics is dominated by a small group of elites and is largely focused on the personal enrichment of that elite class (Kaoma, 2015). Competition does not revolve around ideological lines but is instead primarily focused on gaining control over state resources. The same group of leaders that have dominated politics since the 1990s remains central to Zambian politics. Party allegiances are fluid, with major figures shifting their party identification frequently to maintain access to the central levers of power. For example, Michael Sata, the fifth president of Zambia, was originally a leading figure in the United National Independence Party (UNIP), the authoritarian ruling party, then a minister in the MMD, and finally the MMD's leading opponent as the founder of the Patriotic Front.

In the remainder of the chapter I provide a brief history of Zambia's political environment since independence, then a narrative of the Movement for Multiparty Democracy and the subsequent transition. I focus on the challenge of mobilization, arguing that a lack of continued mobilization and the incorporation of antidemocratic elites (and the attendant sidelining of more democratic MMD leaders) are key in explaining the outcome of the Zambian transition. With few exceptions (notably the struggle between the remnants of the former ruling party UNIP and the MMD around the 1996 election), Zambia also had relatively low levels of transitional maximalism, a positive dynamic for democratic progress. Yet in the context of low levels of public pressure, this positive aspect of Zambia's political culture failed to have a salutary democratizing effect.

Background

Zambia achieved independence in 1964 after a long, largely nonviolent struggle. By the time of independence, the undisputed leader of the independence struggle was Dr. Kenneth Kaunda. Kaunda began as an activist in the Zambian branch of the African National Congress but left the ANC to form his own organization—originally called the Zambian National Congress and later the United National Independence Party—after believing that the ANC was not radical enough in its pursuit of independence. At independence UNIP was the dominant political force in the country, but the ANC continued to have a powerful influence. The country's initial political regime was broadly democratic, with competitive elections and protections for civil liberties. However, the democratic period was short-lived, as partisan divisions on tribal lines provided the primary justification for a move in 1973 from multiparty competition to formalizing UNIP's domination of Zambian politics and making all other parties illegal (Gertzel & Szeftel, 1984; Pettman, 1974).[7] Kaunda and UNIP argued that this decision did not fundamentally undermine Zambia's democracy but simply reshaped it, allowing a means for participation but without partisanship that would damage national unity.[8]

Kaunda's UNIP government followed the model of many other contemporary African nations, perhaps most prominently Julius Nyerere's Tanzania, in pursuing collectivization and a large expansion of the welfare state in tandem with the domination of the state by a single political force. In Zambia's case, this massive expansion of the state was facilitated by the large-scale export of the country's most precious and abundant primary commodity: copper.

The one-party state faced major challenges almost immediately as the 1973 oil crisis led to a sharp increase in the price of imports and the price of copper subsequently declined. As copper revenues decreased throughout the 1980s the government became increasingly incapable of supporting its extensive welfare state, while the parastatal businesses that dominated the economy were increasingly inefficient and ineffective. The creation of the one-party state also significantly taxed state resources by turning UNIP party workers into civil servants, a move of such economic consequence that one former high-level UNIP figure from this period called it the "most memorable failure" of the Kaunda regime.[9]

Zambian political figures pointed to these economic challenges as a critical beginning of the movement that would eventually overthrow the Kaunda regime.[10] In addition, President Kaunda's increasing personalization of power alienated many of the UNIP elites who had been involved in the struggle for independence and subsequently become longtime supporters of his government. The sources of this alienation were areas of significant contention among my interviewees. Many argued that the majority of those dismissed by the Kaunda government were dismissed for good, justifiable reasons. As one former UNIP leader reported:

> There were a lot of people who formed Movement for Multiparty Democracy who Kaunda had fired for some legitimate reasons. For instance, there was Vernon Mwaanga, who later became foreign minister in the first MMD government. He fired him for trafficking in Mandrax. . . . The people who took over as ministers in the Chiluba government were mostly thieves, people Kaunda had fired for some misdemeanor or another.[11]

Others, however, argued that their moves away from the Kaunda government was motivated by conscience—anger at the increasing personalization of power under Kaunda and a desire for meaningful political and economic reforms.[12]

While the government was technically dominated by the political party, along the lines of the one-party regimes of the Soviet Union and Warsaw Pact, in fact power was more and more concentrated in the person of President Kaunda. This concentration was perhaps best captured by the growing cult of personality surrounding Kaunda. A popular slogan often repeated by interviewees was "In heaven, there is God, on earth there is Kaunda." Kaunda was the undisputed leader of UNIP and the one topic on which no dissent or antigovernment expression was tolerated.

Elections, even for the presidency, continued to take place at regular five-year intervals during the period of one-party rule. At the local and parliamentary levels these elections even involved some degree of competition, as various UNIP functionaries competed for the party's nomination (Chikulo, 1988). At the level of the presidency, however, there was no competition. Although Kaunda ran for reelection, he always ran unopposed. Many interviewees recalled presidential elections in which Kaunda would run against a picture of a frog or a rabbit to symbolize the degree to which he controlled Zambian politics.[13]

Struggling against the One-Party State

However, while UNIP firmly controlled Zambian politics during this period, opposition was by no means absent.[14] In the absence of formal opposition parties or civil society organizations beyond those focused on service delivery, sources of opposition common to most stories of resistance to authoritarian rule played a significant role in opposing the Kaunda regime. Student criticism of the government, primarily at the country's flagship institution, the University of Zambia, was frequent and vocal. Many of my interviewees cut their political teeth as student activists organizing student groups against the one-party state.[15]

The Zambian Congress of Trade Unions (ZCTU), originally formed as a UNIP organ to co-opt labor activism into the party structure, emerged as early as the late 1970s and early 1980s as an important counterweight to UNIP influence (Bartlett, 2000; Rakner, 1992). As one former labor leader put it:

> The world was changing... and because of the role the trade unions played in Poland, the unions in Zambia also started thinking that probably we should be advocating for change. Since there were no political parties the labor movement was like a de facto opposition. They were the only voice that was standing up and challenging the government.[16]

ZCTU president Frederick Chiluba organized the union's cadres to oppose the 1980 Local Government Act, a legislative act that would have eliminated the universal franchise for electing local officials and limited voting for local councils to UNIP members. The resistance was intense; between 1981 and 1983 the ZCTU and the Mineworkers' Union of Zambia organized over 200 illegal strikes in opposition to the act (Chiluba, 1994, p. 73). Chiluba himself was briefly sent to prison for his role in organizing this opposition. He also refused the place on the UNIP central committee traditionally reserved for the secretary general of the ZCTU, an act that many of my interviewees reported gave him a great deal of credibility as an opposition leader.

Zambian churches also emerged as an important locus of resistance to the excesses of one-party rule, with church leaders using their significant moral authority to demand greater protection for human rights. The *National Mirror* newspaper, jointly published by Zambia's three largest church bodies—the Evangelical Fellowship of Zambia, the Christian Council of Zambia, and the Zambian Episcopal Conference—was one of the few if not the only major independent media voices by the end of the period of one-party rule. While President Kaunda made many efforts to integrate church leaders into his regime, several issues, particularly UNIP's embrace of a more open policy toward abortion and attempts to implement "scientific socialism," alienated church leaders and led to increasing levels of confrontation (Hinfelaar, 2008).

Many in Zambia's growing intellectual community also criticized the one-party state, the Economics Association of Zambia (EAZ), led by Akashambatwa Mbikusita-Lewanika and Derrick Chitala becoming one early center of critique. The EAZ hosted monthly discussions on economic and political topics which frequently involved criticism of the one-party state and became an important convening forum in which those discontented with the one-party state met and shared ideas.[17]

These disparate centers of opposition to the one-party state—disenfranchised former UNIP elites, trade unions, churches, and intellectuals—came together in 1990 under the banner of a movement that would later become Zambia's new ruling party: the Movement for Multiparty Democracy. A sequence of destabilizing events provided the impetus for them to come together in a single movement.

First, in the late 1980s the Kaunda government began to roll back some of its prior extensive government consumption supports, particularly price supports for the staple foods of mealie meal (corn meal) and cooking oil. The economic downturn created by declining copper prices was the underlying factor behind these rollbacks. Declining amounts of foreign exchange forced the Kaunda government to seek a bailout from the IMF, which demanded significant reductions in government expenditure in return. Even before the subsidies were removed, discontent with President Kaunda's handling of the economy was growing. Many of my interviewees related stories about their difficulties getting access to government price-supported goods at this time. Long lines were the norm to get even basic staples. When the government raised prices, this simmering discontent boiled over into direct disruption and defiance. Food riots broke out in many of the country's major urban centers.

In response to these riots, a small group of Zambian army officers led by Lieutenant Mwamba Luchembe attempted to overthrow the Kaunda government on July 1, 1990. The coup failed, but it was greeted with a great deal of enthusiasm on the streets, providing a powerful signal that the people were no longer supporting the Kaunda government. One interviewee recalled that day this way:

> When I woke up that morning the guard told me, "Oh, there was a coup!" So, I switched on the radio, nothing, until I got BBC and they said there had been an attempt and it has failed. So, I went into town and [just outside] they said, "No, no, no, you can't go into town." I had a van, and they said people were just commandeering vans, just jumping in and celebrating, so I turned around. I saw some people talking, so I started talking to them and I said, "This thing has been foiled." And they were very upset. They were very upset with me! That's what brought a lot of courage. . . . This jolted a lot of people.[18]

This "jolt" inspired significant rethinking on the feasibility of launching a struggle to return to multiparty politics. In line with classic theories on preference falsification in authoritarian regimes (Kuran, 1991), the public reactions to the coup attempt revealed a deep well of discontent with the Kaunda regime. In this context, a group of intellectuals who had been involved in discussions in the EAZ about reforming Zambia's political system began to discuss bringing together the various strands of potential opposition to the one-party state under a single umbrella. Akashambatwa Mbikusita-Lewanika, a member of the Barotse royal family and former president of the EAZ, was the driving force behind organizing a meeting in which a formal discussion of this opposition could take place.

The meeting took place on July 20 and 21, 1990, in the Garden House Hotel in Lusaka. Chaired by the freedom fighter and longtime political player Arthur Wina, the two-day conference featured many people who would later become central in Zambian politics. At the end of the two-day conference, the attendees decided to form an organization, the Movement for Multiparty Democracy, which would advocate for a return to multiparty politics. The organization was explicitly not organized as a party in order to steer clear of violating Zambia's prohibition of parties outside of UNIP. This care went as far as the name of the organization itself. Several of my interviewees who attended the Garden House meeting vividly recalled the debate over this issue. The original name for the organization had been the Alliance for Democracy and Development, but fear that this made the organization sound too much like a party prompted the organizers to change the name.[19]

The various strands of antigovernment activism came together in MMD's early leaders. The founding executive committee included alienated elites from the old regime such as Arthur Wina, Vernon Mwaanga, and Keli Walubita as well as ZCTU chairman Chiluba. Mbikusita-Lewanika and many in the so-called intellectual wing of the opposition dominated the MMD secretariat. One early MMD leader said:

> When we organized MMD, I always say the structure was an African three-legged iron pot. One leg was the intellectuals. The second leg was the workers. The third leg were those whom we could pinch from UNIP, those who had been alienated. Former political leaders who had quarreled with Kaunda, who had been chucked out of Kaunda's government and so on. Those were the three legs. . . . And the process leading up to the formation of MMD provided us with enough of all of them."[20]

MMD was able to rapidly organize opposition to the one-party state. In large part they drew on the preexisting national structures of the ZCTU, a fact that gave ZCTU chairman Chiluba outsized influence (LeBas, 2011). In addition to ZCTU, though, several other semi-autonomous opposition groups had arisen in the previous years. One interviewee described how he joined a small cell in Ndola planning resistance to the one-party state after an informal conversation on a minibus. Their cell met weekly, "only a hundred meters from the police station!"[21] Once the national-level structure of the MMD had been formed, these groups quickly integrated into this structure as well.

MMD's initial goal was to get President Kaunda to allow a return to multiparty politics through a national referendum. However, in late 1990, instead of following his initial plan for a referendum, Kaunda called on the UNIP national assembly to change Article 4 of the constitution (the article banning parties outside of UNIP) and announced that he would cut short his term to allow for a presidential election in 1991. In general my interviewees agreed that this was a strategic move on Kaunda's part (though ultimately it ended up being a strategic blunder). Kaunda was not confident that he would succeed in a referendum, and if the referendum passed, waiting until the next presidential election in 1993 would give nascent opposition forces too much time to mobilize around a single presidential candidate.[22]

With this change in environment, MMD was faced with the question of how to continue to pursue its goals. The organization's leadership decided to repurpose themselves as a party competing with UNIP in the 1991 elections. Some competition among the various leaders of the party eventually resulted in Chiluba becoming the party's candidate for president.

The MMD was now fully repurposed as a party. They developed an extensive nationwide infrastructure and fielded candidates for parliamentary seats across the country. The MMD leaders traveled extensively, holding rallies in urban and rural areas in every province in Zambia. Interviewees reported an electric atmosphere, a feeling of almost boundless optimism over the possibility for change and the country's potential if new leadership could be brought into power.

While there were some scattered incidents of violence against the MMD, on the whole government repression was minimal. President Kaunda attempted to use the machinery and resources of the state to support his own campaign, and the Public Order Act was deployed from time to time to suppress MMD public gatherings, but for the most part elites and ordinary Zambians felt the winds of change, saw the intense popularity of MMD, and rather than resist attempted to work out accommodations with this new political force. In the lead-up to the 1991 election defections from UNIP to MMD were rapid and widespread. One of the most high-profile of these was a future president, Michael Sata, a UNIP MP and longtime party fixer who brought a significant political machinery along with him.

The Chiluba Government: De facto One-Party State

The MMD domination of the 1991 election was staggering. Out of 150 seats in the Zambian national assembly, MMD candidates won 125—even though during the election Kaunda and the UNIP leadership continued to use the state resources at their disposal to improve their electoral prospects. The vote totals for MMD candidates in many constituencies went over 90%. In the presidential contest, Chiluba won the presidency with 76% of the vote. The Zambian electorate had sent an overwhelmingly powerful message demanding change and endorsing the MMD.

So while MMD campaigned as the champions of multiparty democracy, they effectively entered power almost as a new single-party regime, to the extent that some observers described the 1991 election as nothing more than a move from a "*de jure* to [a] *de facto* one party state" (Chikulo, 1993, p. 99). Their domination in the national assembly and the presidency gave them almost unlimited power both to reshape the ranks of government and to change laws and even the constitution. To be effective, any resistance would have to come from within the ranks of the MMD or from forces outside of politics.

Resistance within MMD began to develop around a year after the 1991 election, when a small number of prominent MMD figures, including the convener of the Garden House meeting, Mbikusita-Lewanika, resigned from their positions in the Chiluba government over accusations of corruption. Mbikusita-Lewanika, Baldwin Nkumbula, and others who resigned moved to form an opposition party: the National Party. The pattern was repeated several times throughout the Chiluba presidency. During Chiluba's first term 15 of his original cabinet members were either dismissed or resigned (Baylies & Szeftel, 1997, p. 115), and shortly after the 1996 election the resignations over corruption accusations went as high as Vice President Levy Mwanawasa.[23]

Yet despite this fragmentation of the MMD, no serious opposition emerged from these defections. The MMD defector parties remained small, with little or no ability to directly influence policy and few card-carrying members. As Peter Burnell (1995, p. 680) wrote:

> For the most part [Zambian opposition parties] are little more than one-person bands with "interim" presidents. They have neither formal organizational structures nor credible political and economic programs, and they are bereft of material resources. They do not expand the real scope for effective choice by the electorate.

In part due to this opposition weakness, in the 1996 election MMD in fact expanded its majority, from 125 to 131 seats (Baylies & Szeftel, 1997). The MMD's dominance in the 1996 election was enhanced because the one opposition force not emerging from its ranks, the rump UNIP, chose to boycott the election following the changes to the constitution that barred former president Kaunda, UNIP's leader, from running for the presidency again.

The interaction between the MMD and UNIP during this period provides interesting insights into the maximalism challenge in an environment of low mobilization. After a brief retirement, Kaunda returned as leader of UNIP and began strenuously pushing against the MMD government, rapidly advocating for civil disobedience and even describing the MMD government as a government that "should be fought in the same way UNIP fought the colonial government" (Ihonvbere, 1995b, p. 95). In 1993 several UNIP leaders developed a plan to carry out this fight, the so-called Zero Option plan, which intended to overthrow the government prior to the 1996 elections by fostering divisions within MMD and orchestrating a nationwide campaign of strikes and demonstrations. The plan also called for more sinister attempts to disrupt MMD rule, for instance, by paying unemployed young men to initiate a wave of thefts and other petty crimes in major town centers in order to create a feeling of chaos and insecurity around the country (p. 99). This plan was never implemented but badly shook the MMD government and led to the arrests of 26 UNIP leaders and a brief declaration of a state of emergency.

Following the disruption of the Zero Option plan, Kaunda shifted tactics and began making moves to run against Chiluba in the 1996 presidential election. President Chiluba threw the whole mechanism of the Zambian state against him. The Public Order Act, a holdover from colonial days used throughout Zambian history to suppress political opposition, was employed extensively against UNIP rallies. Kaunda was arrested, and even physically attacked during his political activities. And finally, in early 1996 President Chiluba orchestrated an amendment to the constitution that barred from the presidency all people lacking two parents born in Zambia, anyone who had previously served two presidential terms, and traditional chiefs. This was a "transparent attempt to bar former president Kaunda from again becoming a candidate for President" (Ndulo & Kent, 1996, p. 273) as the only potential contender for the presidency at that time to whom the first two stipulations would apply (and indeed the only person in Zambia to whom the second stipulation would apply) was President Kaunda, while the third stipulation eliminated the UNIP deputy leader Chief Inyambo Yeta.[24]

Formal opposition was largely ineffective in providing a check on the MMD once in power. What of informal political forces from civil society? The return of multiparty democracy doubtless expanded the space for civil society to function, something attested to by many different interviewees involved in civil society during this period. The sheer number of civil society groups expanded significantly, and they put pressure on the MMD government on several different fronts. The Zambian women's movement, for instance, which had played a prominent role in the movement against the one-party state, pushed the new MMD government to implement new protections against discrimination on the grounds of sex, gender, or marital status.[25] A growing free press, perhaps best embodied in the *Post* newspaper, also engaged in significant criticism of the government.

However, these efforts to hold the MMD government accountable were significantly hampered by a lack of grassroots public support. Elite civil society groups were largely reliant on foreign sources of funding and support and had relatively limited levels of success in mobilizing ordinary Zambians to engage in serious activism.

This declining mobilization and level of engagement is evidenced by the fact that, surprisingly, political participation declined from its levels in the one-party state after the transition to multiparty politics. Elections under the one-party state had participation levels estimated at about 39% of the eligible electorate. In the 1996 election this rate dropped to around 30% (Erdmann & Simutanyi, 2003, p. 29). The numbers are even more striking in the elections that took place between these two presidential elections. In local elections in 1992 only 14% of registered voters took part, while parliamentary by-elections between 1991 and 1994 averaged turnout of only 21% of registered voters (Bratton, 1999, p. 555).

The decline in formal political participation was matched by a precipitous decline in informal or noninstitutional methods of participation. While the labor movement did engage in a series of strikes in protest against the MMD's moves to privatize state resources and shrink the size of the state (Ihonvbere, 1995a, p. 16), Zambians as a whole largely eschewed any kind of mass political participation.[26] A 1996 survey found that only 6% of Zambians participated in a single demonstration, march, or rally in the five years between the 1991 and 1996 elections (Bratton, Alderfer, & Simutanyi, 1997, p. 7).

In this mobilizational vacuum, the MMD government steadily moved away from the principles on which the movement had been founded. Perhaps the most visible of these moves was in the area of corruption (Burnell, 1995; van Donge, 2008), to the extent that by the mid-1990s "the letters MMD were commonly said to stand for 'Make Money and Depart'" (Gifford, 1998, p. 372). As one former minister in the Chiluba government put it:

> Among [the members of MMD] were those who had been opposed to President Kaunda and his UNIP government principally because they were unable to steal sufficiently! And those people also came into our government. . . . They had histories of being corrupt, people who should not have been there in the first place took up the big positions in government. So it fell, the project [of democracy in Zambia] fell, and that challenge is still there up to now.[27]

Interviewees disagreed significantly on the pervasiveness of corruption in the Chiluba administration, but almost all agreed that President Chiluba presided over a significant increase in corruption compared to the Kaunda years. To illustrate, Figure 4.2 plots Zambia's annual scores on the Varieties of Democracy project's political corruption index (McMann, Pemstein, Seim, Teorell, & Lindberg, 2016). The period between the dashed lines is the 10 years of the Chiluba presidency, a clear high point in corruption relative to the periods before and after.

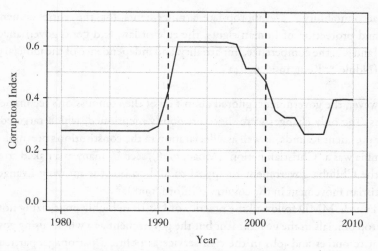

FIGURE 4.2 Corruption before and after the Chiluba Presidency

MMD was also increasingly intolerant of opposition. The attacks on Kaunda and UNIP mentioned earlier were the most prominent but by no means the only example of this. The 1996 election was a significant step down in democratic quality from the 1991 election, in which the MMD had first come to power (Baylies & Szeftel, 1997). In the lead-up to the election the government launched a voter registration effort contracted out to the Israeli company NIKUV that systematically excluded rural voters and was rife with irregularities (Reynolds, 1999, p. 155). The MMD also freely manipulated media coverage in its favor and liberally used the stipulations of the Public Order Act to prevent its rivals from holding public meetings. This manipulation of the political playing field led almost all international and domestic observers of the election to conclude that the election had not been free and fair (National Democratic Institute, 1997).

Third, MMD failed to deliver on its promise of fundamentally reshaping the Zambian political system. While in opposition to the one-party state, the MMD had promised that, once in power, they would rewrite the constitution to encourage greater democracy, particularly by ending the Public Order Act and curtailing the power of the president in appointing government officials. The Chiluba government did appoint a constitutional review commission in 1993 (referred to as the Mwanakatwe Commission after the name of its chairman) with a broad mandate to propose changes to the constitution that would

> ensure that Zambia is governed in a manner that will promote the democratic principles of regular and fair elections, transparency, and

accountability . . . appropriate arrangements for the entrenchment
and protection of human rights, the rule of law, and good governance,
[and] . . . the competence, impartiality, and independence of the judiciary.
(Ndulo & Kent, 1996, p. 242)

However, the government ignored almost all of the commission's recommendations. The only changes were those previously mentioned, which targeted former president Kaunda, as well as a declaration in the constitution's preamble that
Zambia was a "Christian nation" (Mbao, 1998), seen by many as a naked attempt
by the Chiluba government to appeal to and co-opt the growing Evangelical
Christian movement in the country (Gifford, 1998).[28]

Fourth, MMD followed the practice of UNIP in highly politicizing not just
the top officials in the government but the government as a whole, using government resources and jobs in the civil service as political patronage, particularly
for those from Chiluba's home region (Baylies & Szeftel, 1992). One high-placed
insider in the Zambian civil service at the time explained:

The administrative heads of the ministries, some very highly educated and
trained . . . all of them were removed. And then the government appointed
its own supporters. That's what has destroyed the civil service. . . . We still
have that problem up to now. People coming into government look at
these positions as rewards for whatever they did for the political party in
the elections.[29]

Why did the MMD follow these trends? I argue that low mobilization
was a key factor. One interviewee laughed when asked about the challenges of
democratization: "The people who established the MMD were UNIP people,
you know? I didn't expect them to act any differently [than when UNIP was in
power]."[30] While many of the early leaders of the MMD had emerged from civil
society groups, by the time MMD had been in power for a few years it was fully
dominated by elites from the old UNIP government, whose experience in administration and professional norms were overwhelmingly those of a nondemocratic
regime (Baylies & Szeftel, 1992).

These norms and preferences might have been shaped to a greater degree by
popular pressure. After all, many of these leaders defected from UNIP while the
outcome of the struggle for multiparty democracy was by no means fully decided.
They had strongly espoused democratic principles when the Zambian people were
out en masse to push for them. But in the politically demobilized moment of the
first few years of the Chiluba administration, old regime elites found themselves

with a relatively free hand to operate as they pleased. One longtime civil society activist recalled:

> Our attitude was we just want change and that's it, don't talk to us about any of these other things. And in Zambia we had reached that point. We overlooked early warning signs that people were not as they should have been. Maybe we should have been the change we wanted to see instead of entrusting that change to other people.[31]

Or, in the words of a figure prominent in the MMD at the time:

> That was the strength of MMD. We could do the nasty things that Kaunda couldn't do and be trusted. . . . They would have trusted us with anything at that state. Because who was asking questions? I won ninety-two percent [of the vote in the 1991 election]. . . . Who out of that eight percent was going to ask me what I'm doing in a hostile way? Nobody. . . . There wasn't any [popular pushback]. Where would you have gone to push back? UNIP was shot to hell by the time we were finished with them, they had no pulling power at all. There was nobody else.[32]

Why did these patterns occur? Interviewees offered various reasons. Most argued that cultural values related to "patience" were important. "Zambians are a very patient people," one interviewee asserted. "We won't do anything until we are really pushed."[33] There were certainly also active efforts on the part of the government to demobilize potential opposition outside of the MMD, through the liberal use of the Public Order Act and the strategic deployment of patronage. One interviewee involved in opposition politics during the 1990s related an incident in which he was called into President Chiluba's office in the lead-up to the 1996 election. Chiluba told him that his activism was disruptive and offered to give him and his party a specific number of seats in Parliament in the upcoming election if they would agree to stop mobilizing. The man refused and was later attacked by MMD supporters at a rally, suffering significant injuries.[34]

The power of popular mobilization to shape elite preferences appears in another episode of major nonviolent resistance that occurred at the end of President Chiluba's second term in 2001. Many interviewees both from politics and civil society reported concern that no steps were being taken during that time to prepare a successor for the presidency. As 2001 grew closer, President Chiluba began explicitly making moves toward changing the constitution to allow him to run for a third term.

These moves sparked an immediate reaction within civil society. Organizations from the Non-Governmental Organization Coordinating Committee (NGOCC) in the women's movement to the Law Association of Zambia came together to form the Oasis Forum, an alliance of civil society groups that demanded that President Chiluba give up any attempt to run for a third term. The churches, including the evangelical churches, which had been major supporters of Chiluba since his proclamation of Zambia as a Christian nation, joined the Oasis Forum in condemning any attempts by Chiluba to extend his time in office.[35]

These moves powerfully affected President Chiluba's inner circle. Close advisors such as Kaunda-era foreign minister Vernon Mwaanga, who had remained in place throughout the Chiluba presidency, came together to tell Chiluba that his time was up. The master political manipulator, who had made the MMD almost his own personal fiefdom, found his pillars of support collapsing. Faced with the prospect of losing his party's support, President Chiluba ended his attempts to push for a third term and instead supported giving the MMD nomination to his former vice president Levy Mwanawasa, a widely admired person acceptable to the civil society coalition that had orchestrated the movement against the third term.

It is beyond the scope of this analysis to detail Zambia's political history from Mwanawasa's presidency to the present. The relevant aspects of democratic quality and legitimacy have fluctuated in the decades since. Tribalism has become more relevant in recent years, particularly since the rise of President Edgar Lungu. Yet my interviewees overall agreed that the general character of the Zambian regime has remained consistent. The patterns of behavior set up during the transition have been institutionalized and remain in place as of 2019.

Analysis

How does the Zambian case match the predictions of this book's theory and the findings on the impact of mobilization and maximalism from the quantitative research?

That significant demobilization occurred after the MMD's 1991 ascension to power is clear. Interviewees also strongly support the contention that this demobilization gave significant leeway for the failure of the transition to result in a more fully democratic regime. MMD's heavy reliance on old UNIP loyalists to fundraise, mobilize, and campaign on its behalf put into power a great number of people whose primary goal in ousting President Kaunda was not to fundamentally change the Zambian state but who joined the movement in order to gain power and prestige for themselves in an elite semi-democracy. A lack of continued popular pressure on them once they had achieved power allowed these preferences to manifest themselves.

Maximalism, as evidenced by UNIP and the Zero Option plan and by the MMD's attempts to shut President Kaunda out of the political process, also played a role in undermining Zambia's democratic development. This is a surprising element, considering that mobilization was quite low, even for UNIP, and so one might expect maximalism from such a minor force to have a relatively minor impact. The outsized impact can in part be explained by UNIP's history as a ruling party, and particularly by the larger-than-life figure of President Kaunda. Many people involved in the MMD government in the 1990s spoke of the deep paranoia that President Chiluba felt concerning President Kaunda. This may have caused him to overreact to the UNIP threat.

So the patterns of behavior described by this book's theory do seem to have had their expected impacts on Zambia's democratic development. Yet this is, of course, not the key question. The key question is whether these patterns of behavior are simply the result of a natural flow from deeper structural factors. Such determinism was certainly evident in some interviewees' attitudes toward the transition. Many in Zambia have become cynical about the prospects of popular action bringing about any kind of significant change. Several looked back fondly on the Kaunda era, recalling the strict limits on corruption and powerful economic supports that were in place for the Zambian people even during the most dictatorial periods of the Kaunda regime. So was the outcome of the Zambian transition predetermined by structural factors such as Zambia's poverty or tribal divisions?

Poverty, tribal divisions, colonial history, natural resources dependence, and regional context have doubtless shaped the Zambian political system. Cultural attitudes are no doubt also an important factor in shaping the decision-making processes of both elites and ordinary people. Yet the sharp breaks in political continuity and powerful moments of mobilization in Zambia's history belie the plausibility of a simple structural story. Zambia first waged a peaceful struggle for independence under the British. Then in the 1980s until 1991 a panoply of actors engaged in highly effective struggles that brought an end to President Kaunda's single-party rule. Even in the context of a quasi-democratic system under President Chiluba, moments of political action were not absent, as evidenced by the struggle over the third term. While Zambians may be divided by ethnicity and held back by poverty and history, they have shown time and time again that when roused they can use nonviolent tools to achieve astounding changes.

That these moments of intensely powerful nonviolent mobilization have failed to continue through periods of consolidation, leading to a less than perfectly democratic outcome, does not take away from their influence. Instead it suggests powerfully that the strategic challenge of mobilization is itself that: a challenge. When it is not resolved successfully, democratic transitions tend to break down. But when it is resolved, when the people hit the streets, even in conditions of powerful structural disadvantages, major changes can occur.

The resolution of this challenge in the Zambian case did not simply flow from the strategic alignments given by the preexisting economic, social, and cultural structure of Zambia but instead was shaped by the choices made during the period itself. For instance, as Sishuwa Sishuwa (2012, p. 364) writes regarding politics in Zambia during the Chiluba years:

> Opposition leaders . . . played their hands badly. A closer examination of the nature of leadership during this period would reveal that many of the most prominent opposition actors were elitists who failed to take politics out of the boardroom and onto the streets. They lacked a language with which to connect their political agenda with the demands or concerns of the electorate, the majority of whom lived in abject poverty, and so failed to build grassroots support networks.

The outcomes flowed not only from the hand dealt to Zambia by the past but also how this hand was played in the moment by leaders.

What alternative explanations are there for the outcome of the transition in Zambia? The most common is modernization theory. Many interviewees attributed Zambia's failure to democratize to the country's low levels of socioeconomic development. Poverty, according to many of these arguments, played the definitive role in the demobilization that allowed a small group of elites to take control of the Zambian government and turn it to their own ends.

The argument is certainly compelling and captures some central influences on Zambian politics. Yet it leaves several questions unanswered: first, it fails to explain well the most important event of this transitional story, the 1990–91 movement itself. The indicators of modernization are deployed to explain both mobilization and demobilization. On the one hand, the poverty engendered by economic difficulty in the 1980s is used as a factor to explain why the Zambian people were amenable to the mass mobilization necessary to oust Kaunda and bring the MMD to power, while on the other hand it is also deployed to explain why, a few years later, the same group of people were *de*mobilized and unable to hold this new government to account.

Second, data on political participation in Zambia during this period does not support the traditional contention that poverty undermines democratic participation or attitudes. In a 1993 survey Michael Bratton (1999, p. 561) found that poverty had no impact on Zambians' likelihood to participate in politics, and increasing levels of education actually had a negative impact on the likelihood of participation. Similarly, a 1996 survey by Bratton, Phillip Alderfer, and Neo Simutanyi (1997, pp. 17–18) found that traditional socioeconomic measures had inconsistent impacts on political participation. If the modernization story were correct, the data should look very different. We would expect to see low participation and support for democracy among the poor, uneducated segments of Zambian society. That such patterns almost fully fail to obtain suggests that something different is going on.

Clearly poverty plays a significant role in Zambian politics. Economic development or the lack thereof is a central axis of contention. As the literature shows and as I also show in my quantitative testing, modernization plays a significant role in shaping democratization. Yet this role is mediated by a long list of strategic choices and patterns of behavior made by those who come into power and the people who enable them to do so.

Can Zambia's failure to democratize be attributed simply to cultural factors of passivity and a preference for patronage politics? As with poverty, it seems clear from the literature and my own interview research that these factors play an important role in shaping the transitional challenges. Yet the dynamic character of these events also belies the explanatory usefulness of a single focus on culture. Can a passive culture explain Kaunda's ouster? Or the resistance to Chiluba's third term? At the very least Zambian political culture is a complex, involved factor that sometimes can explain some degree of mobilization and at other times can explain a degree of demobilization. Culture helps to set the stage, but patterns of agential behavior make up the play.

While the picture is complex, a close analysis of the Zambian transition generally supports the theory from Chapter 1 and findings from the quantitative research in Chapter 2. Low mobilization and maximalism resulted in a regime that closely approximates an elite semi-democracy. These patterns, while influenced by prior structural factors, are not fully determined by them.

Having covered regimes that approximated my two medial categories of fractious semi-democracy and elite semi-democracy, I now turn to a case of successful democratization in the aftermath of a civil resistance transition: the transition to democracy in Brazil in the 1980s.

5

Mobilization and Moderation in Brazil

THIS FINAL CASE study traces Brazil's transition from military rule to democracy in the 1980s. I selected Brazil to examine my proposed pathway during a civil resistance transition from high mobilization and low maximalism to a successful transition to democracy. The first relevant question is whether Brazil indeed matches this description. Is Brazil a democracy? I argue that it is. In recent years the country has certainly experienced democratic challenges, particularly related to corruption. Since the 2018 election of President Jair Bolsonaro there has been significant concern that Brazil has been a victim of the global trend of democratic backsliding at the hands of right-wing populism (Weizenmann, 2019), and in many parts of the country there have been long-standing problems with police brutality (Muñoz Acebes, 2016), disregard for indigenous rights (Rodrigues, 2002), poor treatment of Afro-Brazilians (Mitchell & Wood, 1998), and other human rights abuses (Ahnen, 2003). Yet since the transition in the 1980s, Brazil's political system has been broadly representative and has maintained largely free and fair elections and general protections for human rights and fundamental freedoms (Freedom House, 2019) and has even pioneered some institutions of participatory democracy (Abers, 2000). The system far exceeds the democratic threshold, though it may fall short of Dahl's (1973) democratic ideal.

Brazil scores quite high on the most highly respected cross-national quantitative measures of democracy. Figure 5.1 replicates the figures from Chapters 3 and 4, showing Brazil's scores on the V-Dem, Polity, and Unified Democracy scores in the 10 years before and after the beginning of the transition in 1985. Even the lowest of these, the Unified Democracy Score, rates Brazil as at least slightly across the threshold of a democratic regime, and Polity and V-Dem rate the regime as quite high on the democratic scale.

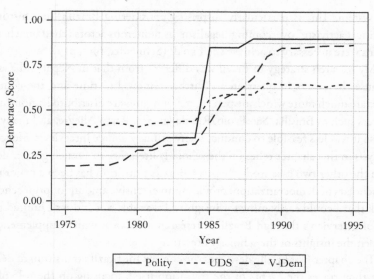

FIGURE 5.1 Brazil's Democracy Index Scores

I argue in this chapter that Brazil closely follows the patterns of mobilization and maximalism that this book's theory argues should push a country toward democracy. Political and social mobilization across many different social and political sectors remained high after the initial democratic breakthrough in 1985. This mobilization took several forms, with the greatest emphasis on advocating for protections to be incorporated in the 1988 constitution. Brazil's labor movement was one major source of this mobilization, both within the constitution-writing process and in day-to-day struggles for greater labor rights and protections (Keck, 1992). But the mobilization went well beyond workers, with significant pushes for progressive constitutional change by students (Langland, 2013), women's groups (Baldez, 2003), and the Catholic church (Mainwaring, 1986), among many others. This mobilization successfully constrained potential antidemocratic forces and helped push the Brazilian transition toward a more full-fledged democratic regime.[1]

Mobilization during the transition also almost universally took nonmaximalist forms, the focus of most major actors being on working within the new constitutional system. Brazil's major political actors, even those associated with the old authoritarian regime, focused their attention not on all-or-nothing grabs for power at the center but on developing cooperative relationships for mutual benefit based on responding to a diverse set of pressures from the broader society. Even formerly maximalist actors such as the Communist Party of Brazil (PCdoB) focused on engaging in institutionalized, electoral politics rather than disrupting the system. This is particularly surprising considering Brazil's long history of "political activism" overcoming "legalism" as numerous actors relied on whatever means were necessary to achieve their goals (Schneider, 1991, p. 9).

My research strategy in Brazil was different from that in Nepal and Zambia because the events in question are further removed in time and the country's elites are much more widely dispersed; major figures are distributed among urban centers such as Brasilia, São Paolo, Rio de Janeiro, Porto Allegre, and many others, so it was less feasible to conduct many primary-source interviews. Hence the analysis in this chapter relies on the scholarly literature to a much greater degree than the other two case study chapters. Brazil's transition has been a major topic for scholars of democratization, providing an extensive amount of prior scholarly work that I could easily mine for insights.[2] I was able to conduct a limited number of interviews through Brazilian research assistants, which supplement and deepen the insights of the scholarly literature.

The chapter first briefly describes the context for Brazil's transition to democracy, then traces the events of the transition itself, focusing on the role played by continued mobilization and the move toward institutionalized politics rather than maximalism. I conclude with an analysis of the role of these challenges in the Brazilian transition and make an argument for their importance.

The Military Regime and the Beginning of the Transition

Brazil's first brief period of democracy lasted roughly 20 years, between the time the quasi-fascist dictator Getulio Vargas was ousted in 1945 and the military coup that overthrew President João Goulart in 1964.[3] The generals who seized power initiated a period of military dictatorship,[4] waging an intense campaign to suppress opposition and concentrate power. However, throughout their rule the regime always maintained a degree of at least nominal adherence to quasi-democratic institutions, prompting Juan Linz (1973) to observe that Brazil did not have an authoritarian regime but rather simply an authoritarian "situation."

In particular, the military regime sought to institutionalize and incorporate its own political opposition. Their primary strategy to achieve this goal was by outlawing all parties in existence before 1964 and establishing a government-mandated two-party system (Kinzo, 1988). In this system the military's conservative allies ruled through the Aliança Renovadora Nacional (ARENA; National Renewal Alliance), and the opposition was represented by the Movimento Democrático Brasileiro (MDB; Brazilian Democratic Movement), the government-sanctioned loyal opposition party. The MDB was permitted to contest elections, and even sometimes to win them, but the electoral and governing institutions were heavily tilted to advantage ARENA and maintain a firm hold on power by elites loyal to the military (Mainwaring, 1988; Sarles, 1982).

Brazil's period of military rule was defined by the various generals who assumed the presidency. The military was heavily factionalized, and the various factions' visions of the goals of military rule diverged widely (Zirker, 1986). Under Presidents Humberto Castelo Branco, Artur da Costa e Silva, and Emilio Médici the regime assumed a set of highly repressive policies, particularly the fifth Institutional Act (AI-5) of 1968, which centralized power in the executive branch, suspended rights of habeas corpus, and severely restricted freedom of the press, freedom of expression, and freedom of assembly.

These extremely repressive measures sparked a backlash. Several different groups attempted to organize violent insurgency-based opposition to the military regime. One of the most prominent of these was a group called the Araguaia Guerrillas, organized by the PCdoB.[5] The PCdoB had broken from the more mainstream Brazilian Communist Party over the question of achieving the goal of a single-party communist state through armed insurrection even prior to the military coup of 1964. The coup provided the impetus for accelerating their efforts and beginning to create cells of guerrillas in the jungles of the Araguaia region. The guerrillas followed the Maoist model of "prolonged popular war," and some had received military training in China. The Brazilian military effectively suppressed this movement. By the early 1970s, through a combination of intensive intelligence operations and application of overwhelming military force, the guerrillas had been almost eliminated, their leaders arrested, killed, or driven into exile (de Souza Pinheiro, 1995).

President Ernesto Geisel initiated a period of liberalization in 1974, lifting some of the heavy restrictions on freedom of assembly and allowing greater civil society mobilization. The goal of this liberalization was primarily to enhance the legitimacy of military rule by allowing the façade of popular participation while still maintaining heavy authoritarian control on the scope of opposition to the government (Lamounier, 1989). The military regime had little fear that such an opening would lead to significant political change because they viewed the opposition as "so weakened through previous repression that it could not present an electoral threat even under conditions of freedom" (Sarles, 1982, p. 45).

The response was a flowering of social movements. The Catholic church played a crucial role in this flowering. Traditionally a conservative force in Brazilian politics, the dynamics of the Catholic church in Brazil, as in much of Latin America, began to change in the aftermath of the Vatican II council in the early 1960s and the Medellín Council of Latin American bishops in 1968 (Mainwaring, 1986). On an elite level, by the 1970s the leadership of the Brazilian Catholic church, organized under the National Conference of Brazilian Bishops, began sponsoring programs for social change, focused on a "centrist defense of civil liberties and human rights" (Della Cava, 1989, p. 146), in particular expressing opposition to torture and other authoritarian excesses. At the grassroots level, radical clergy and laypeople engaged in much more direct activism through the formation of the Ecumenical Base Communities, small local cells that functioned as crucial brokers between the sections of Brazil's emerging civil society (Cavendish, 1994).

The regime still heavily limited the degree to which social organizations could directly question the state, and so few focused directly on democratization. Instead there was a diversity of movement goals, based on the type of organization. One interviewee spoke about how his organization "did not directly call for the end of the military regime. But [they] discussed things that could be worked on in a new system."[6] Yet the overall frame of resisting authoritarianism unified these disparate social movements (Hochstetler, 2000, p. 166). A vast number of neighborhood movements, for example, began as service delivery organizations, but when confronted by the political nature of the challenges facing their communities they escalated their activity to direct advocacy (Mainwaring, 1989). Student groups reemerged to push for greater autonomy in higher education (Langland, 2013). Mothers' groups and neighborhood women's groups also emerged to advocate for the rights of women (Alvarez, 1989) and linked the struggle for women's freedom in the home with freedom from the violence of authoritarian rule (Nelson, 1996), even as a broader feminist movement grew in the 1970s and demanded that the opposition incorporate feminist demands in their programs for democratic reform (Baldez, 2003).

A resurgent labor movement also began to take shape, primarily in the industrial areas of São Paolo State's ABCD region. During the Estado Novo period under President Vargas, the Brazilian government had created a set of labor institutions that severely limited unions' power. Union leaders were more like civil servants whose responsibility was not to advocate for the interests of their union members but to ensure harmony between workers and the government (Keck, 1992). A large portion of union expenses was paid with a union tax collected by the government and distributed to union leaders. The primary responsibility of union leaders was to oversee the distribution of social security benefits, a task that cemented their role as government functionaries and undermined any independent power base (Moisés, 1979).

Thus for much of the time under military dictatorship there was little in the way of labor organizing, even though the regime was explicitly focused on a highly unequal, internationalist mode of development. However, the end of Brazil's "economic miracle" (Fishlow, 1973), when growth rates declined in the late 1970s, along with the government's liberalization process, led to increased levels of organizing activity.[7]

The first major example of organization came in response to the revelation in 1977 that the government had been falsifying inflation-indexing numbers, resulting in a severe underpayment of workers in several different unions (Keck, 1992, pp. 63–64). Luiz Inácio Lula da Silva, the president of the São Paolo Metalworkers Union, revealed the government's deception and demanded that the salary numbers be adjusted.

This resistance by a labor leader helped initiate a massive strike wave in 1978 and 1979. Hundreds of thousands of workers across dozens of industries went on strike over various labor demands. Lula emerged as a touchstone in these strikes, a powerful charismatic figure able to rally huge crowds of workers and to frame the demands of the working class for social, economic, and political change in a way that had not previously been articulated (Moisés, 1979).

The strikes of 1979 coincided with a strategic recalculation by the government. The MDB had successfully used the enforced two-party system as a way of transforming elections into plebiscites on the government's performance. Particularly as Brazil's economic fortunes worsened, this meant that, despite electoral rules that heavily favored ARENA, the MDB was gaining seats in Congress, as well as local positions around the country. As the only legal antigovernment party, MDB aggregated a wide set of diverse social and political forces under its banner. Elections served as referenda on popular support for the military regime (Sarles, 1982). The government sought to disrupt MDB's electoral momentum by changing the laws to allow for the creation of multiple parties. The rules for party creation were still extremely strict: potential parties had to demonstrate a wide degree of geographic dispersion, as well as meet high electoral thresholds, and radical leftist parties such as the PCdoB were still illegal.

Perhaps the most significant long-term consequence of the party liberalization law was the creation of the Partido dos Trabalhadores (PT; Workers' Party) as an outgrowth of the revitalized labor movement under leaders such as Lula. Unlike Brazil's traditional parties, including the MDB (now renamed the Partido do Movimento Democrático Brasileiro [PMDB], or Party of the Brazilian Democratic Movement, in accord with the naming rules in the new law), the PT from the start was a party with a mass base and membership that was deeply invested in party structure. The PT also incorporated a significant degree of intraparty democracy, creating mechanisms in which party members were able to select candidates independent of the preferences of party bosses (Keck, 1992, p. 112).

While the PT and a handful of other parties formed in response to the new party law, the PMDB was initially much more successful in making the case to the Brazilian people that it was the real alternative to military rule. The military was increasingly unpopular, and the appeal of an opposition government was growing. The PMDB's leadership was under pressure to push for a rapid move to civilian government, but under leaders such as Fernando Henrique Cardoso they instead opted to work within the system to gradually assume control rather than more directly confronting the military. Cardoso made the argument that a direct confrontation with the military would lead to bloodshed and that in the long term a democratic government could be achieved only if the military was brought on board with democratic change (Goertzel, 1999).

A crucial turning point in this process of growing PMDB strength occurred in 1982. In the elections that year PMDB candidates assumed the governorships of Brazil's three largest states—a position with significant power and influence in Brazil's federal system—and took many federal deputy and Senate seats.[8]

In 1984 these winds of change broke into a storm as Brazil's opposition movement, including social groups, the PT, and the PMDB, came together in a massive campaign of civil resistance to push for an immediate end to military rule through an amendment to the constitution that would allow for direct elections to the presidency. Brazil's constitution at the time dictated that the president be elected by an indirect electoral college whose members were dominated by military loyalists.

The Diretas Ja (Direct Elections Now!) movement was the largest example of nonviolent resistance in Brazil's history, with millions taking to the streets to push for the amendment's passage (Olivares, 2011). The movement failed in its immediate goal of passing a constitutional amendment. Yet the signaling of popular opposition to military rule forced major reconsiderations of the future among the military and their allies among the political elite. The goal of *abertura*, to create a stable foundation for continued quasi-authoritarian rule dominated by the military, would have to be rethought. Since the beginning of Geisel's presidency the military had justified its rule by claiming that it was gradually preparing the country for democracy, that they did not want to rule indefinitely but that the transition to democracy must be very carefully managed by the traditional military and political hierarchy. It is unclear how exactly the military leadership and their civilian allies intended for this process to take place. Yet it is clear that Diretas Ja signaled that the process would have to adapt to realities on the ground and "spelled the death of authoritarianism in Brazil" (Avritzer, 1995, p. 256).

Perhaps the most consequential outcome of this significant demonstration of popular opposition to continuing authoritarian rule was widespread defections by a number of legislators from the government's party, the Partido Democrático Social (PDS; Democratic Social Party; Martinez-Lara, 1996, p. 34).[9] These legislators, interested in finding a role in what now, because of Diretas Ja, felt like an inevitable move to democratization, formed the center-right Liberal Front and began negotiating with centrists in the PMDB for an acceptable way of transitioning to civilian rule.

Top military leaders also began negotiating with the PMDB. The character of these negotiations remains largely a matter of speculation, but one known demand from the government concerned who the PMDB would elevate as their candidate for president. The PMDB conceded, bypassing its longtime leader and prominent dissident, Ulysses Guimarães, to nominate the much more moderate PMDB governor of the state of Minas Gerais, Tancredo Neves.

The result of these defections and negotiations was that in the electoral college elections for the presidency in January 1985 Tancredo Neves defeated the PDS candidate, Paulo Maluf. The former PDS head and now leader of the Liberal Front José Sarney ran as Neves's vice president, bringing the PDS defectors on board and further assuaging the fear of military leaders of a radical opposition victory.

The continuation of popular opposition during the period leading up to the election served to secure Neves's position. Maluf extended wide patronage guarantees to the members of the electoral college and threatened defectors with retribution (Pang & Jarnagin, 1985). Yet popular opinion polls showed that the Neves ticket had an almost 3-to-1 advantage over Maluf, and mass rallies held by Neves around the country demonstrated the continued willingness of large numbers of people to resist the continuation of military rule, should the military's allies attempt to undermine the PMDB ticket (Schneider, 1991, p. 302). Brazil's first nonmilitary president since the coup of 1964 was set to take office in 1985 and initiate a democratic transition.

The Postelection Transition

A stroke of unkind fate changed the character of the Brazilian transition. Shortly before taking office, Neves was taken ill; he died on April 21, 1985. The next steps were somewhat unclear. Sarney, the former head of ARENA and a longtime military loyalist, was the vice presidential candidate and so had a claim to the presidency. However, since he had not yet been sworn in as the vice president, the legal precedent for his taking office was not straightforward. Were Sarney not to take office, the presidency would fall to the speaker of the House, Guimarães, the more radical leader of the PMDB whom the military had declared unacceptable. To ensure the stability of the transition, Guimarães agreed to not contest the presidency (Goertzel, 1999; Martinez-Lara, 1996, p. 52), and Sarney was elected.

While the level of social mobilization did not reach the peak of the Diretas Ja movement, widespread popular opposition continued under the Sarney government.[10] As Kathryn Hochstetler (2000, p. 163) writes:

Although the mid-1980s did see significant changes in social movements organizing in Brazil, popular and middle-class actors did not retreat from active mobilization. In fact, they launched a new cycle of social movement protest . . . [which showed] social movements to be important and positive contributors to the effort to deepen Brazilian democracy.

For many of the social movements that had struggled against the military regime, the new government was far from what they had wanted, particularly with Sarney at the helm.[11] Furthermore, while the social movements that made up the opposition during the dictatorship had shared a desire for democratization, for many of them a shift to civilian government and direct elections was not the endpoint of their struggle but rather the beginning of their advocacy for more rights (Keck, 1992, p. 2).

Popular movements born in the fires of resistance to authoritarian rule began considering the means by which they could turn the mobilization necessary to fight military rule into the creation of a genuine, fully participatory democracy (Della Cava, 1989, p. 152). Although they had joined hands with the PMDB to resist military rule, these popular movements now for the most part remained autonomous from the PMDB or any other party. This gave them the ability to maintain external sources of pressure over policy goals during the transition (Avritzer, 1995; Mainwaring, 1989, p. 190). The strategies and slogans of resistance to authoritarian rule were repurposed for policy-based movements. For instance, the Diretas Ja slogan of the movement against military rule was repurposed as Planejamento Familiar Ja! (Family Planning Now!) by the Brazilian women's movement (Alvarez, 1989, p. 221).

Civil society movements saw demobilization as a threat and actively sought to counter those tendencies. As Javier Martinez-Lara (1996, p. 86) writes:

[Popular movements] believed that organized efforts should be arranged in order to avoid the demobilizing effects of the "transition through trans-action" and to maximize the prospects of making a break with the past. . . . Aspirations for a more just society could only be achieved if popular pressure and participation were exercised.

Mobilization during the transition was undertaken not just in reaction to immediate needs but as part of a wider vision of advancing a democratic agenda during the uncertain times of the transition.

Within the party system the PT—although they had allied with the PMDB over the issue of direct elections—had even at that time critiqued the PMDB as a bourgeois elite party that did not truly have the interests of workers at heart (Keck, 1992). Under Sarney the labor movement launched a wave of strikes that even exceeded their level of activity in 1978 and 1979 (Skidmore, 1988, p. 294). In 1989 over 3,000 strikes took place around the country, a massive increase even from the peak of pretransition labor activism (Sandoval, 1993, p. 156). Environmental movements, women's movements, neighborhood associations, and others continued their push for their own preferred policy agenda throughout this period (Rothman & Oliver, 1999).

Mobilization was also facilitated by widespread disillusionment with the Sarney government's attempts to address Brazil's economic woes through the so-called Cruzado Plan. This plan involved a series of macroeconomic interventions, including the creation of a new currency and an extensive system of price controls, that were intended to fight inflation and stabilize Brazil's economy. While the Cruzado Plan had some initial success in 1985 and 1986, by 1987 its effectiveness was waning, leading to an increase in popular opposition to President Sarney and his government (Baer & Beckerman, 1989).

High levels of mobilization and political engagement were evidenced by the large turnout in Brazil's first national elections after the return of civilian rule, when almost 95% of registered voters participated (Lamounier & Neto, 2005, p. 175). The elections were particularly crucial as the incoming legislature would also be the constituent assembly writing Brazil's new constitution.

The PMDB dominated the 1986 elections, winning roughly 55% of the seats in the Senate and Chamber of Deputies, an important majority as the rules of the constituent assembly dictated that the constitution would be passed by simply majority (Sa, 2014, p. 87). Yet as the PMDB moved more deeply into government, its social movement allies began to mobilize against it in favor of their preferred policy positions (Martinez-Lara, 1996). Vast numbers of people from different movements came to Brasilia to push the constituent assembly to include in the new constitution items such as greater human rights protections and policies to address Brazil's high levels of poverty and inequality. The PMDB, with its long history of simply being a forum for opposition to the military government, was also highly fragmented and had little capacity to act as a unified front (Hagopian, 1990).

While the constitution was not a full "people's constitution" in the sense that it was largely drafted by Brazil's elites, including a large number of legislators from the old PDS government, the advocacy of labor rights activists, human rights defenders, and others was successful in gaining a number of concessions from the government, leading to the creation, for example, of Brazil's national health service (Martinez-Lara, 1996; Weyland, 1995).

Civil society and social movement groups participated actively and heavily in the drafting of the constitution through the proposal of popular amendments (Benvindo, 2017). The diversity of these amendments and the large numbers of signatures obtained by the organizations pushing for them display the depth and breadth of popular mobilization during the Brazilian transition: 122 popular amendments were sent to the assembly by organizations as diverse as the labor unions, the agricultural cooperative movement, and the National Housewives Association (Sa, 2014).

While there was certainly a diversity of political opinions and strategies, as one might expect in such a large and diverse country, most mainstream Brazilian politicians also pursued institutionalized, nonmaximal strategies for achieving power. Political party and social movement leaders tended to push for their preferred policy agendas within the framework of the constitutional convention and to accept the outcome.

As Wendy Hunter (1997) and others have observed, Brazil's transition, more than perhaps any other in Latin America, maintained the privileged position of the military. The amnesty law of 1979 protected military figures from prosecution for human rights abuses committed during the military regime,[12] and deals that allowed elites to shift parties, for instance through the defection of senators from the PDS to the Liberal Party and the PMDB, allowed many of the old regime elites to stay in power. President Sarney, of course, as an old ARENA hand himself, was friendly to the prerogatives of the military and did not question the military leadership to a significant degree. These bargains struck between the elites who had cooperated closely with the military and those who had labored in the opposition hampered any efforts to clean the slate.

In 1988 the constituent assembly passed and promulgated Brazil's new constitution, formalizing the transition to a democratic regime. The passage of the constitution was followed soon afterward by Brazil's first direct presidential election, in which a divided party space led to the surprise election of Fernando Collor de Mello, a scion of one of Brazil's oldest political families and a man who, like Sarney, had been closely associated with the old regime.

By most measures, and according to the reckoning of most of my interviewees, the election of Collor indicated the end of the transition, as new rules for achieving power had been fully established and put into practice, such that actors' expectations could converge around them.[13] However, because subsequent dramatic events played a role in the establishment of the new regime and evidence the impact of nonviolent resistance on Brazilian democracy, they bear some mention here.

Collor had based his appeal primarily on his youth and a stated commitment to clear out corrupt elites (Valença, 2002). Yet very quickly after beginning his presidential term it became apparent that the president himself was presiding over a deeply corrupt administration, centered around his family members.[14] When these allegations were made public, Brazil's civil society mobilized to demand that the problem be addressed. Nonpartisan mobilization around corruption reached a peak in late 1992, when crowds similar in size to those during the Diretas Ja campaign returned to the public square to demand that Collor be impeached for his corrupt practices (Hochstetler, 2000, p. 171). Brazil's parties responded by uniting in opposition to the president and, following the procedures laid out in the new constitution, impeaching him.

This episode is important as evidence for the power of both high mobilization and low maximalism in Brazil's transitional and posttransitional politics. Even though the rules were relatively untested and a move to more maximalist mobilization would have been eminently understandable, political forces for the most part did not take advantage of this opportunity. Instead they followed the legal, institutionalized process, preserving the new democratic order.[15]

Analysis

How well do mobilization and maximalism explain the Brazilian transition, and how well do they stand up against prominent alternative explanations? The Brazilian transition certainly exhibits both these patterns.

The level of mobilization during the transition was extremely high, with widespread activity on multiple fronts by new political parties, civil society groups, social movements, and a growing labor movement. The diffuse nature and diverse goals of the Brazilian movement for change was frequently cited by interviewees as a key reason for this transitional mobilization.[16] Opposition to the military regime had been situated in a broad set of movements with many different goals. For almost all of these, ending the military regime was only a step along the way. They had broader goals related to the social character of the state, increased rights for workers, greater protection of the environment, and many more. Even the PMDB, which for decades had been almost entirely focused on opposition to military rule, was forced to quickly shift into a political party advocating its own agenda as it rapidly found itself competing for electoral supremacy with the PT and other parties.

Mobilization was also facilitated by the incomplete nature of the 1985 transition. The death of Tancredo Neves and the presidency of José Sarney made most opposition forces deeply suspicious of the government. The PT in particular felt that it was critical to continue to act as a counterbalance to the influence of Sarney and old PDS loyalists (Keck, 1992).

These patterns of mobilization were not predetermined by Brazil's past. Indeed the flowering of civil society and its increasing influence during the transition was a radically new and innovative pattern in Brazilian politics. As Ronald Schneider (1991, p. 13) wrote in the early 1990s, "Mobilization of the populace has been a strikingly ineffective force in Brazilian political life." In the past, clientelist relationships, a strict social hierarchy, and the very diversity of interests across the country's different regions had stymied both the size and the impact of ordinary people's mobilization.[17] We would expect such mobilization to continue to be minimal in size and marginal in impact in this transition. Yet while the old patterns continued to exert an influence, they were heavily influenced by popular mobilization of a greater degree than the country had ever experienced, to the point that by the 1990s former president Itamar Franco suggested the "Diretas Ja and impeachment campaign models" as powerful tools for achieving political goals (Hochstetler, 2000, p. 171). The activation of civil society in the struggle for democracy, and even more in the struggle for a new kind of democracy in the transition after 1985 led to a significant democratization not just of Brazil's politics at a national institutional level but throughout the country as civic actors pushed for and in many cases achieved new participatory governance institutions (Wampler & Avritzer, 2004).

Both tactically and rhetorically the players in Brazil's politics also eschewed maximalism and moved to institutionalize contention. Struggle quickly moved to the forum of the constituent assembly and contention over the degree to which various agendas would be incorporated in the new constitutional structure, and then to the structures put in place by the constituent assembly process. Throughout the transition there was a pattern of compromise and agreement rather than all-or-nothing control of the center. As Schneider (1991, p. 304) writes, "The successful transition owed a great deal to the reasonableness and moderation demonstrated by almost all significant political actors. Those disappointed by the course of events came to accept their setback and eventually assumed a statesman-like stance." Major political players accepted losses and sought to maintain the environment of conciliation among factions. This was perhaps best captured in the way that the transition was initiated, through an agreement between Neves and those PDS leaders who had seen the level of mobilization during the Diretas Ja movement and sought to adapt to the new order. These kinds of agreements continued to be a pattern during the transition. And even when major moves to change power in the center took place, as in the impeachment proceedings against President Collor, these moves took place within the new legal order. Major disruptive noninstitutional action played a minimal role in achieving political changes.

As the transition and later the new democratic regime moved forward, the low maximalism and high degree of institutionalization in Brazil's politics was well captured by the strategies pursued by the PT. Despite its connections to more revolutionary leftist groups, the PT quickly moved to function as a loyal

opposition, articulating its goals and grievances through the realm of institutionalized politics and providing a structured, nonviolent channel of participation for
activists disillusioned with the ways in which Brazil's politics fell short of the ideals they had hoped for when struggling against the military regime (Nylen, 2000).

This type of action has not been typical of Brazilian politics for much of the
country's history. Rather, at least since the beginning of the old republic in the
late 1880s, political competition typically followed much more maximalist lines,
with goals trumping allegiance to legal or normative institutions. The pattern
of politics that the MDB began to articulate during the period of military rule
and that came to the fore during the transition was a new pattern in Brazil, off
the equilibrium path of the past. This sharp divergence speaks to the importance
of actors' agential choices. Culture, economics, and political institutions shape
but do not define the choices that actors make, particularly during the critical
moments of transitions.

What about the major alternative explanations? Because of the situation of
this case in particular, it is important to take a slightly different approach than in
my other case studies. The strongest alternative explanation is that this transition
was not a civil resistance transition at all but instead was solely a matter of military initiative, its terms dictated by the hierarchy of the military leadership. Brazil
is frequently cited as an example of a pacted transition brought about through
top-down initiative; in fact Hunter (1997, p. 26) describes the position of the
Brazilian military at the beginning of the transition as "unassailable." Since this is
the case, is my theory applicable?

That the military leadership's initiative played a key role in Brazil's transition
is undeniable. The decision by President Geisel to initiate the *distensão* (decom-
pression) and later *abertura* (opening) critically shaped the sequence of events
that resulted in Brazil's transition to democracy. It is difficult to imagine the
shape of the transition had such steps not been taken.

But similarly it is difficult to imagine the shape of the Brazilian transition,
or indeed even the occurrence of a transition, with the opposition's sustained
efforts. The *abertura* years were a dialectical process, in which both the government and the opposition felt out how far they could push the other (Skidmore,
1988). The *abertura* process was not only a top-down initiative but reflected
pushes from both above and below. As Scott Mainwaring (1989, p. 196) explains,
"Many changes were not foreseen by the originators of the *abertura*; they rather
reflected an ongoing process of opposition initiatives, followed by subsequent
regime response and initiatives, with occasional negotiating between the two
sides."

When Geisel came to power and took some liberalizing steps his vision was
not of democratization but a gradual move toward increased participation by

"responsible elites." Their steps were designed not to democratize the government but rather to stabilize authoritarian rule, in which elections might occur but pro-government parties would always win (Martinez-Lara, 1996; Skidmore, 1988, p. 164). The military regime opened because they feared the consequences if they remained closed. They feared these consequences at least in part because of the intensity of the opposition, which they anticipated would continue to narrow their range of options if they kept the regime fully closed (Schneider, 1991, p. 270).

Once *abertura* was initiated, resistance by the opposition played a key role in cementing the gains made and pushing for more. Bolivar Lamounier (1989, p. 71) argues, "The importance of movements of so-called civil society . . . was not so much that they forced the beginning of the *abertura,* but that little by little they created informal but effective constraints on the dictatorial exercise of power." Nonviolent resistance prevented a return to dictatorial control and pushed the minimal liberalization envisioned by the military into a democratic transition.

The military did enjoy significant influence over the transition. There was no full breakdown of regime control, and military leaders were able to negotiate significant concessions for themselves in the new regime (Hunter, 1997). But this control was by no means absolute and by the time of Collor's presidency had faded significantly into the background (Zirker, 1993). In the transition military leaders quickly found themselves sidelined by the leaders now in positions of influence. For example, the military had a well-known preference for limiting labor rights in the new democratic regime, and in particular limiting the right to strike (Hunter, 1997, p. 84). Yet well-organized mobilization by the labor movement not only resulted in increased protection of labor rights but even got the right to strike enshrined in the Brazilian constitution (Cook, 2002; Martinez-Lara, 1996). When the military attempted to intervene in strikes during the transition, it sparked such wide societal backlash that the military was forced to significantly scale back its role in labor relations (Hunter, 1997, p. 90). This result fits poorly with a transition managed entirely from above.

Thus it is reasonable to consider Brazil's 1984 transition a civil resistance transition. Civil resistance did not disintegrate the military regime, but disintegration is only one of the mechanisms whereby civil resistance can achieve change. The Brazilian case evidences instead the mechanisms of accommodation, in which the opponent perceives the shifting balance of power brought about through nonviolent resistance and attempts to avoid a worse result by going along with it (Sharp, 1973, pp. 733–40).

So much for the idea that the military leaders in Brazil were solely responsible for the transition and its character. What about broader arguments related to modernization? Brazil had certainly gone through significant socioeconomic development when the transition began in 1985. Yet it is difficult to see the mechanisms of modernization theory at work in this case, primarily because of Brazil's high degree of inequality. While GDP per capita had risen to a level beyond which democratic breakdowns were unlikely, these economic gains were heavily concentrated in the wealthiest classes. A large majority of the Brazilian population still lived (and lives) in extreme poverty (Lopez-Calva & Rocha, 2012).

Increasing levels of economic development, education, and other aspects of modernization were filtered through strategies pursued by the major political actors in Brazil's transition. The economic situation influenced but did not determine the shape those strategies took.

The traditional transitology approach, which was in part inspired by the early stages of the Brazilian transition (Whitehead, O'Donnell, & Schmitter, 1989), certainly fits the transition to some degree. But the fear of popular mobilization and the emphasis on the agency of elites will lead us astray if we focus on them too heavily. The decisions of ordinary people played a central role in shaping the transition's direction, and the mobilization of society to continue to push the transition forward was key in leading Brazil to become not an illiberal quasi-democracy but a relatively liberal democratic political system. Brazil's elites pursued a relatively moderate, democratizing path. But as the evidence presented in this chapter shows, they were kept on that path not by positive, pro-democratic feelings from within but by consistent pressure from without.

So I argue that, while prior theories do a good job of explaining some features of the Brazilian transition, looking at patterns of mobilization and maximalism adds important explanatory power. The transitional dynamics themselves shaped the development of Brazilian democracy, leading to a result that could have been very different had leaders and ordinary people made different choices.

THIS EXAMINATION OF the Brazilian transition concludes the three case studies and the small-*n* analysis component of my nested analysis research design (Lieberman, 2005). In all three cases, while the qualitative examination of the cases reveals potential additional factors to explore, such as the degree of autonomy of mobilization during the transition, the qualitative research supports the quantitative findings. High mobilization and high maximalism in the Nepali case undermined the institutionalization of a new democratic system and led to a fractious semi-democracy. Low mobilization and low maximalism in the Zambian case led to an elite semi-democracy. And high mobilization and low maximalism during the transition in Brazil facilitated a successful transition democracy.

All three case studies reveal that the operation of these strategic challenges is not simple, that other factors play an important role in determining transitional outcomes. However, a close weighing of the various arguments prominent in explanations of these cases reveals an important role played by the resolution of these strategic challenges. There is more work to be done in articulating the more complex interactions of these challenges with other factors identified in these chapters, such as the contrast between independent mobilization and mobilization channeled through political parties. But adding a consideration of the dynamics of mobilization and maximalism is a fruitful starting point from which to begin to understand these complexities.

6

Civil Resistance and Democratization

THIS BOOK HAS examined democratization in transitions initiated by non-violent resistance. The research was motivated by this underlying empirical puzzle: that despite the overall positive influence of nonviolent resistance on democratization, there are still many CRTs that fall short of democratic ideals. What has the evidence shown?

The statistical analysis of 70 years of political transitions and in-depth examinations of the transitions in Nepal, Zambia, and Brazil tell us two important things. First, nonviolent resistance does indeed have a powerful democratizing effect, as argued in the growing literature on this subject. Its effect is stronger and more consistent than many of the other traditionally accepted causes of democratization. Civil resistance is certainly not *less* democratizing than more orderly, elite-led transitions, and in fact seems to be much more democratizing. Therefore the critique of civil resistance as, on average, ushering in regimes in which unstable street politics destroy the potential for establishing consolidated democratic institutions is largely unfounded, at least when compared to all other potential sources for transition (Li, 2014).

Civil resistance stands out as one of the major signs of hope in a period of stalling democratic progress. When transitions are initiated through civil resistance, it alters the balance of power in a democratic direction. These transitions tend to bring to power more democratizing leaders, transform norms of political conflict, and diffuse power from centralized elites to civil society and ordinary people.

However, it is crucial to not be naïve or uncritically optimistic about the relationship between civil resistance and democratization. CRTs can and do break down. Initiating a transition nonviolently, while it may give a country an advantage in the struggle for democratization, is not a panacea. Many CRTs fall short of the high-flown democratic ideals that outside observers often attribute to them at the heights of their mobilization. Such movements as the Arab Spring in Egypt and the nonviolent resistance to the 1991 Soviet hard-liner coup have failed to bring about any significant democratic progress in their wake.

There has been a tendency in the literature to attribute these failures to inevitable structural disadvantages or to culturally or politically contingent factors unique to particular cases. In both cases the preferred explanation leaves little room for individual or group agency. Democracy failed to take hold because the people were simply too poor or their elites too corrupt or their culture too passive. If these critiques are correct, then civil resistance has little to offer a world going through a democratic recession. At best, uprisings on the streets will lead to short-term, unstable political openings, followed by the structurally or culturally inevitable return of autocracy.

In this book I have offered an alternative explanation, backed by both qualitative and quantitative evidence, that recognizes the important shaping role of structure but also opens the democratization causal chain to greater flexibility. When CRTs break down we can understand the systematic sources of that breakdown: they tend to come when either mobilization fails or maximalism triumphs. Both these breakdowns undermine the processes of transformation in leaders, norms, and the distribution of power that sustain the democratizing advantage of civil resistance. Without high transitional mobilization and low transitional maximalism, CRTs will be fraught with difficulty and typically end in a semidemocratic or authoritarian system.

Neither of these patterns of democratizing behavior come easily. Maintaining mobilization during the transition is hampered as the centralizing and unifying figure of the old regime is no longer there to maintain disparate factions' connections (Beissinger, 2013). New elites may also actively discourage mobilization by groups not directly under their control, as happened in Zambia, described in Chapter 4, where when the labor leader Frederick Chiluba became president he rapidly turned against his activist roots and tried to subvert pushes for further democratic progress. And international assistance to civil society that helped fuel the initial breakthrough may wane or redirect itself toward goals disconnected from the needs of ordinary people.

The temptations of maximalism, using the disruptive and destructive potential of nonviolent resistance for narrow ends, is also a major challenge that a country's new leadership often fails to overcome. Without well-established rules of the political game in place to regulate their competition, ambitious elites may seek short-term advantage in burning down the nascent system around them. Polarized publics may follow these elite power plays, destabilizing transitions and making their countries vulnerable to democratic breakdown, as in Nepal, where, as I describe in Chapter 3, the feeling of perpetual crisis has undermined faith in democracy even among the human rights activists who were fundamental to establishing it in the first place.

Yet as evidenced by the many CRTs that have successfully democratized, the avenues to make these choices are always open. As Francisco Weffort (1989, p. 331), one of the protagonists of the democratization struggle in Brazil, asserts:

> It is *always* possible to take different paths of action. . . . Much as the conditions weigh upon the situation, much as the past imposes itself, there are always choices to make. A political action is *par excellence,* an act of freedom. It takes place only in the present and in the face of a future which is always open and uncertain.

In the spirit of this quote, the evidence in this book strongly suggests that structural factors are not able to explain democratization on their own, nor can they fully explain these democratizing patterns of behavior during transitions. While structure constrains, it does not determine. Knowing how poor a country is or whether it has democratic neighbors or its degree of linkage to the democratic West can give us a sense of the extreme bounds of how much democratic progress we may expect, but it does not answer the question of whether a nonviolent revolution will end in a democracy. To get to that answer we must account for the choices made during the period of transition.

These choices, to mobilize or not to mobilize, and whether this mobilization is directed toward maximalist goals, mediate the impact of structural factors. While structure affects both the likelihood of successfully resolving these strategic challenges and the level of democracy, this does not mean that the effects of mobilization and maximalism can be reduced to their structural preconditions. We see this both in the low level of correlation between the structural factors and the mobilization and maximalism variables and in the degree to which adding mobilization and maximalism improves model fit, indicating a significant increase in what we can explain by looking beyond structure. This book's argument and evidence strongly support a more agential and contingent view of democratization. Political actors' choices are meaningful and have important differential impacts.

The quantitative analysis of all CRTs in the post–World War II period finds significant evidence that the theory articulated here accurately and robustly describes the dynamics of CRTs. CRTs with high levels of mobilization and low levels of maximalism almost always cross the minimal threshold of electoral democracy and reach much higher levels of democratic quality, as evidenced by their significantly higher scores on the polyarchy index.

The case studies from Nepal, Zambia, and Brazil provide further evidence that the mechanisms proposed by the theory are in fact what explain the relationship identified in the statistical testing. In all three cases, the choices of political elites and ordinary citizens that together constituted those transitions' patterns of mobilization and maximalism had strong effects on the regimes that emerged at the end of the transition. Taking these patterns of behavior into account explains these transitions' outcomes at least as well as prominent explanations in the literature on the cases themselves and the broader democratization literature.

However, it is important to note that this study's findings come with some significant limitations. First, both my quantitative and qualitative analysis is limited to examining cases of actual transitions, either initiated by civil resistance or not and, if initiated by civil resistance, then characterized by varying degrees of mobilization and maximalism. Thus my findings do not apply to cases of civil resistance that failed to initiate a political transition. There is some evidence from other studies that even such failed campaigns may help improve democratic prospects (Chenoweth & Stephan, 2011), but my research does not speak to this debate.

While the results of the quantitative testing are highly robust to alternative specifications, they do rely on the specific definitions of nonviolent resistance, democracy, mobilization, and maximalism articulated in the introduction and Chapter 1. Other scholars operating with different theoretical priors on the definition of nonviolent action or the essential characteristics of democracy, and thus different procedures for reasonably operationalizing these concepts, may come to radically different conclusions.

Similarly, while I have selected widely divergent cases to attempt to achieve as broad external validity as possible and found broad support for my theory in these differing contexts, it is possible that certain contextual factors in other cases may reduce mobilization and maximalism in the transition to factors of minimal importance. For instance, cases in which direct international intervention overwhelmingly shaped the outcome (such as the transition in East Timor in the 1990s) may fall outside the scope of the theory. To explicitly theorize about such cases is beyond the bounds of this book, but I note it as a limitation of the book's research strategy and leave it as a question for future research.

Significance for Future Research

There are several additional avenues that I hope this book will open for future research. This book is by no means the last word on democratization in CRTs. Instead it is intended to serve as a starting point for a growing research program digging into these dynamics in greater depth than has been possible here. There are three avenues where I see this research most productively continuing: first, articulating additional challenges by continuing to theorize about the incentives implied by the nature of CRTs; second, applying this approach to democratization more generally; and third, looking systematically at the sources of mobilization and maximalism in transitions.

What other challenges might we articulate and test to build better explanations of democratization in CRTs? One insight from the case studies relates to mobilization. Mobilization was most effective in promoting democratization when it was independent from the political parties that came into power after the CRT's success. When mobilization was tied too closely to leaders its democratizing effect was attenuated. In Nepal, for instance, activism has been hampered by the perception that most "independent" civil society actors are in fact simply people from one of the country's major political parties for whom it is not currently convenient to be in office. Attempts to pursue ostensibly nonpartisan, prodemocratic agendas are perceived by major political actors as being strategically deployed for partisan benefit. In Zambia, because the infrastructure of resistance was almost entirely channeled through a single political party, once that party took over there were few powerful countervailing forces to resist its excesses. In Brazil (Chapter 5), in contrast, the opposition had been highly dispersed among different groups with divergent goals. The years of transition were characterized by high levels of pressure from groups that had only tangential connections to political parties and could credibly advocate for their own issue areas.

Therefore an additional challenge in CRTs relates to the organizational structure of resistance both before and during the transition.[1] What are the avenues through which mobilization is pursued? Related to this, a more specific examination of the goals of mobilization could enrich our understanding of the mechanisms whereby mobilization has its positive effect on democratization. Numerous other challenges could also be articulated. The careful blending of qualitative theory building and quantitative testing will be crucial in establishing the applicability and effects of these challenges.

The challenges I have presented also focus primarily on forces that remain outside of the state or that compete for state power. Yet the organs of state power, particularly state security forces, also play an important role in CRTs. And the defection of security forces plays a crucial role in the success of CRTs (Nepstad, 2013). This often makes security forces a decisive actor during the transition, with significant ability to tip the scales when it comes to the transition's political dynamics. Examining the role of security forces in CRTs is an important avenue for further research, with some promising initial studies.[2]

Do maximalism and mobilization have the same effects in other kinds of democratic transitions? I expect that the mechanisms should operate similarly, but with some important divergences. We would expect that popular pressure would generally be positive for democratization and that the disruption caused by maximalist contention would generally be negative. Yet the contextual differences between a CRT and other forms of transition should impact their effects. In a transition initiated by top-down liberalization, popular pressure is less likely to have a causal role in democratic progress since the balance of political power lies so strongly with members of the old regime.

Understanding the sources of mobilization and maximalism in a systematic way will be another crucial way to expand this research agenda. The models in Chapter 2 show that this set of patterns cannot be reduced to any of the usual suspects in democratization theory. For instance, high mobilization during a transition does not automatically occur in countries with high levels of modernization or in those countries that had relatively light authoritarian regimes prior to the transition. Just as civil resistance itself is difficult to predict through structural factors (Chenoweth & Ulfelder, 2017), so are the patterns of behavior during CRTs. Yet, just as I have shown that mobilization and maximalism during the transition matter in defining the transition's conclusion, so it is certainly plausible that strategic factors from before the transition might matter systematically in at least partially explaining these patterns of mobilization and maximalism.

Scholars have already done some initial work in examining these questions. For instance, Charles Butcher and his coauthors (2018) have shown that when certain social groups, particularly labor unions, participate in nonviolent resistance movements, their country's future level of democracy is significantly increased. This occurs because these groups have justifications for functioning that come from quotidian needs that endure beyond the ousting of the old regime. These groups can continue to mobilize once the old regime has been removed. The mechanism here is transitional mobilization, as in this book. Thus examining the connections between the make-up of resistance movements and patterns of mobilization would likely be a fruitful avenue to explore.

Institutions in the old regime may also have an impact on the likelihood of democratization and the level of democracy in the country at the end of the transition. Scholars of the postcommunist transitions in Eastern Europe, for example, have argued that countries that had allowed for even minimal, noncompetitive opposition were better prepared for their democratic transitions than those that had largely suppressed opposition (Ekiert, Kubik, & Vachudova, 2007). One mechanism for this effect to obtain would be by affecting the mobilizational capacity of social and political actors during the transition and making maximalism a less attractive choice.

The insights into the effects of mobilization and maximalism on democratization also speak to several related debates in the nonviolent resistance literature. For instance, there is both a popular and a scholarly debate over the potential benefits of mixing nonviolent resistance with violent tactics. Some argue that any departure from strict nonviolent discipline reduces the chances of campaign success by undermining the mechanisms of nonviolent action (Chenoweth & Schock, 2015), while others argue that mixing some violent with nonviolent tactics protects vulnerable nonviolent protesters, aids in creating the kinds of disruption that make nonviolent resistance effective, and may give the nonviolent segments of a resistance campaign greater appeal and leverage over their opponents (Haines, 1984).

Leaving the question of success aside, my research indicates that the use of violent tactics to overthrow an authoritarian regime likely has a pernicious effect on long-term democratization by encouraging maximalist political dynamics. This was clearest in Nepal, where the fact that Nepal's parties, particularly the Maoists, had armed cadres that they could call upon significantly undermined trust between major political actors, discouraged compromise, and encouraged attempts by all the actors involved to push as much as possible for their own secure power base.

Policy Significance

There are several practical lessons in this work for leaders and ordinary citizens of countries going through CRTs.[3] The necessity for strong, continued popular mobilization beyond the moment of the campaign itself is a clear implication of the work. How can this mobilization be achieved? The case studies have several lessons here. Suspicion of one's own leaders is one lesson. In Zambia mobilization collapsed in large part because of the faith in the new MMD government. In Nepal mobilization continued but became tainted with maximalism as the avenues for mobilization largely followed the dictates of particular leaders. Personalized nonviolent movements with prominent leaders who dictate the character of mobilization to their followers might be one risk factor for a decline in mobilization during a transition. Similarly too close attachment to the fortunes of a leader, rather than to the success of the system, may encourage the kinds of winner-take-all politics characteristic of high maximalism systems.

The findings also speak to the importance of compromise. The sources of maximalism in Nepal, for instance, were given greater salience by a push to fundamentally restructure the state according to the demands of narrowly defined communities. Engaging in maximalism, while it may lead to short-term gains, ultimately undermines the institutional frameworks that support democratic consolidation. Compromise across political opinion is crucial as the foundation for a long-term democratic political order.

The robustness of the democratizing influence of civil resistance also suggests that CRTs may be a particularly potent avenue for intervention by international actors interested in promoting democracy. Democratization is rare in environments that are structurally unfavorable to it. The exception to this rule is a CRT, in which democratic progress often occurs despite hostile conditions.

Intervention requires care and respect for the autonomy of local actors. Social movements and international donors rarely mix well. Yet if international actors respect local actors' connection to their social bases, then there are a few avenues in which this research suggests their assistance may be particularly useful.

Switching focus during transition from maximalist contention to institution-building is one of these. As described in Chapter 1, nonviolent resistance often elevates leaders with more pro-democratic preferences to positions of power and influence. But the very background that may make these leaders more democratically inclined is also likely to have given them little experience in the technicalities of running a modern state and setting up new political institutions. International assistance to give new elites training in understanding and confidence in competing through new political institutions may be a useful way to encourage democratic progress in CRTs.

Keeping transitional elites accountable for protecting freedom of association, and not actively demobilizing their independent civil society, is another avenue through which consistent international pressure can be productive in pushing the democratic progress of CRTs forward. The pressure to demobilize evidenced in the Nepal and Zambia cases was actively encouraged by the new elites struggling for control of the transitional state. International pressure can be a useful avenue with which to discourage this process.

IN CONCLUSION, I RETURN to the words of Hannah Arendt (1963, p. 29) that opened this book: "Liberation may be the condition of freedom but by no means leads automatically to it." Achieving liberation, overthrowing an oppressive regime is only the beginning. Getting from liberation to freedom is a long, arduous, and uncertain journey. I hope that the work done here may light the way for some of the many travelers on that journey.

APPENDIX

Variable Coding, Additional Statistical Tests, and Interview Data

Identifying Transitions and Civil Resistance Transitions

My population of cases, both of transitions as a whole and of CRTs, comes from combining two well-respected data sources: the data on nondemocratic regimes and their types of failure produced by Barbara Geddes, Joseph Wright, and Erica Frantz (2014) and the NAVCO 2.1 data set produced by Erica Chenoweth and Christopher Shay (2019). NAVCO 2.1 is a revised and extended version of the NAVCO 2.0 data set initially produced by Erica Chenoweth and Orion Lewis (2013).

The Geddes et al. data includes every instance of regime breakdown. The data set measures the duration of individual regimes, defined as "the rules that: (1) identify the group from which leaders can come; and (2) determine who influences leadership choice and policy" (Geddes et al., 2014, p. 314). Transitions from one authoritarian regime to another are captured in the data, even if the level of democracy remained almost unchanged from before the transition to after the transition, giving this data set a crucial advantage over other typical data sources used to measure democracy and dictatorship, such as the Polity IV data set. For instance, the Cuban Revolution in 1959 and the Iranian Revolution in 1979, in both of which one authoritarian regime was replaced by another, are captured in the data as transitions from one regime to another rather than continuous periods of nondemocracy.

I first take the entire population of authoritarian regime breakdowns from 1945 through 2011 in the Geddes data. The Geddes data ends in 2010, thus I personally coded the data forward through 2015 to capture any additional regime breakdowns. I detail this process and justify additional regime breakdown codings in the next section. I add to this population all the transitions from colonial rule to independence during this time period. The Geddes data set does not include these transitions since it contains only data on states with formal independence and sovereignty; however, I argue that they are appropriate to include. Colonial rule was an important form of nondemocratic rule for almost the first half of the period that I am including, and there is no inherent theoretical reason why we should expect colonial rule to depart from the general models of transition from authoritarian rule that I have previously described. This process leads to a total population of 331 transitions.

From this population I then determined which cases were CRTs. My first cut at this was to identify all country-years with ongoing nonviolent resistance campaigns in NAVCO 2.1 that correlate with an authoritarian regime breakdown in the Geddes data. I then checked each of these cases individually through an examination of the country-specific scholarly literature to ensure that it met my inclusion criteria. I also added a small number of cases discovered through independent research and by examining the cases included in Pinckney (2014) and Bethke and Pinckney (2019). To determine whether each case warranted inclusion as a CRT I looked at several factors:

1. *Scope.* Was the civil resistance campaign of a size and ubiquity that it would have been almost impossible to ignore? Larger campaigns that were spread more widely across the country are more likely to have had a crucial impact on the subsequent process of political development. I treated campaigns that took place coterminous with regime transitions but were small or concentrated solely in isolated pockets of the country with more skepticism.

2. *Other triggering factors.* As I described earlier, the existence of other crucial factors in explaining a transition does not mean that a transition is excluded from the population of CRTs. However, if in reviewing the secondary literature on a case where a CRT took place I routinely find the civil resistance campaign ignored or its significance downplayed by scholars and other observers, then I treated its inclusion with greater skepticism.

3. *Elapsed time.* If regime breakdown occurred coterminous with or in the immediate aftermath of major civil resistance activity, then I considered the case a more likely candidate for inclusion. If a long period of time elapsed between major nonviolent resistance activities and the regime change, then I considered the case more skeptically.

4. *Counterfactual plausibility.* This is the most powerful criterion even if it is also the most abstract. Can one plausibly argue that the trajectory of regime breakdown would have occurred in the same or a similar way absent the civil resistance campaign? If so, then the case is not a CRT. If, however, the regime breakdown is difficult to imagine absent the civil resistance campaign, then the case is likely a CRT.

Expanding the Authoritarian Regimes Data

I expanded the Geddes data set on authoritarian regimes through 2015 to include new cases of political transition. I checked several sources to ascertain whether a regime change event occurred between 2011 and 2015. For countries that Geddes coded as democracies, my first source to check was the V-Dem polyarchy score (Coppedge et al., 2018). If the score had remained more or less the same as in 2010 (less than a 0.2 decline), I simply coded a democratic regime as continuing through 2015. If there had been a decline in the polyarchy score I then checked the Freedom House (2019a) reports on the country to ascertain the reasons for the declining score. This was typically enough to determine whether a democratic breakdown (as defined by the Geddes codebook) had occurred.

For authoritarian regimes I checked the Archigos data set (Goemans et al., 2009) to determine whether there had been an irregular leader entry or exit between 2010 and 2015. If no irregular leader change had occurred, I simply coded the regime as continuing through 2015. If Archigos did code an irregular leadership change, I checked the Archigos case narratives and other secondary sources to determine the nature of the change.

I also added a prior regime coding of "colonial" to regimes if they entered the data set as a result of obtaining independence from their colonizer (excluding previously colonized countries that became independent prior to 1946). This allowed me to include cases of transition from colonial rule.

I attempted to follow the Geddes coding rules as closely as possible, and unless the empirical evidence was overwhelmingly strong I deferred to their prior codings. Before reading the following case notes I recommend reading the Geddes codebook for context, available at http://sites.psu.edu/dictators/wp-content/uploads/sites/12570/2016/05/GWF-Codebook.pdf.

Specific Case Codings

Afghanistan: I continued Geddes's coding of Afghanistan as *personalistic* from 2009 through 2015. I code a *regime failure* moment at the 2014 election since this fits the definition of regime change, but this did not mark a democratic transition since the election was not free and fair. It is difficult to categorize the current Afghan regime in terms of Geddes's typology; hence for ease of analysis I simply keep it as personalistic. Bosnia: Geddes code Bosnia as *foreign-occupied* because of the power of the high representative to overturn elected government decisions. I follow their coding rule.

Botswana: Geddes code Botswana as a single-party authoritarian regime due to the domination of Botswanan politics by the Botswana Democratic Party. V-Dem gives Botswana a fairly high polyarchy score (roughly 0.7 during the whole 2010–15 period), well above other regimes that Geddes code as democracies. However, for the sake of continuity I deferred to Geddes's coding and coded Botswana as a *single-party authoritarian* regime through 2015.

Burkina Faso: I code the Compaoré regime in Burkina Faso as *ending* in October 2014 with Blaise Compaoré's ouster in the 2014 Lwili Revolution. I code the following regime under interim president Michel Kafando as *provisional* because the regime was explicitly set up to prepare for democratic elections, which did in fact take place in late 2015. Late 2015 marks the *beginning* of a democratic regime. There was an attempted coup in late 2015, but the coup failed to unseat Kafando.

Burundi: Geddes code Burundi as a democracy beginning with the election of 2005. I code this democratic regime as *ending* in 2010 because of the widespread electoral fraud and intimidation of the opposition that characterized the May–July 2010 elections. This follows Geddes's coding rules of an authoritarian regime starting when a leader assumes power in an election that is not free and fair (Geddes codebook, p. 6). I code the following regime as a *party-personal* regime.

Central African Republic: I code the regime in the Central African Republic as *ending* in 2013 with the capture of Bangui by the Seleka militia. I code the subsequent regime under Michel Djotodia as *personalistic*, and code it as *ending* with Djotodia's resignation and the election of Catherine Samba-Panza in 2014.

Egypt: I code the regime that Geddes and her co-authors call "Egypt 52-NA" regime as *ending* with Mubarak's resignation on February 11, 2011. I code the following regime as *provisional*. While it was led by the military, it explicitly took power as a temporary measure leading up to democratic elections, and then did in fact allow the elections to occur in 2012, when Mohamed Morsi was elected. I code Morsi's regime as *democratic* because his election was widely considered to be free and fair. I code the *beginning* of a new regime with the coup that overthrew Morsi in 2013, and the subsequent regime under Abdel Fattah el-Sisi as *military-personalistic*.

Guinea: Geddes code Guinea as *becoming* a democracy following the free and fair election of President Alpha Condé in 2010. Guinea's status as a democracy is certainly problematic; the regime repeatedly delayed holding parliamentary elections until 2013, and the elections themselves were marked by significant violence and allegations of fraud. However, the 2015 presidential election, while characterized by violence, was judged to be relatively free and fair by international observers (Freedom House). According to a strict reading of the Geddes coding rules Guinea should be considered a democracy. I thus code Guinea's regime from the 2010 election through the present as *democratic*.

Guinea Bissau: I code the Guinea Bissau democratic regime as *ending* in 2012 with the coup that took place between the two rounds of the presidential election. I code the following regime as *military*, and *ending* with the agreement that put in place the transitional unity government in early 2013. The transitional government I then code as *ending* in 2014, when relatively free and fair presidential elections took place. I code the subsequent regime as *democratic*.

Honduras: I coded this as a *democratic regime continuing* despite the country's 2009 coup. The coup plotters did not fundamentally change regime rules, and democratic elections (according to Geddes rules) were held in 2010 and 2014.

Iraq: Geddes code Iraq as transitioning from foreign occupation to *autocracy* in the beginning of 2011. I code the subsequent regime as *party-personal*, reflecting the domination by Shia political parties and specifically by Nuri al-Maliki.

Ivory Coast: I code the regime in Ivory Coast as *ending* in 2011 with the arrest of Laurent Gbagbo following the civil war after the 2010 election. While the 2010 election was widely considered acceptably free and fair, and thus the subsequent regime could be coded as a democracy (following Geddes's coding rules), the electoral outcome was ultimately not determinative of the new regime. I code the following regime as *provisional* until 2015, when President Alassane Ouattara won reelection in a race that was widely considered free and fair (Freedom House).

Kyrgyzstan: I coded Kyrgyzstan as *beginning a democratic regime* in 2011. V-Dem codes a jump of around 0.1 in polyarchy score from 2010 to 2011, which is subsequently sustained. Freedom House also codes the country as moving from "not free" to "partly free" and records that the 2010 election was free and fair.

Libya: I code the Muammar el-Qaddafi regime as *ending* with the fall of Surt in November 2011. The subsequent regime by the General National Council I code as *provisional* and as *ending* in 2014 with the beginning of major hostilities between the Tripoli and Tobruk governments.

Macedonia: The country has had some serious democratic backsliding since 2010, particularly related to the 2014 election; however, it is unlikely that this rises to the level of Geddes coding rules for democratic breakdown. While the Geddes data set does consider a "rigged election" one possible start date for an authoritarian regime, it is unclear that the 2014 election would definitively qualify as rigged. See Freedom House 2015 report: https://freedomhouse.org/report/freedom-world/2015/macedonia.

Madagascar: Geddes code the regime of Andry Rajoelina beginning in 2009 as *personalistic*. Rajoelina maintained that his regime was transitional, and he did in fact allow another candidate to take power in 2014. Thus I considered coding the regime as provisional. However, according to a strict reading of Geddes's coding rules, provisional governments are only those charged with conducting elections as "part of a transition to democracy," and coding the Rajoelina regime as autocratic is closer to their rules. I code the regime as *failing* with the assumption of power by democratically elected president Hery Rajaonarimampianina in January 2014.

Mali: I code the Malian democratic regime as *ending* in 2012 with the coup that overthrew President Amadou Toumani Touré. The subsequent regime I code as *military* because the government was first directly in the hands of the military, and then under a nominal civilian administration, which was nonetheless dominated by the military. I code Mali as *returning* to democracy following the 2013 presidential elections, which were judged to be free and fair by international observers (Freedom House).

Myanmar: I considered recoding Myanmar as beginning a *democratic* regime in 2011. V-Dem marks Myanmar's polyarchy score as improving from 0.18 in 2010 to 0.44 in 2015. However, this is still extremely low, and Freedom House codes the country as still "not free" as of the end of 2015. Hence I coded the prior authoritarian regime as *continuing*.

Niger: I code the regime in Niger as *ending* with the 2010 coup that ousted President Mamadou Tandja. The following regime I code as an *authoritarian military* regime that continued until the 2011 presidential elections. These elections were judged as relatively free and fair and initiated a *democratic* regime that continued until the end of 2015.

Thailand: I code the *democratic* regime as ending in 2014 with the military coup that overthrew Prime Minister Yingluck Shinawatra, and a *military regime* in 2015.

Tunisia: I code the Ben Ali regime as *ending* with President Ben Ali's flight from Tunisia on January 14, 2011. I code the following regime as *provisional*, first under Fouad Mebazaa and then under the National Constituent Assembly, which was tasked with running the government until a constitution could be written and democratic elections held. I code this regime as *continuing* until the presidential and parliamentary elections in the fall of 2014, when I code Tunisia as *becoming* a democracy.

Turkey: I strongly considered Turkey as moving to a personalistic regime during this period. However, Freedom House reports that the 2015 election, while certainly contentious, was relatively free and fair. It is possible, indeed likely, that the Recep Tayyip Erdogan regime's crackdown on opposition following the 2016 attempted coup marks Turkey's move away from *democracy*, but it does not appear that this transition occurred prior to 2016.

Ukraine: This is the only place where I directly diverge from a coding by Geddes. They code Ukraine as democratic beginning with its independence from the Soviet Union in 1992. However, by their coding rules autocratic regimes start when an executive achieves power through undemocratic means, that is, elections that are not reasonably competitive. According to experts, the 1999 election of Leonid Kuchma was very far from free and fair, and Kuchma subsequently significantly changed the rules for choosing leaders and policies, centralizing presidential power (Freedom House). I code Ukraine as *autocratic* from 1999 to 2004, when the Orange Revolution defeated Kuchma's successor. I code Ukraine as *democratic* subsequently. V-Dem shows a precipitous decline in Ukraine's polyarchy score following the Euromaidan protests and the ouster of President Viktor Yanukovych. I decided to code a *regime failure event* in 2014, considering the dramatic change in rules for choosing leaders and policies that took place in the aftermath of the Euromaidan protests. However, because Yanukovych's ouster and a free and fair executive election both took place in 2014, the country-years show up as a continuous *democratic* period.

Yemen: I code the Saleh regime as *ending* on November 23 with President Ali Abdullah Saleh's signing of the Gulf Cooperation Council power-transfer agreement.

The following Hadi regime I code as *provisional* because Abdu Rabbu Mansour Hadi was elected in an unopposed election with a mandate to orchestrate a transition to democracy. I code this regime as *ending* in 2014 with the Houthi takeover of Sana'a and subsequent breakout of civil war across Yemen.

Zambia: Geddes code Zambia as a single-party regime from the 1996 ban on major opposition parties through the election of 2011, when the opposition Patriotic Front was allowed to take power, after which they say Zambia was a democracy. I follow their coding and code Zambia as a *democracy* from 2012 to 2015.

Missing Prior Regimes for Civil Resistance Transitions

In addition to expanding the Geddes data through 2015 I filled in some missing values from the Geddes data on regimes in existence prior to the beginning of a CRT. Almost all these codings were straightforward and uncontroversial; however, for the sake of transparency and clarity I include the codings here.

Guatemala 1945: I code the previous regime as *personalistic*. The regime prior to the civil resistance campaign was dominated by the dictator Jorge Ubico. While Ubico emerged from the military he did not rule as part of a military junta or other military structure but rather as a personalistic dictator.

India 1947, Morocco 1956, Ghana 1956, Malawi 1960, Democratic Republic of the Congo 1960, Zambia 1964, and Timor-Leste 2002: I all code as being *foreign ruled* since the prior regime in all these cases was a colonial authority.

Belarus 1991, Latvia 1991, Estonia 1991, Lithuania 1991, and Kyrgyzstan 1991: I code all as being *single-party ruled* since they were all part of the Soviet Union.

Slovenia 1991 I similarly code as being *single-party ruled* since it was part of the single-party communist regime in Yugoslavia.

Guyana 1992: I code the previous regime as *single-party ruled* due to the domination of politics by the People's National Congress party (see Hinds, 2005).

Transitional Endpoints

Determining the endpoint of a political transition is a challenging task, often fully realizable only post facto. Since transitions by definition are periods in which the rules of the political game are in flux, one can tell whether the flux has concluded only by observing recurring patterns over a particular period.

I used the V-Dem polyarchy score to determine my primary measure of transitional endpoints. I first created a variable measuring the annual difference in polyarchy score. I then created two variables to measure what degree of flux was necessary to consider a country "still in transition." These variables measure consider transitions to be ongoing if the level of change in polyarchy score exceeds a cutoff point of either 0.05 or 0.1. These cutoff points are, of course, arbitrary, but reflect the pattern of change in the polyarchy score around these transitional moments.[1] Both measures are highly correlated, with only minor differences. For both measures, the modal length of transition is a single year and the maximum length is 10 years.

I use these measures of transitional endpoints for two purposes. First, I measure my key dependent variables related to levels of democracy at the transitional endpoint rather than at an arbitrary point in the future following the initiation of the transition. Second, I perform tests where I average my independent variables across all years in the transition.

As I described in the main text, I determine the beginnings of transitions by looking at authoritarian regime failures as described in the data on authoritarian regimes produced by Geddes, Wright, and Frantz (2014). I supplement their data with data on civil resistance campaigns that successfully overthrew a nondemocratic regime from Chenoweth and Shay (2019).

A coding challenge arose when considering regime failure events coded by Geddes that fell within periods of time that I had determined, based on the pattern of change in the polyarchy score, to be within a single transition. After careful examination of all the country-years in which this was the case I determined that the best way to address this problem was by dropping these as instances of regime failure and incorporating them as part of the transition already ongoing when they occurred.

My key rationale for making this choice was that, in all these cases, the regimes that were put in place still involved significant fluctuations in the polyarchy score, indicating that they had not truly reached a stable equilibrium point. Thus, considering them as regimes that broke down, initiating their own transitions, did not match well with the actual historical record.

For example, in Haiti in 1986 a primarily nonviolent uprising ousted the authoritarian president Jean-Claude "Baby Doc" Duvalier. Duvalier put in place a transitional government that was tasked with creating a new constitution and holding presidential elections. Elections in 1987 were canceled after widespread violent attacks on voters. Elections in 1988 brought President Leslie Manigat to power, but almost the entire population boycotted the election, giving it little democratic legitimacy. Manigat remained in power only a few months before being ousted in a coup by General Henri Namphy. Namphy ruled until late 1990, when another presidential election brought the Roman Catholic priest Jean-Bertrand Aristide to power. However, Aristide also was ousted in less than a year in a coup led by General Raoul Cédras, who instituted a brief military dictatorship. While military rule in this case lasted somewhat longer than the previous presidencies, it too lasted only until 1994, when an international intervention spearheaded by the United States ousted the military regime and brought Aristide back to power.

After Aristide's return, Haitian politics settled into a more regularized pattern, with Aristide remaining in power until 1996, then handing over power to René Préval, who won the 1996 presidential election. Préval subsequently returned power to Aristide in 2001, and Aristide ruled until 2004, when he was ousted in the 2004 Haitian uprising.

Geddes and her coauthors code regime failures (and thus transitions to a new regime) occurring in 1986 with the overthrow of Duvalier, in 1988 with General Namphy's military coup, in 1990 with the election and almost immediate overthrow of Aristide, and in 1994 with the ousting of the military regime and Aristide's return to power. While I agree with them that each of these moments marked an important turning point, I argue that it makes more theoretical and empirical sense to consider each of these as moments within a lengthy transition rather than as new regimes whose failure in each case initiated a new transition. I base my argument on the definitions of "regime" and "transition."

As I described in the book's introduction, the definition of a regime that I am using in this project is the set of rules and institutions that define who governs in a society and the primary means of political access. These rules must have enough staying power that major political actors' expectations are able to converge around them. Political transitions, the period between regimes, last until these rules become at least somewhat routinized, the point at which "abnormality" no longer characterizes politics (O'Donnell & Schmitter, 1986).

From 1986 until 1994 in Haiti, while many different groups of people governed, in no case were these governments able to establish themselves in a stable way. This was most prominent, of course, for the elected presidents, Manigat and Aristide, whose terms of office lasted only months, but neither were the military regimes characterized by the institutionalization of a new set of governing rules but rather by erratic changes. Only after the 1994 intervention and return of Aristide did Haiti settle into a new, relatively stable pattern of political authority. This pattern broke down as well, but only after a lengthy period of relative stability. Note too that this pattern was not democratic per se, as evidenced by the middling value of the polyarchy score (hovering around 0.45 from 1995 until 2004). Nevertheless it proved able to reproduce itself for a period longer than two or three years, indicating a certain ability to shape actors' expectations.

To illustrate, Figure A.1 shows the polyarchy score for Haiti from 1970 until 2010. The polyarchy score remains almost completely flat for nearly the entire period of the Duvalier regime, then swings significantly back and forth until 1995, when the intervention restores Aristide to power. After 1995 it remains stable until Aristide's 2004 overthrow. Thus, in my counting of transitions and calculation of transitional endpoints I consider this transition in Haiti (and similar cases in a handful of other countries) to have begun in 1986 and ended in 1995, as indicated by the shaded area on the graph.

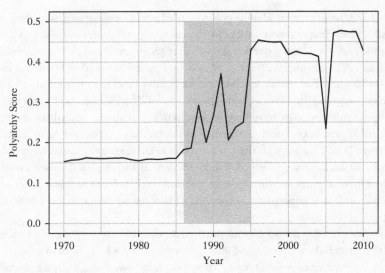

FIGURE A.1 Polyarchy Score in Haiti, 1970–2010

Table A.1 contains the start and end years for all 314 transitions included in my full set of tests, including the 78 civil resistance transitions.

Additional Information on Sources and Variable Construction

In this section I present additional information on all the variables that go into my analysis, including the secondary controls used in robustness checks.

Democracy: The Polyarchy Score

I operationalize my dependent variable using the polyarchy score from the Varieties of Democracy project. I described the polyarchy index in brief in the main text; its goal is to capture, as far as possible, the multidimensional nature of the concept of democracy in a single aggregated index. To that end the polyarchy score is an index of indexes, aggregating different dimensions of democracy that themselves are made up of empirical indicators. To give a better sense of the underlying concept of polyarchy that the creators of V-Dem are seeking to capture through the polyarchy score I quote from the codebook at some length:

> The electoral principle of democracy seeks to embody the core value of making rulers responsive to citizens, achieved through electoral competition for the

Table A.1 All Transitions, 1945–2011

Country	Start Year	End Year	Civil Resistance Transition
Guatemala	1945	1946	Yes
Indonesia	1945	1946	No
Haiti	1946	1946	No
Bolivia	1946	1947	No
Argentina	1946	1947	No
Greece	1946	1947	No
Syria	1946	1955	No
Jordan	1946	1946	No
Philippines	1946	1947	No
Ecuador	1947	1948	No
India	1947	1947	Yes
Pakistan	1947	1947	No
Thailand	1947	1947	No
El Salvador	1948	1950	No
Paraguay	1948	1948	No
Israel	1948	1949	No
North Korea	1948	1949	No
Myanmar (Burma)	1948	1948	No
Sri Lanka	1948	1948	No
Costa Rica	1949	1950	No
German Democratic Republic	1949	1949	No
China	1949	1950	No
Bhutan	1949	1949	No
Turkey	1950	1951	No
Panama	1951	1951	No
Bolivia	1951	1953	No
Libya	1951	1952	No
Nepal	1951	1952	No
Egypt	1952	1954	No
Colombia	1953	1954	No
Cambodia	1953	1955	No
Paraguay	1954	1954	No
Laos	1954	1954	No
Vietnam	1954	1955	No
Panama	1955	1955	No
Argentina	1955	1959	No

(*continued*)

Table A.1 Continued

Country	Start Year	End Year	Civil Resistance Transition
Haiti	1956	1956	Yes
Honduras	1956	1958	No
Peru	1956	1957	No
Morocco	1956	1956	No
Tunisia	1956	1956	No
Sudan	1956	1956	No
Ghana	1957	1957	Yes
Thailand	1957	1957	No
Malaysia	1957	1957	No
Guatemala	1958	1958	No
Colombia	1958	1959	Yes
Venezuela	1958	1959	Yes
Guinea	1958	1958	No
Iraq	1958	1958	No
Syria	1958	1964	No
Pakistan	1958	1958	No
Cuba	1959	1960	No
Cyprus	1960	1961	No
Mali	1960	1960	No
Senegal	1960	1960	No
Benin	1960	1960	No
Mauritania	1960	1960	No
Niger	1960	1960	No
Cote d'Ivoire	1960	1960	No
Burkina Faso	1960	1960	No
Togo	1960	1963	No
Nigeria	1960	1960	No
Gabon	1960	1960	No
Central African Republic	1960	1960	No
Chad	1960	1962	No
Congo—Brazzaville	1960	1960	No
Congo—Kinshasa	1960	1961	Yes
Somalia	1960	1960	No
Madagascar	1960	1961	No
Turkey	1960	1961	No
South Korea	1960	1961	Yes

Table A.1 Continued

Country	Start Year	End Year	Civil Resistance Transition
Myanmar (Burma)	1960	1962	No
Laos	1960	1962	No
Sierra Leone	1961	1962	No
Cameroon	1961	1961	Yes
Tanzania	1961	1961	No
Dominican Republic	1962	1966	Yes
Jamaica	1962	1962	No
Trinidad & Tobago	1962	1962	No
Uganda	1962	1963	No
Burundi	1962	1962	No
Rwanda	1962	1962	No
Algeria	1962	1962	No
Yemen Arab Republic	1962	1962	No
Guatemala	1963	1966	No
Peru	1963	1963	No
Benin	1963	1970	No
Congo—Brazzaville	1963	1964	No
Kenya	1963	1964	No
Iraq	1963	1963	No
Vietnam	1963	1966	No
Bolivia	1964	1966	No
Zambia	1964	1965	Yes
Malawi	1964	1965	Yes
Sudan	1964	1965	Yes
Gambia	1965	1966	No
Central African Republic	1965	1965	No
Zimbabwe	1965	1965	No
Maldives	1965	1965	No
Barbados	1966	1966	No
Guyana	1966	1968	No
Ecuador	1966	1968	No
Argentina	1966	1967	No
Burkina Faso	1966	1967	No
Ghana	1966	1972	No
Burundi	1966	1966	No
Lesotho	1966	1966	No

(continued)

Table A.1 Continued

Country	Start Year	End Year	Civil Resistance Transition
Botswana	1966	1966	No
Indonesia	1966	1966	No
Yemen Arab Republic	1967	1967	No
Yemen People's Republic	1967	1967	No
Equatorial Guinea	1968	1969	No
Mali	1968	1969	No
Sierra Leone	1968	1968	No
Congo—Brazzaville	1968	1968	No
Swaziland	1968	1968	No
Mauritius	1968	1969	No
Iraq	1968	1968	No
Bolivia	1969	1971	No
Libya	1969	1969	No
Guatemala	1970	1970	No
Cambodia	1970	1975	No
Fiji	1970	1970	No
Honduras	1971	1973	No
Uganda	1971	1972	No
Qatar	1971	1971	No
Pakistan	1971	1971	No
Bangladesh	1971	1978	No
Ecuador	1972	1972	No
Madagascar	1972	1975	Yes
Argentina	1973	1976	No
Rwanda	1973	1974	No
Afghanistan	1973	1974	No
Thailand	1973	1975	Yes
Laos	1973	1975	No
Portugal	1974	1976	Yes
Greece	1974	1976	Yes
Guinea-Bissau	1974	1974	No
Niger	1974	1975	No
Ethiopia	1974	1974	No
Yemen Arab Republic	1974	1974	No
Suriname	1975	1975	No
Cape Verde	1975	1975	No
Sáo Tomé and Príncipe	1975	1975	No

Table A.1 Continued

Country	Start Year	End Year	Civil Resistance Transition
Chad	1975	1976	No
Angola	1975	1975	No
Mozambique	1975	1978	No
Comoros	1975	1976	No
Vietnam	1975	1975	No
Spain	1976	1979	No
Seychelles	1976	1978	No
Papua New Guinea	1976	1976	No
Djibouti	1977	1977	No
Pakistan	1977	1978	No
Dominican Republic	1978	1979	No
Mauritania	1978	1979	No
Yemen Arab Republic	1978	1978	No
Afghanistan	1978	1978	No
Nicaragua	1979	1979	No
Ecuador	1979	1980	No
Bolivia	1979	1985	Yes
Ghana	1979	1982	No
Nigeria	1979	1979	No
Central African Republic	1979	1982	No
Chad	1979	1979	No
Uganda	1979	1981	No
Iran	1979	1981	Yes
Iraq	1979	1979	No
Cambodia	1979	1979	No
Solomon Islands	1979	1979	No
Peru	1980	1981	No
Guinea-Bissau	1980	1980	No
Burkina Faso	1980	1982	No
Liberia	1980	1981	No
Zimbabwe	1980	1980	No
Vanuatu	1980	1980	No
Honduras	1981	1982	No
El Salvador	1982	1982	No
Panama	1982	1982	No
Chad	1982	1982	No
Bangladesh	1982	1983	No

(*continued*)

Table A.1 Continued

Country	Start Year	End Year	Civil Resistance Transition
Argentina	1983	1984	Yes
Cameroon	1983	1983	No
Turkey	1983	1984	No
Uruguay	1984	1986	Yes
Guinea	1984	1984	No
Guatemala	1985	1986	No
Brazil	1985	1988	Yes
Uganda	1985	1986	No
Sudan	1985	1986	Yes
Haiti	1986	1995	Yes
Lesotho	1986	1986	No
Philippines	1986	1988	Yes
Burkina Faso	1987	1987	No
Burundi	1987	1988	No
South Korea	1987	1989	Yes
Pakistan	1988	1989	No
Myanmar (Burma)	1988	1989	No
Thailand	1988	1988	No
Panama	1989	1991	Yes
Chile	1989	1990	Yes
German Democratic Republic	1989	1991	Yes
Poland	1989	1991	Yes
Czechia	1989	1991	Yes
Romania	1989	1991	No
Nicaragua	1990	1991	No
Hungary	1990	1990	Yes
Yugoslavia	1990	1992	No
Bulgaria	1990	1991	Yes
Benin	1990	1992	Yes
Liberia	1990	1990	No
Chad	1990	1990	No
Namibia	1990	1990	No
Yemen People's Republic	1990	1990	No
Mongolia	1990	1993	Yes
Bangladesh	1990	1991	Yes
Nepal	1990	1991	Yes
Albania	1991	1992	Yes

Table A.1 Continued

Country	Start Year	End Year	Civil Resistance Transition
Macedonia	1991	1991	No
Slovenia	1991	1991	Yes
Moldova	1991	1991	No
Russia	1991	1992	Yes
Estonia	1991	1992	Yes
Latvia	1991	1993	Yes
Lithuania	1991	1992	Yes
Ukraine	1991	1992	No
Belarus	1991	1997	Yes
Armenia	1991	1991	No
Georgia	1991	1995	Yes
Azerbaijan	1991	1993	No
Mali	1991	1993	Yes
Niger	1991	1993	Yes
Congo—Brazzaville	1991	1992	No
Somalia	1991	1991	No
Ethiopia	1991	1991	No
Zambia	1991	1992	Yes
Turkmenistan	1991	1991	No
Tajikistan	1991	1993	No
Kyrgyzstan	1991	1992	Yes
Uzbekistan	1991	1991	No
Kazakhstan	1991	1991	No
Guyana	1992	1993	Yes
Croatia	1992	1992	No
Bosnia & Herzegovina	1992	1996	No
Sierra Leone	1992	1993	No
Algeria	1992	1995	No
Afghanistan	1992	1992	No
Thailand	1992	1995	Yes
Paraguay	1993	1993	No
Slovakia	1993	1993	No
Nigeria	1993	1993	Yes
Central African Republic	1993	1993	Yes
Burundi	1993	1995	No
Eritrea	1993	1993	No
Lesotho	1993	1995	No

(*continued*)

Appendix

Table A.1 Continued

Country	Start Year	End Year	Civil Resistance Transition
Madagascar	1993	1994	Yes
El Salvador	1994	1994	No
Gambia	1994	1997	No
Rwanda	1994	1995	No
Malawi	1994	1995	Yes
South Africa	1994	1995	Yes
Sri Lanka	1994	1994	No
Guatemala	1995	1995	No
Sierra Leone	1996	1998	No
Afghanistan	1996	1996	No
Liberia	1997	1997	No
Congo—Kinshasa	1997	1997	No
Armenia	1998	1998	No
Guinea-Bissau	1999	1999	No
Niger	1999	2000	No
Côte d'Ivoire	1999	2001	No
Nigeria	1999	1999	Yes
Indonesia	1999	2000	Yes
Mexico	2000	2000	Yes
Peru	2000	2001	Yes
Croatia	2000	2000	Yes
Yugoslavia	2000	2002	Yes
Senegal	2000	2000	Yes
Ghana	2000	2000	Yes
Taiwan	2000	2000	No
Afghanistan	2001	2004	No
Kenya	2002	2003	No
Lesotho	2002	2002	Yes
Madagascar	2002	2002	Yes
Timor-Leste	2002	2002	Yes
Georgia	2003	2004	Yes
Guinea-Bissau	2003	2003	No
Liberia	2003	2006	Yes
Burundi	2003	2005	No
Iraq	2003	2005	No
Haiti	2004	2006	No
Ukraine	2004	2006	Yes

Table A.1 Continued

Country	Start Year	End Year	Civil Resistance Transition
Mauritania	2005	2008	No
Lebanon	2005	2005	Yes
Kyrgyzstan	2005	2005	Yes
Nepal	2006	2008	Yes
Thailand	2007	2008	No
Kosovo	2008	2008	No
Guinea	2008	2010	No
Pakistan	2008	2008	Yes
Bangladesh	2008	2009	No
Afghanistan	2009	2009	No
Iraq	2010	2010	No
Kyrgyzstan	2010	2011	No
Niger	2011	2011	No
Côte d'Ivoire	2011	2011	No
Zambia	2011	2011	No
Tunisia	2011	2012	Yes
Libya	2011	2014	No
South Sudan	2011	2011	No
Egypt	2011	2014	Yes
Syria	2011	2011	No
Yemen Arab Republic	2011	2012	Yes

electorate's approval under circumstances when suffrage is extensive; political and civil society organizations can operate freely; elections are clean and not marred by fraud or systematic irregularities; and elections affect the composition of the chief executive of the country. In between elections, there is freedom of expression and an independent media capable of presenting alternative views on matters of political relevance. In the V-Dem conceptual scheme, electoral democracy is understood as an essential element of any other conception of (representative) democracy—liberal, participatory, deliberative, egalitarian, or some other. (Coppedge et al., 2017, p. 47)

Practically speaking, the polyarchy score is constructed by aggregating the scores from five different indexes: V-Dem's freedom of association index, freedom of expression index, clean elections index, elected officials index, and suffrage index. These indexes are aggregated by taking their weighted average and then adding their multiplicative interaction. This incorporates the ideas that weaknesses along one dimension can be made up for by strengths in another but also that being particularly weak in any one dimension can undermine the strength of the other dimensions. For more detail, see Coppedge et al. (2017, 47–48), as well as Teorell et al. 2016.

Transitional Mobilization

As I describe in Chapter 2, this measure seeks to capture the degree to which political action and engagement continue through the transition. That is to say, how much is the mobilization of the civil resistance campaign carried through once its major goals of regime change have been achieved?

My independent variable is a factor made up of three underlying components, two of which capture more conventional political engagement while the third captures more unconventional, typical civil resistance–type activities. Here I put coding details for each of these three underlying variables, as described in their original data sources.

Engaged Society

This is an expert-coded variable from the V-Dem data set. Experts were asked to code their responses to the question "When important policy changes are being considered, how wide and how independent are public deliberations?" Their answers could take one of six possible ordinal levels, defined as follows:

0: Public deliberation is never, or almost never allowed.
1: Some limited public deliberations are allowed but the public below the elite levels is almost always either unaware of major policy debates or unable to take part in them.
2: Public deliberation is not repressed but nevertheless infrequent and non-elite actors are typically controlled and/or constrained by the elites.
3: Public deliberation is actively encouraged and some autonomous non-elite groups participate, but it is confined to a small slice of specialized groups that tends to be the same across issue-areas.
4: Public deliberation is actively encouraged and a relatively broad segment of non-elite groups often participate and vary with different issue-areas.
5: Large numbers of non-elite groups as well as ordinary people tend to discuss major policies among themselves, in the media, in associations or neighborhoods, or in the streets. Grass-roots deliberation is common and unconstrained. (Coppedge et al., 2017, pp. 202–3).

The V-Dem coders then transform these aggregated ordinal codings from multiple expert coders into a single continuous variable using the V-Dem item response theory methodology (Pemstein et al., 2015).

Civil Society Participation

This is another expert-coded variable from the V-Dem data set. V-Dem asked its country experts to code their responses to the question "Which of these best describes the involvement of people in civil society organizations (CSOs)?" Their answers could take one of four ordinal values:

0: Most associations are state-sponsored, and although a large number of people may be active in them, their participation is not purely voluntary.

1: Voluntary CSOs exist but few people are active in them.

2: There are many diverse CSOs, but popular involvement is minimal.

3: There are many diverse CSOs and it is considered normal for people to be at least occasionally active in at least one of them. (Coppedge et al., 2017, p. 246)

As earlier, the V-Dem coders then transform these aggregated ordinal codings from multiple expert coders into a single continuous variable using the V-Dem item response theory methodology.

Contentious Mobilization

This variable is intended to capture more contentious, confrontational, nonconventional, and yet nonviolent forms of collective action—in short, nonviolent resistance as I defined it in Chapter 1. My primary source is the Phoenix Historical Event Data Set recently released by the Cline Center for Democracy at the University of Illinois and produced in collaboration with the Open Event Data Alliance (OEDA).

Researchers at the Cline Center and the OEDA produced the Phoenix Historical Event Data Set by first collecting a corpus of roughly 14 million news articles from three distinct sources: the *New York Times*, the British Broadcasting Corporation's Summary of World Broadcasts, and the Foreign Broadcast Information Service, produced by the CIA. These articles were then transformed into event data using the second version of the Python Engine for Text Resolution and Related Coding Hierarchy (PETRARCH-2) software, with some minor modifications (Althaus, Bajjalieh, Carter, Peyton, & Shalmon, 2017, pp. 1–2). PETRARCH-2 interprets the information contained in news articles to produce conflict event data following the CAMEO structure of actors performing verbs on targets (Schrodt, Gerner, Yilmaz, & Hermreck, 2005).

As an almost fully automatically collected and coded data set, the Phoenix Data Set has one key advantage and one key disadvantage. Its advantage is its breadth and scope. The greater efficiencies of automated coding allow the project to incorporate a vast amount of data and code a staggering number of events. The complete data set incorporates almost five million events from its three sources from every country in the world for a period of 70 years. To create the same data using human coders would be prohibitively time-consuming and expensive.

Table A.2 Mobilization Factor Loading

Variable	Loading
Public Engagement	0.842
Civil Society	0.844
Phoenix Events	0.023

However, the disadvantage of automated coding is inaccuracy. As the data set's creators readily acknowledge, their process results in significant duplication of events and miscategorization based on their algorithm's misinterpretation of non-conflict-related events. The problem of duplication is particularly problematic when attempting to code over a long period of time, as the quality and scope of coverage has increased over time, and certain countries are almost certainly covered in greater depth than others. Hence the events in Phoenix are best used not as individual units of analysis but as part of a larger trend line, with the biases of uneven coverage over time and space accounted for.

Hence, in transforming this data for my purposes I take three key steps before using the data in analysis. First, I take the annual account of protest events from each country as reported by each of the three different sources in Phoenix and average the three numbers.[2] I then take each annual global cross-section and average the number of events per country reported in that year. I adjust the event counts by subtracting this average from each country's event count in that year to defend against temporal reporting bias. I perform the same operation on each country-specific time series, subtracting the mean from each annual count within that country.

The result is a continuous variable that captures the relative degree of protest activity in a country in a particular year, accounting for some degree of both temporal and geographic reporting bias. These efforts to address potential bias issues and my use of the data in large aggregates rather than in terms of the attributes of single events give me confidence that this is the best data source to use in measuring contention during transitions.

I combine these variables using principal factor analysis with no rotation. Table A.2 reports the factor loading of each of the constitutive variables. As the table shows, the contentious mobilization variable loads weakest onto the factor, indicating a significant amount of divergence from the other two indicators. This is to be expected, as the variable is capturing a significantly different form of mobilization. I maintain this variable as a part of the factor for theoretical reasons, as removing it would significantly limit the scope of mobilization being examined by the factor.

Maximalism

As I describe in Chapter 2, this variable seeks to capture the degree to which the tools of civil resistance are employed in a way that is destructive of the current system and is essentially winner-take-all in its orientation. The maximalism factor that I use in my analysis incorporates four underlying indicators, three from V-Dem and one from the Polity IV data set. I detail the coding rules for each of them here.

Electoral Boycotts

This is an ordinal expert-coded variable. V-Dem asked its country experts to answer the question "In this national election, did any registered opposition candidates or parties boycott?," with the clarification that "a boycott is a deliberate and public refusal to participate in an election by a candidate or a party who is eligible to participate." Coders could give one of five responses:

0: Total. All opposition parties and candidates boycotted the election.
1: Significant. Some but not all opposition parties or candidates boycotted but it is unclear whether they would have constituted a major electoral force.
2: Ambiguous. A few opposition parties or candidates boycotted and they were relatively insignificant ones.
3: Minor. A few opposition parties or candidates boycotted and they were relatively insignificant ones.
4: Nonexistent. No parties or candidates boycotted the elections. (Coppedge et al., 2017, pp. 96–97)

The V-Dem coders transform these aggregated ordinal codings from multiple expert coders into a single continuous variable using the V-Dem item response theory methodology.

Acceptance of Electoral Results

This is also an ordinal expert-coded variable. V-Dem asked its country experts to answer the question "Did losing parties and candidates accept the result of this national election within three months?" Coders could give one of five responses:

0: None. None of the losing parties or candidates accepted the results of the election, or all opposition was banned.
1: A few. Some but not all losing parties or candidates accepted the results but those who constituted the main opposition force did not.
2: Some. Some but not all opposition parties or candidates accepted the results but it is unclear whether they constituted a major opposition force or were relatively insignificant.
3: Most. Many but not all opposition parties or candidates accepted the results and those who did not had little electoral support.
4: All. All parties and candidates accepted the results. (Coppedge et al., 2017, p. 107)

The V-Dem coders transform these aggregated ordinal codings from multiple expert coders into a single continuous variable using the V-Dem item response theory methodology.

Antisystem Movements

This was also an ordinal, expert-coded variable from V-Dem that asked expert coders the question "Among civil society organizations, are there anti-system opposition movements?," with the clarification that

> an anti-system movement is any movement—peaceful or armed—that is based in the country (not abroad) and is organized in opposition to the current political system. That is, it aims to change the polity in fundamental ways, e.g., from democratic to autocratic (or vice versa), from capitalist to community (or vice versa), from secular to fundamentalist (or vice versa). This movement may be linked to a political party that competes in elections but it must also have a "movement" character, which is to say a mass base and an existence separate from normal electoral competition. If there are several movements, please answer in a general way about the relationship of those movements to the regime.

Coders could assign one of five values:

0: No, or very minimal. Anti-system movements are practically nonexistent.
1: There is only a low-level of anti-system movement activity but it does not pose much of a threat to the regime.
2: There is a modest level of anti-system movement activity, posing some threat to the regime.
3: There is a high level of anti-system movement activity, posing substantial threat to the regime.
4: There is a very high level of anti-system movement activity, posing a real and present threat to the regime. (Coppedge et al., 2017, p. 247).

The V-Dem coders transform these aggregated ordinal codings from multiple expert coders into a single continuous variable using the V-Dem item response theory methodology.

Sectarian Political Competition

The next component of my maximalism measure comes from the Polity IV data set, which, among its various components, measures the degree of "regulation of participation" in a political system. This is originally a 5-point scale, from unregulated to regulated. However, each step on the scale has its own detailed description. I determined after examining these descriptions that the closet approximation of maximalism as I had theorized it was the level that the Polity IV authors describe as "sectarian." The complete description of sectarian political competition from the Polity IV codebook is as follows:

> Political demands are characterized by incompatible interests and intransigent posturing among multiple identity groups and oscillate more or less regularly between intense factionalism and government favoritism, that is, when one identity group

Table A.3 Maximalism Factor Loading

Variable	Loading
Electoral Acceptance	0.533
Electoral Boycotts	0.947
Antisystem Movements	0.316
Sectarian Competition	0.082

secures central power it favors group members in central allocations and restricts competing groups' political activities, until it is displaced in turn (i.e., active factionalism). Also coded here are polities in which political groups are based on restricted membership and significant portions of the population historically have been excluded from access to positions of power (latent factionalism, e.g., indigenous peoples in some South American countries). (Marshall, Gurr, & Jaggers, 2016, p. 26)

I created a binary variable measuring whether a country's politics in a particular year were coded as sectarian by Polity IV.

I combined these four variables using principal factor analysis with no rotation. The factor loadings, averaged across the five Amelia imputations, are reported in Table A.3.

Modernization

My measure of modernization is a factor variable made up of four underlying elements: GDP per capita, urbanization, education, and infant mortality. I present details on each of these underlying elements below.

GDP per Capita (Logged)

I import this variable from V-Dem and transform it using the natural logarithm. The variable's original source is the Maddison Project. For details on their data collection process, see Bolt and van Zanden (2014) as well as the project's website: http://www.ggdc.net/maddison/maddison-project/home.htm.

Urbanization

This variable is the ratio of the total urban population to the country's total population. Urban population is defined according to "the criteria of each area of country." I import this variable from V-Dem. The original data comes from the Clio-Infra project at the International Institute of Social History in the Netherlands. V-Dem then fills in missing years of data through linear interpolation. For more detail, see the Coppedge et al. (2017, p. 391–92), or the Clio-Infra project website: https://www.clio-infra.eu/.

Education

This variable is the average number of years of education received for those over the age of 15, with some years of missing data imputed using a linear model based on sources that measure the average years of educational attainment, primary school completion rate, secondary school enrollment rate, and literacy rate. I import this variable from V-Dem. They base the variable on several original sources—primarily Clio Infra but also data from the World Bank and others. For more detail, see Coppedge et al. (2017, p. 369), or the Clio Infra website: https://www.clio-infra.eu/.

Infant Mortality

This base variable is the number of deaths prior to age 1 per 1,000 live births in a year. I invert the variable so that the good outcome of lower infant mortality is at the high end of the variable, and thus the variable can be incorporated into a modernization factor. I import the variable from V-Dem. They draw the data for the variable from Gapminder and Clio Infram and linearly interpolate missing data within a time series. For more detail, see Coppedge et al. (2017, p. 389–90), and the Clio Infra and Gapminder websites: https://www.clio-infra.eu/ and www.gapminder.org.

I combine these four variables using principal factor analysis without rotation. The variable loadings are in Table A.4.

Trade

My data on trade used in generating the Western linkage control variable comes from the IMF's Direction of Trade Statistics. I sum the annual flow of exports and imports for each country from the United States, United Kingdom, Canada, Australia, and the euro area, and then divide by the country's GDP.

INGO Membership

An additional measure of Western linkage is the degree to which countries are embedded in the international network of INGOs. A common way of measuring INGO

Table A.4 Modernization Factor Loading

Variable	Loading
GDP per Capita (logged)	0.814
Urbanization	0.814
Education	0.872
Infant Mortality	0.852

presence is by using the absolute count of the number of INGOs in which the country is either a member or has offices in that country. However, as Paxton et al. (2015) argue, INGO membership is not the same for all countries because the global set of INGOs constitute a network that links states in relative positions of network centrality. Two states may have the same absolute number of INGO memberships but be at radically different positions in this network.

I follow Paxton and her coauthors in using a measure of network centrality, a country's eigenvector score, as a more theoretically informed alternative to the absolute count score. Eigenvector scores measure the degree to which countries are connected to other highly connected countries, capturing their proximity to the "center" of the global network.

Paxton and her coauthors generate their scores by recording country-level memberships in over 5,000 INGOs at 11 points in time from 1950 until 2008. They then convert these into eigenvector scores. I use linear interpolation for scores in intervening years, and linear extrapolation to determine the scores from 1945 to 1949 and 2009 to 2016. I logically bound my extrapolations at 0 and 1, with any extrapolated values above or below these limits set at the liminal value.

Percentage Muslim Population

I use the World Religion Dataset (WRD) produced by Zeev Maoz and Errol Henderson (2013) to generate the percentage of a country's population that is Muslim. The finding that a large Muslim population decreases the likelihood of democratization is highly contested, with various arguments that the finding is spurious because of the effects of oil wealth (Ross, 2012) or of unique regional dynamics in the Middle East (Solingen, 2009). Thus I do not include this variable in my main tests. However, I do include it in some additional models that I run for the sake of robustness checking.

WRD's National Religion data set contains estimates of the numbers of adherents of each of the world's main religions in every country in the international system from 1945 to 2010. The data is collected at five-year intervals. The data set reports both the raw numbers of adherents as well as an estimate of the percentage of the total population that adheres to a faith. For my testing I use WRD's "isgenpct" variable, which measures the total number of Muslims in a country. These numbers do not vary much from year to year, so I use linear interpolation to fill in the missing years and linear extrapolation for the years 2011 to 2016. As with the INCS scores, I logically bound my extrapolations at 0 and 1, with any extrapolated values above or below these limits set at the liminal value.

Inequality: Gini Coefficient

For my measure of inequality, I employ the most commonly used measure in academic work on inequality: a country's Gini coefficient. The Gini coefficient is a mathematical measure derived from the Lorenz curve, a graphical tool for depicting the distribution of income or expenditure in a society. The Lorenz curve plots the percentage of the country's population against the percentage of income that that portion of the population possesses. A perfectly straight Lorenz curve line moving at a 45-degree angle from 0 to 100 would depict a society with perfectly equal distribution of income. The Gini coefficient measures the two-dimensional space between a 45-degree Lorenz curve and the actual Lorenz curve, divided by the total area beneath the 45-degree line.

Many different academics and public policy professionals have sought to measure Gini coefficients globally, yet the practicalities of measuring individual or household-level income in methodologically robust ways, particularly in developing countries, means that obtaining a global timeseries of Gini coefficients stretching back for a significant period of time is almost impossibly costly.

The most comprehensive data set on Gini coefficients globally is the United Nations University World Income Inequality Database (WIID). WIID aggregates many different data collection measures for 182 countries around the world. It includes data on income distribution from the World Bank, the Organization for Economic Cooperation and Development, Eurostat, and a wealth of different academic studies, including, for example, the Deininger and Squire (1996) data on inequality that Carles Boix (2003) used in his influential book *Democracy and Redistribution*.

While WIID contains many thousands of observations, the irregular and aggregative nature of the data set means that it does not simply report a simplified country-year time series cross-sectional data set. Thus to use it for my purposes some adaptation was necessary. First, I averaged the different measures of the Gini coefficient for the same country-year, only dropping those measures that WIID reports to be of low quality. The WIID creators caution against this, since different data sources employ different methods of calculating the Gini coefficient. However, I believe this to be a reasonable procedure since what I am seeking to measure is the general underlying degree of inequality rather than any specific type of inequality. It is reasonable to assume that different measures of the Gini coefficient all capture some degree of inequality and that the actual measure is somewhere in between them.

Simply averaging the scores is a crude method of getting at this underlying aspect of inequality. Factor analysis or item response theory measures would be a more methodologically robust way of doing so. However, the spottiness of the different data sources made these more robust measures impractical. Since I am limited to this method, the results I report with Gini coefficients should thus be taken with a grain of salt. It bears mentioning, however, that results from other well-respected academic studies that use the Gini coefficient over a lengthy period are subject to the same critique. Inequality is simply something difficult to measure.

After creating these country-year average scores, I then use linear interpolation to fill in missing years, and linear extrapolation for up to a five-year window back from the earliest and forward from the latest scores where necessary. Reported Gini coefficients tend to remain within a narrow band, without dramatic changes over time; thus I find the assumptions of the linear interpolation and extrapolation to be reasonable. However, since over the longer term the likelihood of a stochastic shock to inequality becomes more likely, I do not extrapolate beyond five years from the known data.

In addition, because of the limited range of variation in the observed Gini coefficients, I put bounds on the maximum extent to which the linear extrapolation can diverge from the known data. In no country does the maximum or minimum observed score exceed more than 2.6 standard deviations from the mean. Hence my logical bounds for the extrapolated Gini scores are 2.6 country-specific standard deviations from the mean observed Gini coefficient.

Additional Results Not Reported in the Main Text

Effects of Civil Resistance on Posttransition Democracy

In this section I present additional tests, primarily robustness checks, not reported in the main text. Figure A.2 shows residuals versus fitted plots for my two OLS models looking at the entire population of transitions from 1945 to 2011. Model 1 includes a binary measure of whether the transition was a civil resistance transition, while Model 2 contains only my primary structural variables.

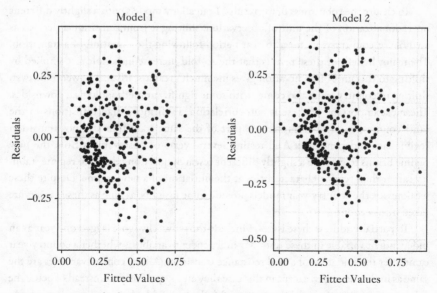

FIGURE A.2 Residual against Fitted Value (RVF) Plots for Models of CRT Impact on Posttransition Democracy

Table A.5 Variance Inflation Factors in CRT Models

Variable	Model 1	Model 2
Modernization	1.7217	1.6661
Old Polyarchy Level	1.1052	1.0941
Democratic Neighbors	1.3160	1.3149
INCS Score	1.4248	1.3239
Trade Linkage	1.0012	1.0011
CRT	1.2271	

Table A.5 shows the variance inflation factor (VIF) scores for each of the variables included in these two models, a standard way of testing for the possibility of multicollinearity between the independent variables affecting the outcome. As the table shows, VIF scores are universally low for each of the independent variables, with the highest falling just short of a score of 2—well below the standard cutoff point of 10.

The RVF plots and VIF tables I reproduce here are from regression models run on the first of my five Amelia imputations rather than averages of regressions run on all five Amelia imputations. I report only results from this single imputation for the sake of brevity and clarity; tests run on regression models in the other four imputations are substantively identical to the results reported here.

To ensure the robustness of my results, I ran all my models with a slightly different operationalization of the unit of observation, shifting it from transitional periods as a whole to country-years for a 10-year period following the initiation of a transition. The major benefit of these tests is that the 10-fold increase in sample size implied by shifting to this unit of observation gives me much greater statistical power. However, shifting to country-years also comes with some significant methodological downsides. The most important of these is autocorrelation. Even more than transitions in the same country, country-years that are part of the same transition and posttransition regime lack independence. And testing several years of observations from the new regime begins to get into a slightly different research question related to regime stability rather than regime characteristics at the initiation of a new regime. Despite these weaknesses, the country-year models provide some insights, as long as these caveats are taken into account.

To partially address these issues, I include the polyarchy score lagged one year as an independent variable in these tests. My independent variable is whether a country-year came after the initiation of a civil resistance transition. All my control variables are the same as in the main text, except in this case they are lagged one year instead of being the values at the beginning of the transition. Model 1 in Table A.6 reports the results. As expected, autocorrelation dominates the results, with most of the variation explained

Table A.6 Country-Year Tests of Civil Resistance Impact

	Model 1 OLS	Model 2 OLS	Model 3 Logistic	Model 4 Logistic
Civil Resistance Transition	0.0201***		0.1037**	
	(0.0050)		(0.0468)	
Modernization	0.0097***	0.0093***	−0.0683**	−0.0548**
	(0.0032)	(0.0027)	(0.0266)	(0.0268)
Trade Linkage	0.0031	0.0021	−0.2505***	−0.2545***
	(0.0102)	(0.0101)	(0.0724)	(0.0567)
INGO Score	0.0285**	0.0384***	0.3342***	0.3197***
	(0.0119)	(0.0106)	(0.1137)	(0.1037)
Democratic Neighbors	0.0309***	0.0267***	0.0244	0.0380
	(0.0090)	(0.0081)	(0.0925)	(0.0913)
Lagged Polyarchy Score	0.9153***	0.9325***	1.4815***	1.5787***
	(0.0122)	(0.0094)	(0.1130)	(0.0965)
Constant	0.0181***	0.0165***	−0.2749***	−0.2626***
	(0.0048)	(0.0041)	(0.0390)	(0.0362)
Observations	2,634	2,917	2,397	2,666
R^2/AUC	0.9287	0.9269	0.9484	0.9416

* $p < 0.05$, ** $p < 0.01$, *** $p > 0.001$

by the lagged polyarchy score. However, civil resistance remains a significant and positive predictor of greater democracy, with the effect size somewhat reduced because of the different unit of analysis.[3]

I also ran these models showing the impact of CRTs relative to other forms of transition using my alternative definition of a transitional endpoint. In the main tests this is when the fluctuation in the polyarchy score declines below 0.1. In these alternative tests, reported in Table A.7, the transitional endpoint is defined as when the fluctuation in the polyarchy score declines below 0.05 for a period of at least two years.

I also replicated the same model using my primary transitional endpoint but substituting the Polity IV score for the V-Dem polyarchy score. Models 1(3) through 4(3) report the results. The effect of a civil resistance transition is similar, highly significant both in improving the linear predicted Polity score and in improving the likelihood of crossing the democratic threshold (in this case set at the common standard of a Polity score of 6 or higher). The control variables also have effects of similar size and direction as in the polyarchy score tests, though levels of significance are somewhat different for some controls.

**Table A.7 Effects of Civil Resistance on Posttransition Democracy
(Alternative Endpoint)**

	Model 1 (2) OLS	Model 2 (2) OLS	Model 3 (2) Logistic	Model 4 (2) Logistic
Civil Resistance	0.1813***		1.7733***	
Transition	(0.0218)		(0.3692)	
Democratic	0.2046***	0.2154***	2.0009	2.0966*
Neighbors	(0.0496)	(0.0543)	(1.0624)	(1.0414)
INGO Network	0.0574	0.1838**	2.7263**	3.5169***
Centrality	(0.056)	(0.0599)	(0.972)	(0.9317)
Modernization	0.0762***	0.0926***	0.2438	0.3851
	(0.0129)	(0.0145)	(0.2224)	(0.2103)
Old Polyarchy	0.4864***	0.4284***	3.9509**	3.1744**
Level	(0.0654)	(0.072)	(1.2381)	(1.1693)
Trade Linkage	0.0375	0.0242	−1.0762	−0.9437
	(0.0675)	(0.0735)	(1.3088)	(1.0856)
Constant	0.1576***	0.1892***	−2.5823***	−2.1352***
	(0.0245)	(0.0272)	(0.4774)	(0.4413)
N	329	329	302	302
r2/AUC	0.5672	0.4731	0.831	0.7913

* p < 0.05, ** p < 0.01, *** p < 0.001

Finally, I ran the same set of models using data that had not been put through the Amelia multiple imputation process. Instead all observations with missing data on any of the variables were removed using listwise deletion. The results are robust to this reduction in sample size. Table A.9 reports the coefficients and standard errors from these models. These results show that the findings reported in the main chapter are robust to several different specifications, and not a statistical artifact of the Amelia process.

Additional Tests of The Two Transitional Challenges

Figure A.3 contains scatterplots of mobilization and maximalism during transitions plotted against the polyarchy score at the conclusion of the transition. Clear patterns of correlation can be observed for both factors, with a positive relationship between

Table A.8 Effects of CRTs on Posttransition Democracy (Polity IV Score)

	Model 1 (3) OLS	Model 2 (3) OLS	Model 3 (3) Logistic	Model 4 (3) Logistic
Civil Resistance Transition	3.721*** (0.7786)		1.6695*** (0.348)	
Democratic Neighbors	7.6867*** (1.6591)	7.8813*** (1.7235)	3.3195*** (0.8911)	3.1557*** (0.8825)
INGO Network Centrality	3.5155 (2.1157)	6.0313** (2.0683)	1.4884 (0.9352)	2.2908* (0.9123)
Modernization	0.9855* (0.4724)	1.333** (0.4987)	0.2168 (0.2269)	0.3965 (0.2156)
Old Polyarchy Level	11.0913*** (2.2873)	9.9571*** (2.3692)	2.3992* (1.1599)	1.6967 (1.0957)
Trade Linkage	1.6309 (2.3501)	1.35 (2.45)	−0.1907 (1.0942)	−0.2708 (1.011)
Constant	−5.275*** (0.8809)	−4.6058*** (0.9098)	−2.779*** (0.4707)	−2.2519*** (0.4335)
N	320	320	294	294
r2/AUC	0.3631	0.3151	0.8198	0.7738

* $p < 0.05$, ** $p < 0.01$, *** $p < 0.001$

mobilization and posttransition democracy and an inverse relationship between maximalism and democracy.

Figure A.4 shows the residuals versus fitted values plots for Models 9 and 10 from the main text, that is to say tests of the impact of the two transitional challenges on the posttransition level of democracy in addition to structural factors in CRTs (Model 9) and the impact of structural factors alone on posttransition democracy in CRTs (Model 10). As the figure shows, there is no clear pattern in the plot, indicating no homoscedasticity.

Table A.10 reports VIF scores for all independent variables in both these models as well. The VIF scores are well below 10, indicating no problematic multicollinearity among the variables.

As a robustness check, I ran country-year models looking at the 10-year period following the end of a CRT (results reported in Table A.11). As in my tests of the impact of a CRT relative to a non-CRT, I use one-year lagged control variables and include the one-year lagged polyarchy score to control for autocorrelation. The

Table A.9 Effects of CRTs Relative to Non-CRTs (Non-Amelia Data)

	Model 1 (4) OLS	Model 2 (4) OLS	Model 3 (4) Logistic	Model 4 (4) Logistic
Civil Resistance Transition	0.185***		2.106***	
	(0.026)		(0.454)	
Modernization	0.096***	0.110***	0.125	0.210
	(0.023)	(0.026)	(0.394)	(0.362)
Democratic Neighbors	0.281***	0.325***	3.678**	3.850**
	(0.066)	(0.073)	(1.380)	(1.319)
INGO Network Centrality	0.058	0.175	3.135*	3.966**
	(0.083)	(0.091)	(1.519)	(1.411)
Trade Linkage	0.185	0.258	−0.638	0.366
	(0.160)	(0.179)	(2.726)	(2.330)
Old Polyarchy Level	0.257**	0.211*	2.571	1.779
	(0.091)	(0.101)	(1.695)	(1.497)
Constant	0.221***	0.250***	−2.756***	−2.259**
	(0.045)	(0.050)	(0.811)	(0.736)
N	198	198	195	195
R^2/AUC	0.585	0.474	0.839	0.783

* $p < 0.05$, ** $p < 0.01$, *** $p < 0.01$

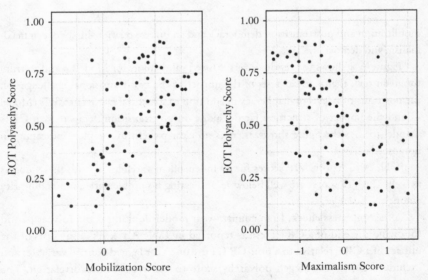

FIGURE A.3 Scatterplots of Mobilization/Maximalism and Posttransition Democracy

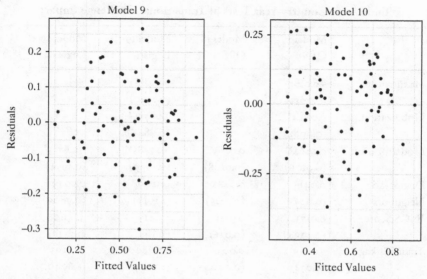

FIGURE A.4 RVF Plots for Models 9 and 10

Table A.10 Variance Inflation Factor Scores from Models 9 and 10

	Model 9	Model 10
Modernization	1.3561	1.7908
Old Polyarchy Level	1.2347	1.4813
Democratic Neighbors	2.1136	1.3425
INCS Score	1.5140	1.0374
Trade Linkage	1.3995	1.0520
Mobilization	1.0641	
Maximalism	1.1498	

values for mobilization and maximalism are the same as those used in my main models.

As with my first set of country-year models, autocorrelation accounts for much of the variation, with lagged polyarchy the most substantial coefficient in all models. However, the mobilization and maximalism variables still play an important explanatory role. In the OLS models the mobilization variable is the most highly significant predictor behind the lagged polyarchy score. The mobilization and maximalism factors are the only independent variables whose sign and significance remain the same across the OLS and logistic regression models.

Table A.11 Country-Year Tests of Transitional Challenge Impact

	Model 17 OLS	Model 18 OLS	Model 19 Logistic	Model 20 Logistic
Maximalism	−0.0181***		−0.4802**	
	(0.0053)		(0.2347)	
Mobilization	0.0344***		1.0670**	
	(0.0082)		(0.4848)	
Modernization	0.0262**	0.0285***	−0.7383**	−0.6735*
	(0.0106)	(0.0108)	(0.3677)	(0.3954)
Democratic	0.0469*	0.0282	0.3849	0.2049
Neighbors	(0.0248)	(0.0215)	(1.1597)	(0.9609)
INCS Score	0.0175	0.0311	2.6419	3.2560*
	(0.0294)	(0.0261)	(1.6590)	(1.7710)
Trade Linkage	−0.0193	0.0032	−2.6800*	−1.5293
	(0.0346)	(0.0402)	(1.3964)	(1.6049)
Lagged Polyarchy	0.7279***	0.8408***	8.9129***	11.9356***
Score	(0.0428)	(0.0341)	(1.6742)	(1.7143)
Constant	0.1023***	0.0706***	−4.2400***	−5.1338***
	(0.0227)	(0.0202)	(0.8660)	(0.9362)
N	746	746	726	726
r2/AUC	0.8934	0.8864	0.9391	0.9319

* $p < 0.05$, ** $p < 0.01$, *** $p > 0.001$

Robust standard errors, clustered by country code, in parentheses.

I ran all four models on data that had not been put through Amelia. The OLS models, displayed as Models 9(2) and 10(2) in Table A.12, show the same relationship as in the Amelia data, with similar coefficient sizes and relative levels of statistical significance, as well as similar increases in the model's r^2 relative to the purely structural model. However, as would be expected, the significantly decreased number of observations results in somewhat decreased levels of statistical significance overall.

In the logistic regression models, the loss of statistical power means that the maximalism variable loses its statistical significance. However, its coefficient becomes more substantive, suggesting that what is happening here is not that the relationship is being undermined but rather just that the relatively small n makes it impossible to find a significant effect of this size.

I ran these primary models again with the alternative definition of the transitional endpoint (less than 0.05 change in polyarchy for at least two years). As shown in Table A.13, changing the endpoint definition does not result in any significant change

Table A.12 Main Tests on Non-Amelia Imputed Data

	Model 9 (2) OLS	Model 10 (2) OLS	Model 11 (2) Logistic	Model 12 (2) Logistic
Mobilization	0.168***		4.790*	
	(0.043)		(2.158)	
Maximalism	−0.077*		−1.141	
	(0.033)		(1.049)	
Modernization	0.062	0.115*	0.353	0.912
	(0.040)	(0.046)	(1.430)	(0.987)
Democratic Neighbors	0.226*	0.123	0.414	−0.152
	(0.097)	(0.116)	(4.383)	(2.898)
INGO Network Centrality	0.066	0.174	1.190	1.697
	(0.131)	(0.156)	(4.674)	(3.426)
Trade Linkage	0.234	0.454	16.079	53.252
	(0.224)	(0.269)	(62.338)	(61.373)
Old Polyarchy Level	−0.128	0.073	0.013	3.309
	(0.141)	(0.158)	(4.944)	(3.921)
Constant	0.443***	0.448***	1.071	0.490
	(0.073)	(0.088)	(2.745)	(2.019)
Observations	50	53	50	53
R2	0.637	0.496	0.927	0.806

* $p < 0.05$, ** $p < 0.01$, *** $p < 0.001$

in coefficient size, sign, or significance in the OLS models. In the logistic regression models of binary democracy, the maximalism variable loses its significance though the mobilization variable remains significant. The inclusion of the two strategic challenges also significantly increases the r^2 and area under the ROC curve (AUC) over a purely structural model.

Next I shifted my measurement of the dependent variable from the polyarchy score to the Polity IV score. As described in Chapter 2, I consider this to be an inferior measure to the polyarchy score, with less reliable and theoretically satisfying definitions of democracy and democraticness. However, it offers a meaningful way of providing additional robustness to my results.

Using the Polity score as my measurement of posttransition democracy leads to similar results in terms of sign, coefficient size, and significance. In the linear tests maximalism loses its significance but remains negatively signed.

Finally, I ran the models including the secondary control variables: logged area in square kilometers, British colonialism, military regime, the Gini coefficient, the Muslim

Table A.13 Models of Mobilization and Maximalism (Alternative Endpoint)

	Model 9 (3) OLS	Model 10 (3) OLS	Model 11 (3) Logit	Model 12 (3) Logit
Maximalism	−0.0636**		−0.8697	
	(0.0197)		(0.5017)	
Mobilization	0.1714***		2.5879**	
	(0.0278)		(0.8826)	
Democratic Neighbors	0.1914*	0.1	4.1589	2.7201
	(0.0771)	(0.0996)	(2.8948)	(2.7054)
INGO Network	−0.0118	0.056	2.4595	2.9906
Centrality	(0.0723)	(0.0919)	(2.0787)	(1.7378)
Modernization	0.0906***	0.1475***	−0.9979	−0.1566
	(0.0227)	(0.0268)	(0.6197)	(0.463)
Old Polyarchy Level	−0.1236	0.1036	1.353	3.601
	(0.1174)	(0.1414)	(3.813)	(3.0966)
Constant	0.3859***	0.4339***	−1.6048	−0.9822
	(0.0401)	(0.0509)	(1.2466)	(1.0113)
Trade Linkage	0.1358	0.3444	−2.9095	0.3058
	(0.1854)	(0.2396)	(5.1854)	(4.5659)
N	78	78	76	76
r2/AUC	0.704	0.5017	0.8679	0.7342

population, and oil and gas rents. I report the results in Model 9(5) in Table A.15. The mobilization and maximalism variables remain significant and with coefficients of similar size in the OLS model. I am unable to replicate the logistic regression models with the full set of controls because the model does not converge, leading to meaningless coefficients and standard errors.

In Table A.15 I also report the results of running this extended structural model through a stepwise deletion process, that is to say, running the model iteratively while deleting the least significant independent variable in each iteration until only variables with a p value below a certain threshold remain. I chose an elimination threshold of p > 0.1. Comparing Models 9(5) and 10(5) with the stepwise deletion models shows the robustness of the mobilization and maximalism measures relative to structural predictors. For instance, the democratic neighbors variable is insignificant in Model 10(5) but significant in both models that include mobilization and maximalism. In contrast to these fluctuating levels of significance for structural factors, throughout the stepwise deletion process the mobilization and maximalism measures remain highly significant and are often the most significant predictors by an order of magnitude.

Table A.14 Maximalism and Mobilization Tests with
Polity Dependent Variable

	Model 9 (4) OLS	Model 10 (4) OLS	Model 11 (4) Logistic	Model 12 (4) Logistic
Maximalism	−0.5727		−1.0233*	
	(0.6826)		(0.4954)	
Mobilization	4.8657***		1.8287**	
	(0.9348)		(0.6634)	
Democratic Neighbors	6.1801*	3.9512	3.766	2.0204
	(2.6567)	(3.0536)	(2.411)	(2.0428)
INGO Network Centrality	−0.6914	1.3081	1.0841	1.2378
	(2.5177)	(2.8033)	(1.8597)	(1.5682)
Modernization	0.602	1.7579*	−0.1796	0.5281
	(0.8037)	(0.8244)	(0.5781)	(0.4653)
Old Polyarchy Level	−3.6648	2.5641	0.1263	2.0737
	(3.8795)	(4.3242)	(3.0314)	(2.3502)
Trade Linkage	0.6081	6.69	7.211	7.8603
	(6.5957)	(7.6305)	(11.1384)	(9.5498)
Constant	0.8712	2.0225	−1.6213	−0.7596
	(1.3767)	(1.5692)	(1.0706)	(0.8748)
N	78	78	78	78
r2/AUC	0.4026	0.1766	0.8625	0.7523

Case Study Research Additional Materials

List of All Interviewees

Because of the ongoing political relevance of many of the events discussed in the case study chapters, the human subjects protection protocol for this project called for acknowledging the participation of individual interviewees but for specific quotations to remain anonymous. The human subjects protection protocol is University of Denver Institutional Review Board Protocol 962008-2. The complete list of interviewees as well as their titles and the dates of their interviews are provided in Tables A.16, A.17, and A.18.

Questionnaire for Semistructured Interviews

The following questionnaire served as a guide for all the interviews performed for the three case studies for this book. As described in the introduction to the case study

Table A.15 Models with Secondary Controls and Stepwise Deletion

	Model 9 (5) OLS	Model 10 (5) OLS	Model 9 (6) OLS
Maximalism	−0.0585*		−0.0564*
	(0.0251)		(0.0215)
Mobilization	0.175***		0.1836***
	(0.0336)		(0.0255)
British Colony	−0.0378	−0.018	
	(0.0445)	(0.0534)	
Democratic Neighbors	0.2027*	0.0816	0.2*
	(0.0902)	(0.11)	(0.0779)
Gini Coefficient	0.0592	−0.0573	
	(0.0875)	(0.108)	
Military Regime	0.0293	0.0215	
	(0.0419)	(0.0521)	
INGO Network	−0.0127	0.1025	
Centrality	(0.125)	(0.1502)	
Modernization	0.0824*	0.1503***	0.0713***
	(0.0321)	(0.0359)	(0.0207)
Area (logged)	0.0066	0.0046	
	(0.0127)	(0.0158)	
Oil Revenue	−0.0088	−0.0154	
	(0.0091)	(0.0113)	
Muslim Population	−0.0586	−0.0364	−0.1163*
	(0.0596)	(0.073)	(0.0455)
Old Polyarchy Level	−0.0745	0.1327	
	(0.1352)	(0.1642)	
Trade Linkage	0.161	0.347	
	(0.2032)	(0.2488)	
Constant	0.3018	0.4337*	0.3783***
	(0.157)	(0.1931)	(0.0303)
N	67	67	78
r2	0.6772	0.487	0.715

Table A.16 Complete Nepal Interview List

Name		Position	Interview Date
Aditya	Adhikari	Journalist, *Kathmandu Post*	22.12.2016
Indra	Adhikari	Deputy executive director, Institute of Foreign Affairs	14.12.2016
Rabindra	Adhikari	Member of Parliament, CPN-UML	07.12.2016
Govinda Sharma	Bandi	Advocate, Supreme Court of Nepal	18.12.2016
Lok Raj	Baral	Executive chairman, Nepal Center for Contemporary Studies	12.12.2016
Basanti	Basatoli	Journalist, *Sancharika Samuha*	14.12.2016
Binod	Bhattarai	Founding president, Inter-Party Society of Nepal (IPAS-Nepal)	12.12.2016
Rajan	Bhattarai	Member of Parliament, CPN-UML	08.12.2016
Meena	Bishwakarma	Central Committee member, Nepali Congress	05.12.2016
Rem Bahadur	Biswokarma	President, Collective Campaign for Peace	10.12.2016
Shobhakar	Budathoki	Independent NGO contractor and human rights activist	01.12.2016
Devraj	Dahal	Nepal country director, Friedrich-Ebert Stiftung	06.12.2016
Khim Lal	Devkota	Spokesman, Naya Shakti Party	11.12.2016
Daman Nath	Dunghana	Former speaker of the House, Nepali Congress	05.12.2016
Yubraj	Ghimire	Editor, *Annapurna Post*	17.12.2016
Yogendra	Ghising	Member of Parliament, CPN-MC	17.12.2016
Dipak	Gyawali	Former minister and academician, Nepal Academy of Science and Technology	07.12.2016
Vijay	Karna	Professor of political science, Tribhuvan University	11.12.2016
Ajaya	Khanal	Former editor, *Himalayan Times*	14.12.2016

(continued)

Table A.16 Continued

Name		Position	Interview Date
Muma Ram	Khanal	Central Committee member, Communist Party of Nepal (Maoist), 1996–2004	09.12.2016
Sridhar	Khatri	Professor of foreign affairs, Tribhuvan University	13.12.2016
Suresh Ale	Magar	Secretariat member, CPN-MC	23.12.2016
Pancha	Maharjan	Professor, Center for Nepal and Asian Studies, Tribhuvan University	01.12.2016
Bharat	Nepali	Executive director, Feminist Dalit Organization	13.12.2016
Krishna	Pahadi	Founding chair, Human Rights and Peace Society	13.12.2016
Devendra Raj	Pandey	Convener, Citizen's Movement for Democracy and Peace	21.12.2016
Kamal	Pangeni	Member of Parliament, Nepali Congress	18.12.2016
Krishna Man	Pradhan	Executive director, Nepal Law Society	06.12.2016
Prateek	Pradhan	Editor-in-chief, *Bharapuri Online Newspaper*	09.12.2016
Charan	Prasai	Coordinator, Accountability Watch Committee	15.12.2016
Subodh Raj	Pyakurel	Chairperson, Informal Sector Service Center	02.12.2016
Sushil	Pyakurel	Special advisor to the president, Government of Nepal	20.12.2016
Gaurav	Rana	Chief of general staff, Nepal Army, 2012–15	21.12.2016
Uday Shamsher	Rana	Member of Parliament, Nepali Congress	13.12.2016
Minendra	Rijal	Former minister and member of Parliament, Nepali Congress	16.12.2016
Hari	Rokka	Independent analyst in political economy	09.12.2016
Bishnu	Sapkota	Country director, FHI 360 Nepal	22.12.2016

Table A.16 Continued

Name		Position	Interview Date
Om Prakash	Sen	Director, Advocacy Forum–Nepal	16.12.2016
Abhishek Pratap	Shah	Member of Parliament, Federal Socialist Forum	20.12.2016
Tula	Shah	Executive director, Nepal Madhes Foundation	02.12.2016
Min Bahadur	Shahi	Chairperson, Human Rights Alliance	15.12.2016
Bala Nanda	Sharma	General (Ret.), Nepal Army	15.12.2016
Hari	Sharma	Director, Alliance for Social Dialogue	20.12.2016
Prakash Mani	Sharma	Senior advocate, Pro Public	20.12.2016
Sumit	Sharma	Executive director, Nepal Transition to Peace Initiative	12.12.2016
Kapil	Shrestha	Professor, Tribhuvan University	03.12.2016
Sabin	Shrestha	Executive director, Forum for Women, Law, and Development	19.12.2016
Shyam	Shrestha	Member of Parliament, CPN-MC	15.12.2016
Renu	Sijapati	General secretary, Feminist Dalit Organization	13.12.2016
Malla K	Sundar	Founding member, Nepal Federation of Indigenous Nationalities	14.12.2016
Padam	Sundas	Chairperson, Samata Foundation	29.11.2016
Ujjwal	Sundas	Managing director, Samata Foundation	29.11.2016
Deepak	Thapa	Director, Social Science Baha	16.12.2016
Dinesh	Tripathi	Advocate, Supreme Court of Nepal	04.12.2016
Padma Ratna	Tuladhar	Independent left politician	08.12.2016
Dina	Upadhyay	Member of Parliament, Nepali Congress	19.12.2016
Bishnu	Upreti	Director, Nepal Center for Contemporary Research	13.12.2016
George	Varughese	Nepal country representative, The Asia Foundation	08.12.2016

Table A.17 Complete Zambia Interview List

Name		Position	Interview Date
Darison	Chaala	Former general secretary, Civil Servants and Allied Workers of Zambia Union	31.03.2017
Theresa	Chewe	Administrator, Southern Africa Center for Constructive Resolution of Disputes	10.04.2017
McDonald	Chipenzi	Former executive director, Foundation for Democratic Process, 2011–16	28.03.2017
Chris	Chirwa	Director, Image Publishers Limited	28.03.2017
Mbita	Chitala	Founding deputy secretary, Movement for Multiparty Democracy	05.04.2017
Mark	Chona	Founding permanent secretary, Zambian Ministry of Foreign Affairs	04.04.2017
Rodger	Chongwe	Former president, Law Association of Zambia	22.03.2017
Bright	Chunga	Presidential chief of staff, Government of Zambia, 1990–91	27.03.2017
Jacob	Goma	General secretary, Forum for Democracy and Peace	20.03.2017
Lee	Havasonda	President, Transparency International Zambia; former executive director, Southern Africa Center for Constructive Resolution of Disputes	27.03.2017
Batuke	Imenda	Former member of Parliament, National Assembly of Zambia	12.04.2017
Jack	Kalala	Foreign Service of Zambia, 1992–99	25.03.2017
Austin	Kaluba	Journalist, *National Mirror*	03.04.2017
Enoch	Kavindele	Vice president of Zambia, 2001–3	28.03.2017

Table A.17 Continued

Name		Position	Interview Date
Sarah	Longwe	Chair, NGO coordinating committee	29.03.2017
Bradford	Machila	Former minister for lands, Government of Zambia	06.04.2017
Peter	Machungwa	Former home affairs minister, Government of Zambia	11.04.2017
Amos	Malupenga	Permanent secretary, Ministry of Local Government and Housing	24.03.2017
John	Mambo	Chairperson, Civil Society Constitutional Agenda	04.04.2017
Akashambatwa	Mbikusita-Lewanika	Founding national secretary, Movement for Multiparty Democracy	18.03.2017
Chibeza	Mfuni	Founding president, Social Democratic Party	31.03.2017
Stanley	Mhango	Former president, Foundation for Democratic Process	10.04.2017
Laura	Miti	Executive director, Alliance for Community Action	30.03.2017
Jotham	Momba	Associate professor of political science, University of Zambia	12.04.2017
Alfred	Mudenda	Deputy secretary general, Zambian Congress of Trade Unions	23.03.2017
Gilbert	Mudenda	Founding member, Movement for Multiparty Democracy	09.04.2017
Teddy	Mulonga	Former deputy secretary to the cabinet, Government of Zambia; founding member, Movement for Multiparty Democracy	24.03.2017
Mike	Mulongoti	President, People's Party	23.03.2017
Christine	Munalula	Program manager, CARE International	22.03.2017
Charity	Musamba	Lecturer in development studies, University of Zambia	04.04.2017

(*continued*)

Appendix

Table A.17 Continued

Name		Position	Interview Date
Frederick	Mutesa	Founder, Zambians for Empowerment and Development Party	06.04.2017
Lucy	Muyoyeta	Former chairperson, NGO coordinating council	12.04.2017
Vernon	Mwaanga	Founding vice chair for publicity, Movement for Multiparty Democracy; minister of foreign affairs, Government of Zambia	27.03.2017
Maureen	Mwanawasa	First lady of Zambia, 2002–8	11.04.2017
Tentani	Mwanza	President, National Democratic Party	21.03.2017
Lewis	Mwape	Executive director, Zambia Council for Social Development	03.04.2017
Raphael	Nakacinda	National secretary, Movement for Multiparty Democracy	11.04.2017
Bizeck	Phiri	Professor of political science, University of Zambia	03.04.2017
Sketchley	Sacika	Former secretary to the cabinet, Government of Zambia	07.04.2017
Richard	Sakala	Editor, *Daily Nation Newspaper*	29.03.2017
Guy	Scott	Acting president of Zambia, 2014–15	14.04.2017
Fackson	Shamenda	Former president, Zambian Council of Trade Unions	30.03.2017
Emily	Sikazwe	Commissioner, Electoral Commission of Zambia	31.03.2017
Neo	Simutanyi	Executive director, Center for Policy Dialogue	05.04.2017
Ludwig	Sondashi	President, Forum for Democratic Alternatives	29.03.2017
Keli	Walubita	Founding vice chair for security and intelligence, Movement for Multiparty Democracy	21.03.2017

Table A.17 Continued

Name		Position	Interview Date
Sikota	Wina	Former minister (various portfolios), Government of Zambia	01.04.2017
Simon	Zukas	Founding member, Movement for Multiparty Democracy; former member of Parliament, National Assembly of Zambia	29.03.2017
Ballard	Zulu	Outreach director, Indaba Agricultural Policy Research Institute	13.04.2017

Table A.18 Complete Brazil Interview List

Name		Position	Interview Date
Jaime	Almeida	Professor, University of Brasilia	07.06.2017
Criméia	Almeida	Activist, Comissão de Familiares de Mortos e Desaparecidos	28.06.2017
Ademar	Bertucci	Former president, Caritas	06.06.2017
Carlos Henrique	Cardim	Ambassador, Brazilian Ministry of Foreign Affairs	20.06.2017
Athos Magno	Costa e Silva	Founding member, PT	09.06.2017
Antonio Carlos Alves	Coutinho	Brigadier general, Escola Superior de Guerra	31.05.2017
Alvaro	Dias	Senator, PMDB	01.06.2017
Helio	Doyle	Founding member, PT	19.06.2017
Helio	Duque	Constituent assembly member	30.06.2017
Elio	Gaspari	Journalist, *O Globo/Folha de S. Paulo*	14.06.2017
Eliana Magalhães	Graça	Sociologist, Special Secretariat on Women's Politics	29.06.2017
Ada	Lemos	Political analyst, PMDB	23.06.2017
Ivan	Marx	Federal attorney, Transitional Justice Working Group	30.06.2017

(*continued*)

Table A.18 Continued

Name		Position	Interview Date
Delano	Menezes	Brigadier general; director, Escola Superior de Guerra	26.05.2017
Vera	Mercucci	Lobbyist, Health Professionals Syndicate	20.06.2017
Elimar	Nascimento	Former student activist and PCdoB militant	03.07.2017
Bolívar	Pêgo	Researcher, Institute for Applied Economic Research	07.06.2017
Daniel	Reis	Founding member, PT	06.07.2017
Isaac	Roitman	Professor, Brazilian Society for the Advancement of Science	20.06.2017
Maria Aparecida Guimarães	Skorupski	Former student activist	26.06.2017
Tin	Urbinatti	Founder, Grupo Forja; cultural advisor, Sáo Paolo Worker's Movement	20.06.2017

chapters, the interviews were semistructured. Therefore each interview did not necessarily include all the questions, nor does the questionnaire include every question asked of each interviewee. Instead the interviews were tailored to fit the background and knowledge of the interviewee in question. However, all interviews followed the general pattern laid out in the questionnaire.

The Pretransition Movement

- First, I'm going to ask you some questions about the events that led up to your country's political transition. I am interested in anything you can tell me about how [**country-specific references to the movement that initiated the country's political transition—referred to hereafter as "the movement"**] worked and how things that happened during the movement may have affected the political transition.
- Tell me about the movement. What were its major events?
- Follow-up: And what was your role and the role of your organization in this movement?
- How did the movement get started? And why did people choose to start it at that particular time?

- Was establishing democracy[4] a key goal of the movement? What other goals were there?
- How did people in the movement deal with people from the old government who wanted to join? How welcome were they?
- What were the things that helped make the movement successful? What were the biggest challenges that it faced?
- How did people in the movement talk about the political transition? What challenges did you anticipate facing if you were successful in removing the old government from power?
- What kind of plans did people in the movement make for the political transition? Did people in the movement plan to continue protests and other activism during the political transition?
- Would you say that the movement succeeded in achieving its goals?

Transitional Challenges

- Now I'm going to ask you some questions about the political transition after the old government was removed. I am interested in understanding what challenges there were in moving your country toward democracy and how you and other people from the movement tried to address these challenges.
- Tell me about the transition. What were the major events? How did things change and how did they stay the same?
- What aspects of your country's politics made establishing democracy easier? What things made it harder?
- Specifically, how did your role and your organization's role change?
  - Follow-up if necessary: For example, did you enter politics? Did you try to pursue different kinds of policies? Did you organize new protests or strikes?
  - Follow-up: Why did you and your organization pursue this path? What did you want to accomplish?
- Did other people from the movement or other political groups still organize protests, strikes, or other kinds of extreme political action?
  - Follow-up if yes: Who organized these kinds of actions?
  - Follow-up if yes: What kinds of tactics did they use?
  - Follow-up if yes: What kinds of goals did they pursue?
  - Follow-up if yes: What was the reaction to this kind of action from people who were now in power?
- Were people from the old government punished in any way for abuses they had committed while in power? Why or why not?
  - Follow-up if yes: What kind of punishment was there? Who did it apply to and how heavy were the penalties?
  - Follow-up if yes: How did the people from the old government facing punishment react? Did they try to prevent the punishment in any way?

- How much agreement or disagreement was there between groups within the old movement about what the new political system should look like? Were disagreements resolved, and if so how?
- What were the most important political divisions during the transition?
  - Follow-up: For example, divisions over ethnicity, religion, economic class, or political ideology.
- Who got to participate in making political decisions during the transition? Who was left out?
  - Follow-up: How did people who were left out respond? How did they try and get people to listen to their agenda?
- How did the new people in power deal with members of the old government? Who was allowed to stay in politics? Who was not allowed to stay in politics?
  - Follow-up: If people from the old government could participate in politics, what was their role? How central were they in the new government?
- How democratic would you say your country is today? Completely democratic, mostly democratic, a little democratic, or not democratic at all?
  - Follow-up (if not fully democratic): What is keeping your country from being fully democratic?
  - Follow-up (if fully democratic): What are the things that support your country's democratic system?
- What else should I know about your country that we haven't talked about yet?

Notes

INTRODUCTION

1. Interview 55. To protect confidentiality, as required by the human subjects protection protocol for this project, all specific statements from interviewees for this project will be referred to by a randomly assigned number. The complete list of interviewees is available in the appendix (Tables A16–A.18).
2. Transitions calculated using the "Regimes of the World" indicator from the Varieties of Democracy data set (Coppedge et al., 2018). All countries' regime type measured in 2018.
3. Frequently referred to as a "nonviolent revolution."
4. I discuss the logic of nested analysis in more detail in the introduction to Chapters 3–5.
5. "Highly democratic" here is defined as having a polyarchy score of 0.75 or higher, "minimally democratic" as having a polyarchy score of 0.5 or higher, and "autocratic" as scoring less than 0.5.
6. See Chapter 2 for an in-depth discussion of how all these concepts are operationalized.
7. For major works of modernization theory, see, for example, Barro (1999); Bollen and Jackman (1985); Diamond (1992); Jackman (1973).
8. Although see critiques from Acemoglu et al. (2008); Robinson (2006).
9. See, for example, Ballou (1910); Thoreau (2016); Tolstoy (1894).
10. For an excellent selection of some of Gandhi's primary writings on nonviolent resistance, see Gandhi (2019).
11. See also Ackerman and DuVall (2000); Ackerman and Kruegler (1994); Roberts and Ash (2009); Zunes, Asher, and Kurtz (1999); and many others.
12. See, for example, Belgioioso (2018); Braithwaite, Braithwaite, and Kucik (2015); Butcher, Gray, and Mitchell (2018); Butcher and Svensson (2016); K. G. Cunningham, Dahl, and Fruge (2017); Dahlum (2019); Kristian S. Gleditsch and

Rivera (2017); Petrova (2019); Pinckney (2016); Svensson and Lindgren (2011); Thurber (2018).

13. Other terms commonly used for civil resistance are "nonviolent resistance," "nonviolent action," and "peaceful resistance." Less common terms are "passive resistance" and "satyagraha." I use "nonviolent resistance" and "nonviolent action" interchangeably with "civil resistance."

14. When aggregated to the level of a campaign, few nonviolent resistance movements are exclusively nonviolent. Movements often struggle to maintain "nonviolent discipline" in the face of provocation. What makes it meaningful to describe these movements as nonviolent resistance is the preponderance of nonviolent tactics over violent tactics (Pinckney, 2016).

15. A process that is often made more difficult by observational biases that tend to focus outside knowledge of contention on its violent elements and downplay nonviolent elements (Day, Pinckney, & Chenoweth, 2015).

16. See, for example, Fernandes (2015), which examines this relationship by comparing the Spanish and Portuguese transitions to democracy.

17. For example, consider the examination of the labor movement in Latin America in Collier and Collier (1991). While labor initially functioned in opposition to the political order, when repression failed to suppress the movement Latin American elites engaged in various strategies to incorporate the demands of labor into routinized politics, a shift that had important consequences for contentious politics across the region for decades following the initial incorporation.

18. For example, see seminal works by Acemoglu and Robinson (2001); Bratton and Van de Walle (1994); Collier (1999); Di Palma (1990); Mohamedou and Sisk (2016); O'Donnell and Schmitter (1986); Rustow (1970).

CHAPTER 1

1. The literature on this subject is large and growing. Some of the most important works to date are Bayer, Bethke, and Lambach (2016); Celestino and Gleditsch (2013); Chenoweth and Stephan (2011); Johnstad (2010); Karatnycky and Ackerman (2005).

2. For more on Havel as both activist and president, see Keane (2000) and Kriseova (1993).

3. Political power is a complex and contested concept. I use it here simply to indicate an ability to affect political outcomes, considered in terms of Easton's (1954) classic formulation of politics, discussed earlier. For classic discussions of the concept, see Dahl (1957); Lukes (1986); Weber (1978).

4. For more on this, see the discussion of "movement culture" in Tufekci (2017).

5. This contrasts with victorious rebel movements, which, while their victory may lead to more democratization than in government victories in civil war (Toft, 2010),

often lead to consolidation of authoritarian rule under a strong rebel successor party (Lyons, 2016).

6. See France24, "Arrestation des leaders de Y'en a marre et du Balai citoyen à Kinshasa," March 3, 2015, http://www.france24.com/fr/20150316-rd-congo-kinshasa-arrestation-balai-citoyen-yen-a-marre-senegal-burkina-faso.

7. See, for example, Burrowes (1996).

8. Thanks to Colin Beck for suggesting this term.

9. This model of radicalization of politics follows a logic similar to Rabushka and Shepsle's (1972) analysis of politics in "plural" societies.

10. Some seminal versions of the strong structural argument applicable here do exist, though. For instance, Skocpol's (1979) explanation of revolutions approaches the strong structural argument. And many classic Marxist approaches to revolution and social change approach fully deterministic accounts, with the economic base determining the social and political superstructure "independent of [the] will" (Marx 1859/1977), though see critiques of a deterministic interpretation of Marx in Gilbert (1979) and Harman (1986).

11. For seminal contributions, see Archer (2003); Berger and Luckmann (1966); Bhaskar (2014); Giddens (1984).

12. The biographies of key participants in the Hungarian roundtable talks powerfully illustrate this point. For brief summaries of the varied life stories of these participants, see Bozoki (2002, 385–409).

13. An examination of the democratization literature quickly shows this to be true. Jan Teorell (2010, p. 158), in one of the most comprehensive examinations of various arguments in the democratization literature, concludes, "Even the broadest and most inclusive statistical models perform dismally poorly in trying to predict short-term development of democracy." Quantitative studies of democratization based on various structural characteristics tend to have very low measures of model fit, indicating limited explanatory power (for example, note the r^2 measures reported in Fish, 2002; Przeworski, 2000; or Stradiòtto and Guo, 2010). Even findings with good model fit from a single scholar are often difficult for later scholars to replicate. For example, while Boix's (2003) *Democracy and Redistribution* finds a strong relationship between low levels of economic inequality and democratization, later studies by Dutt and Mitra (2008), Houle (2009), and Teorell (2010) were unable to replicate this finding.

14. See, for instance, Haggard and Kaufman (2016a) and Teorell (2010).

15. This finding has been replicated numerous times and in numerous ways. See, for example, Brinks and Coppedge (2006); Cederman and Gleditsch (2004); Doorenspleet (2004); Gleditsch and Ward (2006); Leeson and Dean (2009); Starr (1991).

16. See Simmons, Dobbin, and Garrett (2006) for an enumeration of this and other potential mechanisms of democratic diffusion.

17. See Teorell (2010) for a discussion of this.

CHAPTER 2

1. My primary sources for transitions are the Authoritarian Regimes data set by Barbara Geddes and her coauthors (2014) and the various versions of the NAVCO data project from Erica Chenoweth and her co-authors (Chenoweth and Lewis, 2013; Chenoweth and Shay, 2019). I used the first data set to identify instances of transition and the second as my primary source for identifying whether a transition was a civil resistance transition. I detail my reasons for selecting these data sources as opposed to other potential data sources on transition, as well as my logic in identifying civil resistance transitions, in the appendix.

2. Multiple transitions can occur and have occurred in single countries, such as Madagascar and Zambia. I do not exclude transitions from countries that have previously appeared in the data, since new transitions occur in very different contexts and in response to very different regimes.

3. I am simplifying Linz and Stepan's (1996) definition for the sake of brevity. They also include several caveats related to the de facto authority of the elected government, etc. For all the details on their definition, see Linz and Stepan (1996, p. 1).

4. Though, as Schedler (2002) points out, the evaluation of "freedom and fairness" is shot through with many challenges as the powerful seek to break various points in the "chain of democratic choice." Even here consistent cross-national evaluation is difficult.

5. For example, Svolik (2008) examines the effects of economic factors such as recessions on the likelihood of democratic breakdowns, and Bayer, Bethke, and Lambach (2016) examine the effects of nonviolent resistance on the durability of democratic regimes.

6. My primary definition of "dramatic" fluctuation is a change of at least 0.1 in the polyarchy score. I also run robustness checks defining a "dramatic" fluctuation as a change of 0.05 in the polyarchy score. The two measures are highly correlated, and changing the definition of the transitional endpoint does not significantly affect the analysis that I perform in subsequent sections of this chapter. I report results using the alternative measure of transitional endpoints in the appendix. In the large majority of transitions the difference in final polyarchy scores across endpoint definitions is minimal.

7. The best known of these is likely the Polity data set from Monty Marshall and his coauthors (2016). Other well-known measures include the Freedom House (2019a) Freedom in the World scores and the Unified Democracy scores (Pemstein, Meserve, & Melton, 2010).

8. There are numerous data sets that measure the occurrence of free and fair elections. For the sake of consistency with my data on transitions, I lift this measure from the Geddes et al. (2014) data set on authoritarian regimes.

9. To code this variable, V-Dem asked country expert coders to characterize a country's level of public involvement in civil society on a 4-point scale ranging from a

characterization of "most associations are state-sponsored . . . participation is not purely voluntary" at one end to "there are many diverse [civil society organizations] and it is considered normal for people to be at least occasionally active in one of them" at the other end (Coppedge et al., 2017).

10. Country experts coded this variable based on a 6-point scale from values equivalent to "public deliberation is never allowed" to "large numbers of non-elite groups as well as ordinary people tend to discuss major policies among themselves, in the media, in associations or neighborhoods, or in the streets. Grassroots deliberation is common and unconstrained (Coppedge et al., 2017, pp. 202–3)

11. For validity of inference it was also crucial to choose indicators from V-Dem that were not a part of the aggregation process for creating the polyarchy score. V-Dem includes other measures that could plausibly be included in a mobilization factor, but these are almost all included in one of the indexes that V-Dem's creators then use to construct the polyarchy score.

12. I describe the details of this adjustment process and provide greater detail on the Phoenix data, in the appendix.

13. Factor loading tables for all factors are in the appendix.

14. See Black and Kingsley (2013).

15. See, for example, Laver, Benoit, and Garry (2003); Pauwels (2011); Proksch and Slapin (2010).

16. For instance, one of the most comprehensive efforts to map political positions is the Manifesto Project (formerly the Comparative Manifestos Project), yet this is limited to parties' formal manifestos and only covers roughly 50 countries. See the Project's website, https://manifesto-project.wzb.eu/, for more information.

17. Many previous democratization scholars, particularly Przeworski (1991), have argued similarly that willingness to accept unfavorable electoral results is *the* fundamental underlying democratic norm.

18. For more on the back-and-forth protests of these two movements, see Forsyth (2010); Hewison (2014); Thabchumpon (2016).

19. This is a four-level ordinal variable that ranges from "no parties or candidates boycotted the elections" to "all opposition parties and candidates boycotted the elections" (Coppedge et al., 2017, pp. 96–97).

20. This is also a four-level ordinal variable with values ranging from "no candidates accepted the results of the election" to "all parties and candidates accepted the results" (Coppedge et al., 2017, p. 107).

21. This variable is originally coded with values ranging from "anti-system movements are practically non-existent" to "there is a very high level of anti-system movement activity, posing a real and present threat to the regime" (Coppedge et al., 2017, p. 247).

22. The four indicators that make up the modernization factor are GDP per capita, urbanization, the infant mortality rate, and the number of years of education for

children older than 15. When run through principal factor analysis these four measures yield a single factor with an eigenvalue above 1. This factor is my measure of modernization. See the appendix for the sources and coding details of the component variables.

23. I calculate the percentage of democracies in a region using definitions of regions from Haber and Menaldo (2011). The measure of export and import flows specifically is the total exports and exports between the country in question and the United States, United Kingdom, Canada, Australia, and the euro area, divided by GDP. The measure comes from the International Monetary Fund and follows Levitsky and Way's (2010) suggestion for one key measure of Western linkage. The measure of INGO connectedness is the INGO network centrality score (INCS), developed by Melanie Hughes and her coauthors (2009) and later expanded by Pamela Paxton and her coauthors (2015). The INCS is a theoretical innovation built on the common practice of using an absolute count of a country's INGO memberships as a way of measuring a country's linkage to the Western-dominated world system (e.g., Landman, 2005; Murdie, 2009). The INCS is created by using countries' common membership in INGOs to construct a global INGO network. Country scores are then assigned using the Bonacich (1987) measure of eigenvector network centrality, which measures not just a country's connections but how closely they are linked to other highly linked countries. See the appendix for more details.

24. The theoretical inspiration for most of these variables comes from Teorell's (2010) study of democratization. There are various data sources. I describe each of these data sources and the specific transformations of the variables used in testing in the appendix.

25. I also ran robustness checks with a new binary measure of democracy, transforming the linear polyarchy score into a binary score. This transformation relied on the traditional democratic threshold of a Polity score of 6 or higher. I ran an OLS model regressing the Polity score on the polyarchy score, then used the predictions of that model to define a polyarchy score equivalent to a Polity score of 6. In the full V-Dem and Polity data sets, this came to a value of roughly 0.624. I then coded every polyarchy score equal to or above this value as democracies and all those below it as nondemocracies.

26. To provide additional support for my arguments, in the appendix I run a set of tests that shift the unit of observation from the country to the country-year for a 10-year period following a transition's initiation.

27. I considered incorporating tests using simultaneous equations to address the concerns over endogeneity in my independent variables; however, after an examination of the econometrics literature I determined that this would not be appropriate (Hausman, 1983; Mills & Patterson, 2006). A simultaneous equations model is intended to address a situation in which some of the independent variables are

caused by the dependent variable, creating a correlation between the independent variable and the error term of the regression model. In my case, however, I am not dealing with endogeneity in this sense, but rather endogeneity in the sense of my independent variables being part of a larger system of causation—steps along the way from remote causal variables to a future dependent variable. Thus the relationship I am modeling is one not of simultaneity but of mediation, as I discuss in the previous chapter.

28. For an in-depth description of Amelia II's methodology and use in time series cross-sectional data, see Honaker and King (2010). I ran the Amelia II algorithm with country-specific intercepts and time dependencies assumed.

29. The Amelia procedure is computationally intensive, particularly when one adds country-specific intercepts and time dependencies to one's data, as I did. Hence I was able to run only my core independent, dependent, and control variables through the Amelia process. I did not include the other control variables—the logged geographic area, Muslim percentage of the population, Gini coefficient, British colonialism, and prior military regime—in the Amelia process, hence some data is missing and the total number of observations in models that include these measures is limited.

30. I defined these four categories by breaking down the continuous 0 to 1 polyarchy score into four bins, with 0 to 0.25 defined as "very autocratic," 0.25 to 0.5 defined as "slightly autocratic," 0.5 to 0.75 defined as "slightly democratic," and 0.75 to 1 defined as "very democratic."

31. Because the variable is binomial, the marginal effect is equivalent to the beta coefficient.

32. VIF testing shows no problematic multicollinearity between the independent variables. The highest VIF for one of the variables is around 3, well below the standard point of concern at 10. Examination of a residual against fitted values (RVF) plot shows no visible pattern of heteroscedasticity. I show a representative example of the RVF plot from one Amelia imputation in the appendix.

33. I selected the genetic matching algorithm because it had the best performance in creating balanced samples of control and treated cases. I compared the algorithm to nearest neighbor matching, optimal matching, full matching, and coarsened exact matching. For details on the genetic matching algorithm program, see Sekhon (2011).

34. I report these numbers, as well as tests for heteroscedasticity in the residuals of all OLS models, in the appendix.

35. Matching procedures tend to be based around a binary assignment of treatment. This is not practical here because both the mobilization and maximalism variables are continuous. However, numerous statistical techniques exist to perform the same balancing for continuous variables. For this test, I used a dose-response model with propensity score matching for each of my independent variables using Hirano and

Imbens's (2004) procedure for incorporating matching with a continuous treatment. This procedure adjusts for imbalance in covariates at different levels of the independent variable, producing a generalized propensity score (GPS) which can then attenuate the bias caused by imbalanced covariates. As in the propensity score matching for civil resistance transitions, I generated the GPS using the same set of control variables incorporated in my main predictive models: modernization, trade linkage, international non-governmental organization network centrality, the percentage of democratic neighbors, and the pretransition polyarchy level.

36. I report the results of all these alternative models in the appendix. See tables A.11–A.15 in the appendix.

INTRODUCTION TO CASE STUDY CHAPTERS

1. Nested analysis has been widely recognized as one of the most meaningful ways of combining the insights of quantitative and qualitative research (Gerring, 2007; Hafner-Burton & Ron, 2009). However, the method is not without its weaknesses. It is critically important that the complementary strengths of the two research methods not undermine the researcher's case in within-method validation of their research strategy, absent which nested analysis can lead to even worse outcomes than a single-method research design (Rohlfing, 2008). For example, I validate my quantitative findings with extensive robustness checks and model fit tests and present extensive arguments as to why my case studies are appropriate examples of the dynamics that I argue they represent.

2. I was also limited in terms of time and resources. It bears mentioning that the only case of a civil resistance transition ending with a polyarchy score lower than 0.25 at the end of the transition in the past 20 years is the Arab Spring transition in Egypt. For more on the Egyptian transition, see Ketchley (2017).

3. In Nepal my primary partner was the Nepal Peacebuilding Initiative. In Zambia I partnered with the Foundation for Democratic Process and researchers at the University of Zambia. In Brazil I partnered with the Department of Political Science at the University of Brasilia.

4. The questionnaire that structured these interviews is in the appendix.

5. In Nepal and Zambia I conducted all of the interviews personally. In Brazil I hired a team of Brazilian graduate students as research assistants who conducted the interviews on my behalf and translated them from Portuguese to English.

6. My interview research methodology builds on insights from McCracken (1988), Spradley (1979), and Aberbach and Rockman (2002), among others.

CHAPTER 3

1. All indexes were rescaled from 0 to 1 for comparability.

2. Terminology can be somewhat confusing when it comes to distinguishing the Nepali ethnolinguistic identity and the national identity of citizens of Nepal.

I follow the convention common in Nepal of using "Nepali" to refer to members of the ethnolinguistic group that speaks the language commonly referred to as "Nepali," "Gorkha," or "Khaskura" and the term "Nepalese" to refer to a citizen of the country of Nepal of no particular ethnolinguistic identity group.

3. Interview 30.

4. Interview 12.

5. The links with this earlier mobilization are strong enough that while the typical term for referring to the 2006 uprising is the "Second People's Movement," some refer to it as the "Third People's Movement" (Interview 12).

6. See discussion of this period in Whelpton (2005, 86–121).

7. Interview 43.

8. See the discussion of the contested role of "constitutional monarchy" in Bhandari (2014, pp. 8–12).

9. For an excellent overview of many of the challenges associated with Nepal's incomplete democratization in 1990 and the connections between disillusionment with the 1990 dispensation and the onset of the Maoist rebellion in 1996, see Pfaff-Czarnecka (2004).

10. Even this number may dramatically understate the number of identity groups in Nepal. Nepal's Central Bureau of Statistics (2014, pp. 1–2) reported that actual responses to the 2011 census question on ethnic/caste identity amounted to over 1,200 distinct identity groups. The Bureau then parsed these actual responses down into 125 categories. Their report does not specific the methodology used to make these determinations.

11. Brahmins and Chhetris are the highest caste groups in the traditional caste hierarchy of Nepal. The term "Madhesi" encompasses a diverse group of ethnic and linguistic groups that are native to Nepal's southern plains. This region is commonly referred to as "Madhesh," a term meaning "middle country," and also as "the Tarai," a term that is roughly equivalent to "plains" or "lowlands" in English. The Nepalese Central Bureau of Statistics (2014, p. 3) makes these divides somewhat differently, splitting the Nepalese population into nine categories: "(1) The caste-origin Hill groups, (2) Hill Adibasi/Janajati groups, (3) Hill Dalit, (4) Madhesi caste-origin groups (Level 1), (5) Madhesi caste origin groups (Level 2), (6) Madhesi caste-origin low caste groups or Dalits (Level 3), (7) Tarai (Madhesi) Adibasi/Janajati, (8) Musalman or Muslims, and (9) other cultural groups."

12. Interview 43.

13. For a detailed breakdown of the various factional struggles within the Nepalese communist movement that led to the emergence of the Communist Party of Nepal (Maoist Center), see Thapa (2004).

14. For example, Baburam Bhattarai, one of the Maoists' long-term leaders, described the causes of their rebellion as being rooted in five distinct class problems: domination by upper economic classes over the lower classes, by high-caste Hindus over

lower castes and *janajatis*, by *pahadis* over Madhesis, by non-Dalits over Dalits, and by men over women (quoted in Ogura 2008, 11).

15. The Maoists' choice to engage in armed struggle had many organizational factors driving it as well. Ches Thurber (2019, 9) points to the lack of ties to other social and political groups beyond the Maoists' "geographically and linguistically isolated base of support," a point that was reinforced to me by Interview 47.

16. While the royal massacre did not directly precipitate the subsequent events, its role in unraveling the Nepali monarchy is important to emphasize. As Interview 48 said, "The moment the king was assassinated with his whole family in the mind of a citizen like me, who has worked in the *panchayat* system, has known the king, to me Nepal's monarchy was done that day. It was done away with because then it was the usurper king that was in power."

17. The specific narrative here is contested. Most accounts describe the dissolution of the Parliament in 2002 as a royal power grab. However, those more sympathetic to the monarchy point out that the prime minister at the time requested the dissolution of Parliament in order to hold elections (Interview 4). For a detailed accounting of the specific sequence of events, see Whelpton (2005, pp. 218–21).

18. Interview 43.

19. Interview 43.

20. Interview 48.

21. Interview 47.

22. The creation of a constituent assembly had been a long-time demand of Nepal's communist parties, going back to the initial democratic opening at the end of the Rana regime in 1951 (Adhikari, 2014; P. Jha, 2014; Thapa, 2004).

23. Interview 47.

24. Interviews 4 and 59 in particular.

25. Interview 48.

26. Interview 47.

27. Interview 65.

28. For an overview of the differing visions of the 2006 political regime, see Pandey (2010).

29. Interview 59.

30. Interview 43.

31. Interview 48.

32. As Interview 81 described it, "How do you expect Prachanda, who contributed directly to the deaths of fifteen thousand Nepalese . . . if you just have one election for him in 2008 . . . he was a rebel leader until 2006, so is he suddenly going to be democratic after having killed for ten years? No he's not! Do you think he doesn't fear the International Criminal Court? That's what motivates him every day. He wants someone who will come to power and protect him forevermore."

33. This understanding of the reasons behind the breakdown of the Rayamajhi Commission is supported by Sigdel's (2014) research on the subject.

34. Interview 81 in particular.

35. See, for example, Bandi (2017); Ghimire (2018).

36. A report by the International Commission of Jurists (2017) concluded, "More than ten years after the Comprehensive Peace Agreement was signed in 2006, there has been near absolute impunity for those responsible for serious crimes under international law during Nepal's conflict, and few victims have had access to an effective remedy and reparation for the abuses they have suffered."

37. For an excellent overview of the background and dynamics of the 2007 Madhesi movement, see P. Jha (2014).

38. Interviews 65 and 93 emphasized this point in particular.

39. Interview 93.

40. *Pahadi* is a Nepali term that literally translates as "hilly person" and is commonly used to refer to people whose ethnic background is from the Himalayan foothills.

41. India is Nepal's largest trading partner by far, accounting for roughly 60% of both Nepal's imports and exports in 2017, and a trade deficit between the two countries of roughly $6 billion (World Integrated Trade Solution, 2017).

42. Interview 30.

43. Interview 106.

44. For more detail on the election violence and the general dynamics of the 2008 election, see International Crisis Group (2008).

45. See reports by the Carter Center (2008), which deployed 62 election observers, and the Asian Network for Free Elections, which deployed over 100 election observers (Cooper, 2008).

46. Interview 12 in particular, a figure associated with the Nepali Congress, emphasized this point.

47. See discussion of these events in Whelpton (2005, pp. 86–121).

48. Interview 29.

49. Interview 108.

50. Interview 13.

51. Prachanda was also facing dissension within his own party. Indeed Housden (2010, p. 72) claims, "Prachanda . . . attempted to sack the former chief of staff Katawal because by overhauling the army leadership—a reform that all Maoist cadres [were] calling for—he could consolidate unity within the politburo."

52. See Gellner (2014) for an overview of the process leading up to the elections and the electoral results.

53. Interview 106.

54. Though some claim the conspiracies benefited the Maoists, by tampering with the results to ensure that certain party leaders, including Prachanda, would not lose their seats (Interview 43). I was unable to confirm these rumors.

55. Interview 96.
56. Interview 48.
57. Interview 104.
58. Interview 91.
59. Interview 79.
60. For example, one interviewee sympathetic to the Nepali Congress and CPN-UML described the 2008 election in this way: "[The 2008 election] took place on the Maoist agenda . . . 99% of the agenda. People felt intimidated by the Maoists. . . . They had an army, they had goons, and the backing of all opportunists. [And the] Maoists did not allow other political parties to launch campaigns. They physically intimidated the activists of the other parties . . . and then, see, the voters list was *so* scientific that my own name appeared in four places! So that gave a lot of room for multiple votings" (Interview 106).
61. Interview 47.
62. Interview 93.
63. See, for example, Skocpol (1979, p. 18).
64. Such delegitimization has a long history. Before it was a frame used to delegitimize the Madhesi movement, it was commonly deployed to delegitimize activism by the Nepali Congress against the king (Acharya, 2009; Hachchethu, 1992).
65. Thanks to Kristian Skrede Gleditsch for suggesting this point.
66. Interview 4.
67. In this there is a certain degree of continuity with politics in Nepal from the 1990 First People's Movement until the royal seizure of power in the early 2000s. As Genevieve Lakier (2007, p. 251) writes, "Almost as soon as the rubble of the People's Movement of 1990 cleared, new protest programmes were announced by groups who threatened 'to take to the streets' (*saddakma orlanu*) if they could not achieve their objectives any other way. Street protests, ranging in forms from the simple rally to the national strike, played a major role in almost all important political struggles in the democratic period."
68. Interview 15.
69. Interview 91, a civil society leader, particularly emphasized this point.
70. Interview 47 in particular discussed the possibility of disillusionment with the political parties giving rise to space for a populist challenge from the right, in which a conservative leader with army backing could plausibly seize power and unravel many of the democratic protections of the transition.
71. Interviews 8 and 13.
72. Interview 4.
73. Interview 30.
74. Interview 43.
75. Interview 4.

76. Purchasing power parity GDP per capita in constant 2011 international dollars from the World Bank World Development Indicators (www.databank.worldbank.org).

77. For instance, Interview 108 said that if current political trends continue, "not even God can prevent Nepal from plunging into an ethnic war." Interview 43 also claimed, "We are very, very quickly heading to a new round of conflict.... We made the new constitution a fertile ground for conflict."

CHAPTER 4

1. Interview 2.
2. Interview 68.
3. Interviews 72, 32, and 62.
4. Interview 35.
5. Interviews 87 and 37 in particular emphasized this point.
6. See also similar analyses in Cheeseman and Larmer (2015); van Donge (1995); Erdmann and Simutanyi (2003); Ihonvbere (1995); Mbikusita-Lewanika (2003).
7. The move to the one-party system was long in coming. As Interview 39, a long-standing political insider, reported, "The declaration of the one-party state actually officialized the political attitude of those leaders who led us to independence. In other words, they did not really believe that equally patriotic people, equally knowledgeable people, can have different political opinions or that they should have. Maybe they can have them, but they shouldn't. This was declared a nuisance in decision-making."
8. Interview 80.
9. Interview 61.
10. Interview 39 in particular emphasized this point: "People were quite prepared to trade in their personal freedom and particularly other people's freedom if they could get jobs.... After Zambia's independence, it was a paradise where anybody who graduated from even lower primary school could find a job.... But that didn't last long. Before long these jobs were no longer that available. And therefore the unequal power structure which led to the one-party state meant that those who were in power or whose relatives had influence, whatever, began to be the only ones with access.... So within five years, six years, that gate which could make you forget that there's no freedom was now not accessible."
11. Interview 61. Mandrax is a combination sedative and euphoric commonly used as a recreational drug. The specific accusation against Vernon Mwaanga recorded here is not unique to Interview 61. Mwaanga was arrested and found guilty of drug trafficking by a government commission. See Bartlett (2000).
12. Interview 52.
13. Interview 7.

14. The many strands of opposition politics during this period are comprehensively detailed in Larmer (2016).

15. Interview 2 in particular, who went on to become a major civil society leader, emphasized the importance of student activism.

16. Interview 25.

17. Interview 57.

18. Interview 36.

19. Interview 107. Though apparently this move was fairly transparent to the regime. As Interview 39, an early MMD leader, said, "President Kaunda, to his credit, saw through it immediately. He said this is not a movement, this is a party . . . almost before we even formed it!"

20. Interview 39.

21. Interview 55.

22. Interview 32.

23. This incident is discussed in depth in Malupenga (2009).

24. In an ironic twist, though, it is possible that the constitutional provision would have actually disqualified Chiluba himself, as Zambian media revealed significant evidence that Chiluba's parents originally came from the Democratic Republic of the Congo (Reynolds, 1999, p. 154).

25. Interview 2.

26. An important point here is that, while the trade union movement played an important role in the organization of the MMD, trade union participation in Zambia is quite low. In a 1993 survey only 2% of respondents reported membership in any kind of trade union (Bratton, 1999, p. 560).

27. Interview 57.

28. This amendment to the constitution followed a longtime strategy by President Chiluba. He made the initial public declaration of Zambia as a Christian nation within just two months of his election as president in 1991 and frequently encouraged and even organized evangelistic "crusades." Paul Gifford (1998, p. 371) reports one incident in particular in which Chiluba opened an evangelistic convention with a sermon in which he "insisted that when he made mistakes, true believers should not try to remove him, but pray for him. The prayers of Christians had brought him to power without violence. Subsequent problems had arisen because Christians had stopped praying—thus Chiluba implied that Zambia's difficulties were their fault, not his."

29. Interview 72.

30. Interview 72.

31. Interview 87.

32. Interview 68.

33. Interview 98.

34. Interview 32. I cannot confirm that this interview took place.

35. For an excellent overview of the anti-third term struggle, see Chella and Kabanda (2008).

CHAPTER 5

1. Though see Hagopian (1990) for an alternative perspective that emphasizes the elite dimensions of the Brazilian transition and downplays the role of civil society and the opposition.

2. Some of the seminal works that I rely on throughout this chapter are Hunter (1997); Keck (1992); Mainwaring (1999); Martinez-Lara (1996); Stepan (1988, 1989).

3. For a detailed account of the events leading up to the 1964 military intervention, see Parker (1979).

4. See Skidmore (1988) for a definitive account of the politics of the authoritarian regime in Brazil.

5. For more on the Araguaia Guerrillas and other violent opposition to the military regime, see Almeida (2015) and de Almeida Teles (2017).

6. Interview 126.

7. Economic crisis also helped bring together the left and right wings of the opposition in a "pragmatic convergence" (Markoff & Baretta, 1990).

8. For more on the importance of the 1982 election, particularly the gubernatorial elections, see Samuels and Abrucio (2000).

9. The successor to ARENA after the party reform of 1979.

10. Though many grassroots movements did struggle to adapt to the new democratic dispensation (Foweraker, 2001).

11. Interview 129.

12. An issue that has only recently begun to be addressed (Gugliano & Gallo, 2013).

13. Interview 119.

14. For more on the Collor corruption and impeachment, see Flynn (1993) and Rosenn and Downes (1999).

15. As Interview 114 put it, "The first test was the process of impeachment of Collor. It was a moment in which the population demonstrated great outrage with the country, and the process was rigorously conducted according to the norms of the constitution. The constitution was tested and it worked."

16. Interviews 119 and 112.

17. As Timothy Power (1988, p. 254) puts it, "Brazil's practice of democracy has always appeared mediocre: participation has been more restricted, representative institutions like the Congress have been much less effective, the public bureaucracy has functioned less well, regional and center-local relations have been contentious, and the military has intruded into political life on numerous occasions. These factors augur poorly for democracy."

CHAPTER 6

1. There is growing research on the organizational structure of resistance movements and their links to democratization. See, for example, Pinckney, Butcher, and Braithwaite (2018).

2. See, for example, Neu (2018).
3. For a detailed examination of these lessons, see Pinckney (2018).

APPENDIX

1. The mean change in polyarchy score in the year of a CRT is 0.13. The mean annual change in polyarchy score over a five-year period following a CRT is 0.62.
2. "Protest" events are those with a CAMEO root code of 14. The broad category contains more specific categories, such as "demonstrate or rally," "conduct hunger strike," "conduct strike or boycott," "obstruct passage, block," and "protest violently, riot" (Althaus, Bajjalieh, Carter, Peyton, & Shalmon, 2017, pp. 19–20).
3. The results for all the independent variables are inconsistent in this model. Including a second lagged polyarchy score reduces the significant of the CRT variable to $p < 0.1$, and including a third lagged polyarchy score makes the coefficient insignificant (though still positive).
4. If necessary, I defined "democracy" for respondents as follows: "For this study, I am looking at democracy as a political system where the government responds fairly to the needs and wishes of the people. Countries can be more or less democratic depending on how well the government responds. The key thing separating democracies from non-democracies is that at least leaders are chosen in elections that are free of interference and fair to all participants."

Works Cited

Abdalla, Nadine. 2016. "Youth Movements in the Egyptian Transformation: Strategies and Repertoires of Political Participation." *Mediterranean Politics* 21(1): 44–63.

Aberbach, Joel D., and Bert A. Rockman. 2002. "Conducting and Coding Elite Interviews." *PS: Political Science and Politics* 35(4): 673–76.

Abers, Rebecca Neaera. 2000. *Inventing Local Democracy: Grassroots Politics in Brazil.* Boulder, CO: Lynne Rienner Publishers.

Aboultaif, Eduardo Wassim. 2019. *Power Sharing in Lebanon: Consociationalism Since 1820.* Abingdon-on-Thames, UK: Routledge.

Acemoglu, Daron, Simon Johnson, James A. Robinson, and Pierre Yard. 2008. "Income and Democracy." *American Economic Review* 98(3): 808–42.

Acemoglu, Daron, and James A. Robinson. 2001. "A Theory of Political Transitions." *American Economic Review* 91(4): 938–63.

Acemoglu, Daron, and James A. Robinson. 2005. *Economic Origins of Dictatorship and Democracy.* New York, NY: Cambridge University Press.

Acharya, Ina. 2009. "Working under Monarchy: Political Leadership and Democracy in Nepal." *Asian Politics & Policy* 1(1): 127–41.

Achen, Christopher H. 2002. "Toward a New Political Methodology: Microfoundations and ART." *Annual Review of Political Science* 5: 423–50.

Achen, Christopher H. 2005. "Let's Put Garbage-Can Regressions and Garbage-Can Probits Where They Belong." *Conflict Management and Peace Science* 22: 327–39.

Achen, Christopher H., and Larry M. Bartels. 2016. *Democracy for Realists: Why Elections Do Not Produce Responsive Government.* Princeton, NJ: Princeton University Press.

Ackerman, Peter, and Jack DuVall. 2000. *A Force More Powerful: A Century of Non-Violent Conflict.* London, UK: Palgrave Macmillan.

Ackerman, Peter, and Christopher Kruegler. 1994. *Strategic Nonviolent Conflict: The Dynamics of People Power in the Twentieth Century.* Boston, MA: Praeger.

Adhikari, Aditya. 2012. "Revolution by Other Means: The Transformation of Nepal's Maoists in a Time of Peace." In *Nepal in Transition: From People's War to Fragile Peace*, ed. Sebastian Von Einsiedel, David M. Malone, and Suman Pradhan. New York, NY: Cambridge University Press, 265–86.

Adhikari, Aditya. 2014. *The Bullet and the Ballot Box: The Story of Nepal's Maoist Revolution*. Brooklyn, NY: Verso.

Aditya, Anand. 2016. "Minorities on March—Turbulent Tarai-Madhes: Reshaping Party Image and Renurturing Nepali Politics." In *The Role of Political Parties in Deepening Democracy in Nepal: A Study of Party Image, Issues at Stake, and Agenda Building*, ed. Anand Aditya and Chandra D. Bhatta. Kathmandu, Nepal: Friedrich Ebert Stiftung, 1–114.

Ahnen, Ron. 2003. "Between Tyranny of the Majority and Liberty: The Persistence of Human Rights Violations under Democracy in Brazil." *Bulletin of Latin American Research* 22(3): 319–39.

Akcinaroglu, Seden. 2012. "Rebel Interdependencies and Civil War Outcomes." *Journal of Conflict Resolution* 56(5): 879–903.

Almeida, Thamyris F. 2015. *Araguaia: Maoist Uprising and Military Counterinsurgency in the Brazilian Amazon*. Amherst, MA: University of Massachusetts–Amherst.

Althaus, Scott, et al. 2017. *Cline Center Historical Phoenix Event Data Variable Descriptions*. Champaign, IL: Cline Center for Democracy. http://www.clinecenter.illinois.edu/data/event/phoenix/ (retrieved February 11, 2020).

Alvarez, Sonia E. 1989. "Politicizing Gender and Engendering Democracy." In *Democratizing Brazil: Problems of Transition and Consolidation*, ed. Alfred C. Stepan. New York, NY: Oxford University Press, 205–51.

Archer, Margaret S. 2003. *Structure, Agency and the Internal Conversation*. New York, NY: Cambridge University Press.

Arendt, Hannah. 1963. *On Revolution*. New York, NY: Penguin Books.

Ash, Timothy Garton. 2014. *The Magic Lantern: The Revolution of '89 Witnessed in Warsaw, Budapest, Berlin and Prague*. London, UK: Atlantic Books Ltd.

Avritzer, Leonardo. 1995. "Transition to Democracy and Political Culture: An Analysis of the Conflict between Civil and Political Society in Post-Authoritarian Brazil." *Constellations* 2(2): 242–67.

Baer, Werner, and Paul Beckerman. 1989. "The Decline and Fall of Brazil's Cruzado." *Latin American Research Review* 24(1): 35–64.

Baldez, Lisa. 2003. "Women's Movements and Democratic Transition in Chile, Brazil, East Germany, and Poland." *Comparative Politics* 35(3): 253–72.

Ball, Stephen J. 1994. "Political Interviews and the Politics of Interviewing." In *Researching the Powerful in Education*, ed. G. Walford. London, UK: UCL Press, 96–115.

Ballou, Adin. 1910. *Christian Non-Resistance in All Its Important Bearings: Illustrated and Defended*. 2nd ed. Philadelphia, PA: Universal Peace Union.

Bandi, Govinda Sharma. 2017, July 17. "Search for Justice." *Kathmandu Post*. https://kathmandupost.com/opinion/2017/07/17/search-for-justice (retrieved October 25, 2019).

Baral, Lok Raj. 1994. "The Return of Party Politics in Nepal." *Journal of Democracy* 5(1): 121–33.

Barker, Colin, Alan Johnson, and Michael Lavalette. 2001. "Leadership Matters: An Introduction." In *Leadership in Social Movements*, ed. Colin Barker, Alan Johnson, and Michael Lavalette. Manchester, UK: Manchester University Press, 1–23.

Barro, Robert J. 1999. "Determinants of Democracy." *Journal of Political Economy* 107(S6): S158–S183.

Bartlett, David M. C. 2000. "Civil Society and Democracy: A Zambian Case Study." *Journal of Southern African Studies* 26(3): 429–46.

Bauer, Gretchen, and Scott D. Taylor. 2011. *Politics in Southern Africa: Transition and Transformation*. Boulder, CO: Lynne Rienner Publishers.

Bayer, Markus, Felix S. Bethke, and Daniel Lambach. 2016. "The Democratic Dividend of Nonviolent Resistance." *Journal of Peace Research* 53(6): 758–71.

Baylies, Carolyn, and Morris Szeftel. 1992. "The Fall and Rise of Multi-party Politics in Zambia." *Review of African Political Economy* 19(54): 75–91.

Baylies, Carolyn, and Morris Szeftel. 1997. "The 1996 Zambian Elections: Still Awaiting Democratic Consolidation." *Review of African Political Economy* 24(71): 113–28.

Beardsworth, Nicole, Nic Cheeseman, and Simukai Tinhu. 2019. "Zimbabwe: The Coup That Never Was, and the Election That Could Have Been." *African Affairs* 118(472): 580–96.

Beissinger, Mark R. 2013. "The Semblance of Democratic Revolution: Coalitions in Ukraine's Orange Revolution." *American Political Science Review* 107(3): 574–92.

Belgioioso, Margherita. 2018. "Going Underground: Resort to Terrorism in Mass Mobilization Dissident Campaigns." *Journal of Peace Research* 55(5): 641–55.

Benvindo, Juliano Zaiden. 2017. "The Forgotten People in Brazilian Constitutionalism: Revisiting Behavior Strategic Analyses of Regime Transitions." *International Journal of Constitutional Law* 15(2): 332–57.

Beresford, Alexander, Marie E. Berry, and Laura Mann. 2018. "Liberation Movements and Stalled Democratic Transitions: Reproducing Power in Rwanda and South Africa through Productive Liminality." *Democratization* 25(7): 1231–50.

Berger, Peter L., and Thomas Luckmann. 1966. *The Social Construction of Reality*. New York, NY: Anchor Books.

Berry, Jeffrey M. 2002. "Validity and Reliability Issues in Elite Interviewing." *PS: Political Science & Politics* 35(4): 679–82.

Bethke, Felix S., and Jonathan Pinckney. 2019. "Nonviolent Resistance and the Quality of Democracy." *Conflict Management and Peace Science* Onlinefirst. https://journals.sagepub.com/doi/10.1177/0738894219855918 (retrieved February 11, 2020).

Bhandari, Surendra. 2014. *Self-Determination and Constitution Making in Nepal.* Singapore: Springer Singapore. http://link.springer.com/10.1007/978-981-287-005-6 (retrieved October 24, 2019).

Bhaskar, Roy. 2014. *The Possibility of Naturalism: A Philosophical Critique of the Contemporary Human Sciences.* London, UK: Routledge.

Bia, Michela, and Alessandra Mattei. 2008. "A Stata Package for the Estimation of the Dose-Response Function through Adjustment for the Generalized Propensity Score." *The Stata Journal* 8(3): 354–73.

Bishwakarma, Mom. 2019. *Political Transformations in Nepal: Dalit Inequality and Social Justice.* London, UK: Routledge.

Black, Ian, and Patrick Kingsley. 2013, August 16. "Egypt: Resentment towards Brotherhood Fuels Crackdown Support." *The Guardian.* https://www.theguardian.com/world/2013/aug/16/egypt-nationalism-muslim-brotherhood-crackdown (retrieved July 9, 2018).

Bob, Clifford, and Sharon Erickson Nepstad. 2007. "Kill a Leader, Murder a Movement? Leadership and Assassination in Social Movements." *American Behavioral Scientist* 50(10): 1370–94.

Boix, Carles. 2003. *Democracy and Redistribution.* New York, NY: Cambridge University Press.

Boix, Carles, and Susan C. Stokes. 2003. "Endogenous Democratization." *World Politics* 55(4): 517–49.

Bollen, Kenneth A., and Robert W. Jackman. 1985. "Political Democracy and the Size Distribution of Income." *American Sociological Review* 50(4): 438–57.

Bolt, Jutta, and Jan Luiten van Zanden. 2014. "The Maddison Project: Collaborative Research on Historical National Accounts." *The Economic History Review* 67(3): 627–51.

Bonacich, Phillip. 1987. "Power and Centrality: A Family of Measures." *American Journal of Sociology* 92(5): 1170–82.

Bondurant, Joan V. 1958. *Conquest of Violence: The Gandhian Philosophy of Conflict.* Princeton, NJ: Princeton University Press.

Boserup, Anders, and Andrew Mack. 1975. *War without Weapons: Non-violence in National Defence.* New York, NY: Schocken Books.

Bozoki, Andras, ed. 2002. *The Roundtable Talks of 1989: The Genesis of Hungarian Democracy—Analysis and Documents.* Budapest, Hungary: Central European University Press.

Braithwaite, Alex, Jessica Maves Braithwaite, and Jeffrey Kucik. 2015. "The Conditioning Effect of Protest History on the Emulation of Nonviolent Conflict." *Journal of Peace Research* 52(6): 697–711.

Bratton, Michael. 1999. "Political Participation in a New Democracy: Institutional Considerations from Zambia." *Comparative Political Studies* 32(5): 549–88.

Bratton, Michael, Phillip Alderfer, and Neo Simutanyi. 1997. *Political Participation in Zambia, 1991–1996: Trends, Determinants and USAID Program Implications.* Washington, DC: U.S. Agency for International Development.

Bratton, Michael, and Nicolas Van de Walle. 1994. "Neopatrimonial Regimes and Political Transitions in Africa." *World Politics* 46(4): 453–89.

Bratton, Michael, and Nicholas Van de Walle. 1997. *Democratic Experiments in Africa: Regime Transitions in Comparative Perspective.* New York, NY: Cambridge University Press.

Brinks, Daniel, and Michael Coppedge. 2006. "Diffusion Is No Illusion: Neighbor Emulation in the Third Wave of Democracy." *Comparative Political Studies* 39(4): 463–89.

Bruns, Stephan B., and John P. A. Ioannidis. 2016. "P-Curve and p-Hacking in Observational Research." *PLoS One* 11(2): e0149144.

Bueno De Mesquita, Bruce. 2005. *The Logic of Political Survival.* Boston, MA: MIT Press.

Bunce, Valerie J. 2003. "Rethinking Recent Democratization: Lessons from the Postcommunist Experience." *World Politics* 55(2): 167–92.

Bunce, Valerie J., and Sharon L. Wolchik. 2011. *Defeating Authoritarian Leaders in Postcommunist Countries.* New York, NY: Cambridge University Press.

Burnell, Peter. 1995. "The Politics of Poverty and the Poverty of Politics in Zambia's Third Republic." *Third World Quarterly* 16(4): 675–90.

Burrowes, Robert J. 1996. *Strategy of Nonviolent Defense: A Gandhian Approach.* New York, NY: SUNY Press.

Butcher, Charles R., John L. Gray, and Liesel Mitchell. 2018. "Striking It Free? Organized Labor and the Outcomes of Civil Resistance." *Journal of Global Security Studies* 3(3): 302–21.

Butcher, Charles R., and Isak Svensson. 2016. "Manufacturing Dissent: Modernization and the Onset of Major Nonviolent Resistance Campaigns." *Journal of Conflict Resolution* 60(2): 311–39.

Camerer, Colin F. 2003. "Behavioural Studies of Strategic Thinking in Games." *Trends in Cognitive Sciences* 7(5): 225–31.

Carothers, Thomas. 2002. "The End of the Transition Paradigm." *Journal of Democracy* 13(1): 5–21.

Carter Center. 2008. *Observing the 2008 Nepal Constituent Assembly Election.* Atlanta, GA: The Carter Center. https://www.cartercenter.org/resources/pdfs/news/peace_publications/election_reports/finalreportnepal2008.pdf (retrieved February 11, 2020).

Cavendish, James C. 1994. "Christian Base Communities and the Building of Democracy: Brazil and Chile." *Sociology of Religion* 55(2): 179–95.

Cederman, Lars-Erik, and Kristian Skrede Gleditsch. 2004. "Conquest and Regime Change: An Evolutionary Model of the Spread of Democracy and Peace." *International Studies Quarterly* 48: 603–29.

Celestino, Mauricio Rivera, and Kristian Skrede Gleditsch. 2013. "Fresh Carnations or All Thorn, No Rose? Nonviolent Campaigns and Transitions in Autocracies." *Journal of Peace Research* 50(3): 385–400.

Central Bureau of Statistics. 2014. II *Population Monograph of Nepal: Social Demography.* Kathmandu, Nepal: Government of Nepal. http://old.cbs.gov.np/

image/data/Population/Population%20Monograph%200f%20Nepal%202014/
Population%20Monograph%200f%20Nepal%202014%20Volume%20I%20
FinalPrintReady1.pdf (retrieved February 11, 2020).

Che, Yi, Yi Lu, Zhigang Tao, and Peng Wang. 2013. "The Impact of Income on Democracy Revisited." *Journal of Comparative Economics* 41(1): 159–69.

Cheeseman, Nic, and Miles Larmer. 2015. "Ethnopopulism in Africa: Opposition Mobilization in Diverse and Unequal Societies." *Democratization* 22(1): 22–50.

Chella, Chomba, and Simon Kabanda. 2008. *Lessons in Effective Citizen Activism: The Anti–Third Term Campaign in Zambia*. Johannesburg, South Africa: South African Institute of International Affairs.

Chenoweth, Erica. 2015. "Trends in Civil Resistance and Authoritarian Responses." In *Is Authoritarianism Staging a Comeback?*, ed. Mathew Burrows and Maria J. Stephan. Washington, DC: The Atlantic Council, 53–62.

Chenoweth, Erica, and Orion A. Lewis. 2013. "Unpacking Nonviolent Campaigns: Introducing the NAVCO 2.0 Dataset." *Journal of Peace Research* 50(3): 415–23.

Chenoweth, Erica, and Kurt Schock. 2015. "Do Contemporaneous Armed Challenges Affect the Outcomes of Mass Nonviolent Campaigns?" *Mobilization: An International Quarterly* 20(4): 427–51.

Chenoweth, Erica, and Christopher Shay. 2019. "NAVCO 2.1 Dataset." https://doi.org/ 10.7910/DVN/MHOXDV, Harvard Dataverse, V2 (Retrieved February 11, 2020).

Chenoweth, Erica, and Maria J. Stephan. 2011. *Why Civil Resistance Works: The Strategic Logic of Nonviolent Conflict*. New York, NY: Columbia University Press.

Chenoweth, Erica, and Jay Ulfelder. 2017. "Can Structural Conditions Explain the Onset of Nonviolent Uprisings?" *Journal of Conflict Resolution* 61(2): 298–324.

Cheung, Yin-Wong, and Daniel Friedman. 1997. "Individual Learning in Normal Form Games: Some Laboratory Results." *Games and Economic Behavior* 19(1): 46–76.

Chikulo, Bornwell C. 1988. "The Impact of Elections in Zambia's One Party Second Republic." *Africa Today* 35(2): 37–49.

Chikulo, Bornwell C. 1993. "End of an Era: An Analysis of the 1991 Zambian Presidential and Parliamentary Elections." *Politikon* 20(1): 87–104.

Chiluba, Frederick. 1994. "Democratisation in Zambia" (Unpublished master's thesis). Warwick, UK: University of Warwick.

Clarke, Kevin A. 2005. "The Phantom Menace: Omitted Variable Bias in Econometric Research." *Conflict Management and Peace Science* 22(4): 341–52.

Collier, David, and Steven Levitsky. 1997. "Democracy with Adjectives: Conceptual Innovation in Comparative Research." *World Politics* 49(3): 430–51.

Collier, Ruth Berins. 1999. *Paths toward Democracy: The Working Class and Elites in Western Europe and South America*. New York, NY: Cambridge University Press.

Coller, Ruth Berins, and David Collier. 1991. *Shaping the Political Arena: Critical Junctures, the Labor Movement, and Regime Dynamics in Latin America*. Princeton, NJ: Princeton University Press.

Cook, María Lorena. 2002. "Labor Reform and Dual Transitions in Brazil and the Southern Cone." *Latin American Politics and Society* 44(1): 1–34.

Cooper, Adam. 2008. *Nepal: The Constituent Assembly Election 2008*. Bangkok, Thailand: The Asian Network for Free Elections.

Coppedge, Michael, et al. 2017. *V-Dem Codebook V7*. Gothenburg, Sweden: Varieties of Democracy (V-Dem) Project.

Coppedge, Michael, et al. 2018. *V-Dem Country. Year Dataset V8*. Varieties of Democracy (V-Dem) Project.

Cunningham, David E. 2006. "Veto Players and Civil War Duration." *American Journal of Political Science* 50(4): 875–92.

Cunningham, Kathleen Gallagher. 2013. "Actor Fragmentation and Civil War Bargaining: How Internal Divisions Generate Civil Conflict." *American Journal of Political Science* 57(3): 659–72.

Cunningham, Kathleen Gallagher, Marianne Dahl, and Anne Fruge. 2017. "Strategies of Resistance: Diversification and Diffusion." *American Journal of Political Science* 61(3): 591–605.

Dahl, Robert Alan. 1957. "The Concept of Power." *Systems Research and Behavioral Science* 2(3): 201–15.

Dahl, Robert Alan. 1973. *Polyarchy: Participation and Opposition*. New Haven, CT: Yale University Press.

Dahlum, Sirianne. 2019. "Students in the Streets: Education and Nonviolent Protest." *Comparative Political Studies* 52(2): 277–309.

Day, Joel, Jonathan Pinckney, and Erica Chenoweth. 2015. "Collecting Data on Nonviolent Action: Lessons Learned and Ways Forward." *Journal of Peace Research* 52(1): 129–33.

de Almeida Teles, Janaína. 2017. "The Araguaia Guerrilla War (1972–1974): Armed Resistance to the Brazilian Dictatorship." *Latin American Perspectives* 44(5): 30–52.

Deininger, Klaus, and Lyn Squire. 1996. "A New Data Set Measuring Income Inequality." *The World Bank Economic Review* 10(3): 565–91.

Della Cava, Ralph. 1989. "The 'People's Church,' the Vatican, and Abertura." In *Democratizing Brazil: Problems of Transition and Consolidation*, ed. Alfred C. Stepan. New York, NY: Oxford University Press, 143–67.

Della Porta, Donatella. 2014. *Mobilizing for Democracy: Comparing 1989 and 2011*. New York, NY: Oxford University Press.

Deming, Barbara. 1971. *Revolution and Equilibrium*. New York, NY: Penguin Books.

Diamond, Alexis, and Jasjeet S. Sekhon. 2013. "Genetic Matching for Estimating Causal Effects: A General Multivariate Matching Method for Achieving Balance in Observational Studies." *Review of Economics and Statistics* 95(3): 932–45.

Diamond, Larry. 1992. "Economic Development and Democracy Reconsidered." *American Behavioral Scientist* 35(4–5): 450–99.

Diamond, Larry. 2002. "Elections without Democracy: Thinking about Hybrid Regimes." *Journal of Democracy* 13(2): 21–35.

Diamond, Larry. 2015. "Facing Up to the Democratic Recession." *Journal of Democracy* 26(1): 141–55.

Diamond, Larry Jay. 1999. *Developing Democracy: Toward Consolidation*. Baltimore, MD: Johns Hopkins University Press.

Di Palma, Giuseppe. 1990. *To Craft Democracies: An Essay on Democratic Transitions*. Berkeley, CA: University of California Press.

Dixit, Kanak Mani. 2006. "The Spring of Dissent: People's Movement in Nepal." *India International Centre Quarterly* 33(1): 113–25.

Doorenspleet, Renske. 2004. "The Structural Context of Recent Transitions to Democracy." *European Journal of Political Research* 43(3): 309–35.

Drury, John, et al. 2005. "The Phenomenology of Empowerment in Collective Action." *British Journal of Social Psychology* 44: 309–28.

Dutt, Pushan, and Devashish Mitra. 2008. "Inequality and the Instability of Polity and Policy." *The Economic Journal* 118(531): 1285–314.

Easton, David. 1954. *The Political System*. New York, NY: Alfred A. Knopf.

Ekiert, Grzegorz, and Jan Kubik. 2001. *Rebellious Civil Society: Popular Protest and Democratic Consolidation in Poland, 1989–1993*. Ann Arbor, MI: University of Michigan Press.

Ekiert, Grzegorz, Jan Kubik, and Milada Anna Vachudova. 2007. "Democracy in the Post-Communist World: An Unending Quest?" *East European Politics and Societies* 21(1): 7–30.

Erdmann, Gero, and Neo Simutanyi. 2003. *Transition in Zambia: The Hybridisation of the Third Republic*. Lusaka, Zambia: Konrad-Adenauer-Stiftung.

Fernandes, Tiago. 2015. "Rethinking Pathways to Democracy: Civil Society in Portugal and Spain, 1960s–2000s." *Democratization* 22(6): 1074–104.

Findley, Michael, and Peter Rudloff. 2012. "Combatant Fragmentation and the Dynamics of Civil Wars." *British Journal of Political Science* 42(4): 879–901.

Fish, M. Steven. 2002. "Islam and Authoritarianism." *World Politics* 55(1): 4–37.

Fishlow, Albert. 1973. "Brazil's Economic Miracle." *The World Today* 29(11): 474–81.

Flynn, Peter. 1993. "Collor, Corruption and Crisis: Time for Reflection." *Journal of Latin American Studies* 25(2): 351–71.

Fordham, Benjamin O., and Victor Asal. 2007. "Billiard Balls or Snowflakes? Major Power Prestige and the International Diffusion of Institutions and Practices." *International Studies Quarterly* 51(1): 31–52.

Forsyth, Tim. 2010. "Thailand's Red Shirt Protests: Popular Movement or Dangerous Street Theatre?" *Social Movement Studies* 9(4): 461–67.

Foweraker, Joe. 2001. "Grassroots Movements and Political Activism in Latin America: A Critical Comparison of Chile and Brazil." *Journal of Latin American Studies* 33(4): 839–65.

Freedom House. 2019a. *Freedom in the World 2019*. Washington, DC: Freedom House. https://freedomhouse.org/sites/default/files/Feb2019_FH_FITW_2019_Report_ForWeb-compressed.pdf (retrieved October 3, 2019).

Freedom House. 2019b. "Freedom in the World 2019: Brazil." https://freedomhouse.org/report/freedom-world/2019/brazil (retrieved November 1, 2019).

Freedom House. 2019c. "Freedom in the World 2019: Zambia." https://freedomhouse.org/report/freedom-world/2019/zambia (retrieved October 28, 2019).

Freedom House. 2019d. "Syria." https://freedomhouse.org/report/freedom-world/2019/syria (retrieved October 7, 2019).

Galtung, Johan. 1969. "Violence, Peace, and Peace Research." *Journal of Peace Research* 6(3): 167–91.

Gandhi, Mohandas K. 2019. *The Power of Nonviolent Resistance: Selected Writings*, ed. Tripid Suhrud. New York, NY: Penguin Books.

Ganz, Marshall. 2009. *Why David Sometimes Wins: Strategic Capacity in Social Movements*. New York, NY: Oxford University Press.

Garcia-Ponce, Omar, and Leonard Wantchekon. 2017. "Critical Junctures: Independence Movements and Democracy in Africa." *George Washington University Working Paper*. http://omargarciaponce.com/wp-content/uploads/2013/07/critical_junctures_may_2017.pdf (Retrieved February 11, 2020).

Gasiorowski, Mark J., and Timothy J. Power. 1998. "The Structural Determinants of Democratic Consolidation: Evidence from the Third World." *Comparative Political Studies* 31(6): 740–71.

Geddes, Barbara. 1999. "What Do We Know about Democratization after Twenty Years?" *Annual Review of Political Science* 2(1): 115–44.

Geddes, Barbara, Joseph Wright, and Erica Frantz. 2014. "Autocratic Breakdown and Regime Transitions: A New Data Set." *Perspectives on Politics* 12(2): 313–31.

Gellner, David. 2014. "The 2013 Elections in Nepal." *Asian Affairs* 45(2): 243–61.

Gerring, John. 2004. "What Is a Case Study and What Is It Good For?" *American Political Science Review* 98(2): 341–54.

Gerring, John. 2007. "Is There a (Viable) Crucial-Case Method?" *Comparative Political Studies* 40(3): 231–53.

Gertzel, Cherry J., and Morris Szeftel. 1984. *The Dynamics of the One-Party State in Zambia*. Manchester, UK: Manchester University Press.

Ghimire, Binod. 2018, November 21. "12 Years on, Political Leadership Still Dithers on Transitional Justice." *Kathmandu Post*. https://kathmandupost.com/national/2018/11/21/12-years-on-political-leadership-still-dithers-on-transitional-justice (retrieved October 25, 2019).

Giddens, Anthony. 1984. *The Constitution of Society: Outline of the Theory of Structuration*. Oakland, CA: University of California Press.

Gifford, Paul. 1998. "Chiluba's Christian Nation: Christianity as a Factor in Zambian Politics 1991–1996." *Journal of Contemporary Religion* 13(3): 363–81.

Gilbert, Alan. 1979. "Social Theory and Revolutionary Activity in Marx." *American Political Science Review* 73(2): 521–38.

Gleditsch, Kristian Skrede, and Mauricio Rivera. 2017. "The Diffusion of Nonviolent Campaigns." *Journal of Conflict Resolution* 61(5): 1120–45.

Gleditsch, Kristian Skrede, and Michael D. Ward. 2006. "Diffusion and the International Context of Democratization." *International Organization* 60(4): 911–33.

Goemans, Henk E., Kristian Skrede Gleditsch, and Giacomo Chiozza. 2009. "Introducing Archigos: A Dataset of Political Leaders." *Journal of Peace Research* 46(2): 269–83.

Goertzel, Ted George. 1999. *Fernando Henrique Cardoso: Reinventing Democracy in Brazil*. Boulder, CO: Lynne Rienner Publishers.

Gregg, Richard B. 1935. *The Power of Nonviolence*. Hartford, ME: Greenleaf Books.

Grzymala-Busse, Anna. 2010. "The Best Laid Plans: The Impact of Informal Rules on Formal Institutions in Transitional Regimes." *Studies in Comparative International Development* 45(3): 311–33.

Gugliano, Alfredo Alejandro, and Carlos Artur Gallo. 2013. "On the Ruins of the Democratic Transition: Human Rights as an Agenda Item in Abeyance for the Brazilian Democracy." *Bulletin of Latin American Research* 32(3): 325–38.

Gunitsky, Seva. 2014. "From Shocks to Waves: Hegemonic Transitions and Democratization in the Twentieth Century." *International Organization* 68(3): 561–97.

Guo, Sujian, and Gary A. Stradiotto. 2014. *Democratic Transitions: Modes and Outcomes*. Abingdon-on-Thames, UK: Routledge.

Gurung, Anne Mary. 2017. *The Madhesi Movement in Nepal: A Study on Social, Cultural, and Political Aspects, 1990–2015* (Unpublished dissertation). Sikkim University.

Gyanwali, Pradip. 2016. "Managing Intra-party Clash and Strengthening Democracy." In *The Role of Politial Parties in Deepening Democracy in Nepal*, ed. Anand Aditya and Chandra D. Bhatta. Kathmandu, Nepal: Friedrich Ebert Stiftung—Nepal, 145–59.

Haber, Stephen, and Victor Menaldo. 2011. "Do Natural Resources Fuel Authoritarianism? A Reappraisal of the Resource Curse." *American Political Science Review* 105(1): 1–26.

Hachchethu, Krishna. 1992. "Mass Movement 1990." *Contributions to Nepalese Studies* 17(2): 177–201.

Hafner-Burton, Emilie M., and James Ron. 2009. "Seeing Double: Human Rights Impact through Qualitative and Quantitative Eyes." *World Politics* 61(2): 360–401.

Haggard, Stephan, and Robert R. Kaufman. 2016a. "Democratization during the Third Wave." *Annual Review of Political Science* 19: 125–44.

Haggard, Stephan, and Robert R. Kaufman. 2016b. *Dictators and Democrats: Masses, Elites, and Regime Change*. Princeton, NJ: Princeton University Press.

Hagopian, Frances. 1990. "'Democracy by Undemocratic Means'? Elites, Political Pacts, and Regime Transition in Brazil." *Comparative Political Studies* 23(2): 147–70.

Haines, Herbert H. 1984. "Black Radicalization and the Funding of Civil Rights: 1957–1970." *Social Problems* 32(1): 31–43.

Harman, Chris. 1986. "Base and Superstructure." *International Socialism* 2(32): 3–44.

Harsch, Ernest. 2017. *Burkina Faso: A History of Power, Protest, and Revolution*. London, UK: Zed Books.

Harsch, Ernest. 2018, April 19. "How Burkina Faso Took to the Streets to Remove a Dictator, Then Stayed There." *African Arguments*. http://africanarguments.org/2018/04/19/how-burkina-faso-took-to-the-streets-to-remove-a-dictator-then-stayed-there/ (retrieved May 24, 2018).

Hausman, Jerry A. 1983. "Specification and Estimation of Simultaneous Equation Models." *Handbook of Econometrics* 1: 391–448.

Head, Megan L., et al. 2015. "The Extent and Consequences of P-Hacking in Science." *PLoS Biology* 13(3): e1002106.

Helmke, Gretchen, and Steven Levitsky. 2004. "Informal Institutions and Comparative Politics: A Research Agenda." *Perspectives on Politics* 2(4): 725–40.

Helvey, Robert L. 2004. *On Strategic Nonviolent Conflict: Thinking about the Fundamentals*. Boston, MA: Albert Einstein Institute.

Hewison, Kevin. 2014. "Thailand: The Lessons of Protest." *Asian Studies* 50(1): 1–15.

Higley, John, and Michael G. Burton. 1989. "The Elite Variable in Democratic Transitions and Breakdowns." *American Sociological Review* 54(1): 17–32.

Higley, John, and Michael R. Burton. 2006. *Elite Foundations of Liberal Democracy*. Lanham, MD: Rowman & Littlefield.

Hill, Daniel W. 2010. "Estimating the Effects of Human Rights Treaties on State Behavior." *The Journal of Politics* 72(4): 1161–74.

Hinds, David. 2005. "Problems of Democratic Transition in Guyana: Mistakes and Miscalculations in 1992." *Social and Economic Studies* 54(1): 67–82.

Hinfelaar, Marja. 2008. "Legitimizing Powers: The Political Role of the Roman Catholic Church, 1972–1991." In *One Zambia, Many Histories*, ed. Marja Hinfelaar, J. B. Grewald, and G. Macola. Leiden, Netherlands: Brill, 127–43.

Hipsher, Patricia L. 1998. "Democratic Transitions as Protest Cycles: Social Movement Dynamics in Democratizing Latin America." *The Social Movement Society: Contentious Politics for a New Century*, ed. David S. Meyer and Sidney Tarrow. Lanham, MD: Rowman & Littlefield Publishers, Inc., 153–72.

Hirano, Keisuke, and Guido W. Imbens. 2004. "The Propensity Score with Continuous Treatments." In *Applied Bayesian Modeling and Causal Inference from Incomplete-Data Perspectives*. Hoboken, NJ: Wiley-Blackwell, 73–84.

Hochstetler, Kathryn. 2000. "Democratizing Pressures from Below? Social Movements in the New Brazilian Democracy." In *Democratic Brazil: Actors, Institutions, and*

Processes, ed. Peter Kingstone and T. J. Power. Pittsburgh, PA: University of Pittsburgh Press, 167–84.

Högström, John. 2013. "Does the Choice of Democracy Measure Matter? Comparisons between the Two Leading Democracy Indices, Freedom House and Polity IV." *Government and Opposition* 48(2): 201–21.

Honaker, James, and Gary King. 2010. "What to Do about Missing Values in Time-Series Cross-Section Data." *American Journal of Political Science* 54(2): 561–81.

Honaker, James, Gary King, and Matthew Blackwell. 2011. "Amelia II: A Program for Missing Data." *Journal of Statistical Software* 45(7): 1–47.

Houle, Christian. 2009. "Inequality and Democracy: Why Inequality Harms Consolidation but Does Not Affect Democratization." *World Politics* 61(4): 589–622.

Housden, Oliver. 2010. "Nepal's Elusive Peace." *The RUSI Journal* 155(2): 70–77.

Hughes, Melanie M., Lindsey Peterson, Jill Ann Harrison, and Pamela Paxton. 2009. "Power and Relation in the World Polity: The INGO Network Country Score, 1978–1998." *Social Forces* 87(4): 1711–42.

Hunter, Wendy. 1997. *Eroding Military Influence in Brazil: Politicians against Soldiers*. Chapel Hill, NC: University of North Carolina Press.

Huntington, Samuel P. 1993. *The Third Wave: Democratization in the Late Twentieth Century*. Norman, OK: University of Oklahoma Press.

Ihonvbere, Julius O. 1995a. "From Movement to Government: The Movement for Multi-party Democracy and the Crisis of Democratic Consolidation in Zambia." *Canadian Journal of African Studies* 29(1): 1–25.

Ihonvbere, Julius O. 1995b. "The 'Zero Option' Controversy in Zambia: Western Double Standards vis a vis Safeguarding Security?" *Africa Spectrum* 30(1): 93–104.

International Commission of Jurists. 2017. *Achieving Justice for Gross Human Rights Violations in Nepal: Baseline Study, October 2017*. Geneva, Switzerland: International Commission of Jurists. https://www.icj.org/wp-content/uploads/2017/10/Nepal-GRA-Baseline-Study-Publications-Reports-Thematic-reports-2017-ENG.pdf (retrieved February 11, 2020).

International Crisis Group. 2008. *Nepal's Election: A Peaceful Revolution*. Brussels, Belgium: International Crisis Group.

Ioannidis, John P. A. 2005. "Why Most Published Research Findings Are False." *PLoS Medicine* 2(8): 696–701. https://doi.org/10.1371/journal.pmed.0020124.

Iyer, Raghavan N. 1973. *The Moral and Political Thought of Mahatma Gandhi*. New York, NY: Oxford University Press.

Jackman, Robert W. 1973. "On the Relation of Economic Development to Democratic Performance." *American Journal of Political Science* 17(3): 611–21.

Jarernpanit, Thannapat. 2019. "The Contestation of 'Good Politics': Explaining Conflict and Polarisation in Thailand." *Asian Studies Review* 43(4): 1–17.

Jeffery, Renée. 2017. "Nepal's Comprehensive Peace Agreement: Human Rights, Compliance and Impunity a Decade On." *International Affairs* 93(2): 343–64.

Jha, Kalpana. 2017. *The Madhesi Upsurge and the Contested Idea of Nepal.* Singapore: Springer.

Jha, Prashant. 2014. *Battles of the New Republic: A Contemporary History of Nepal.* New York, NY: Oxford University Press.

Jimenez-Diaz, Jose, and Santiago Delgado-Fernandez. 2016. *Political Leadership in the Spanish Transition to Democracy (1975–1982).* Hauppage, NY: Nova Science Publishers.

Johnstad, Petter Grahl. 2010. "Nonviolent Democratization: A Sensitivity Analysis of How Transition Mode and Violence Impact the Durability of Democracy." *Peace & Change* 35(3): 464–82.

Kaoma, Kapya J. 2015. *Raised Hopes, Shattered Dreams: Democracy, the Oppressed, and the Church in Africa (The Case of Zambia).* Trenton, NJ: Africa World Press.

Karatnycky, Adrian, and Peter Ackerman. 2005. *How Freedom Is Won: From Civic Resistance to Durable Democracy.* Washington, DC: Freedom House.

Karl, Terry Lynn, and Philippe C. Schmitter. 1991. "Modes of Transition in Latin America, Southern and Eastern Europe." *International Social Science Journal* 128(2): 267–82.

Kathmandu Post. 2015, August 29. "PM Koirala Pledges to Fulfill Dalit Demands."

Keane, John. 2000. *Vaclav Havel: A Political Tragedy in Six Acts.* New York, NY: Basic Books.

Keck, Margaret E. 1992. *The Worker's Party and Democratization in Brazil.* New Haven, CT: Yale University Press.

Ketchley, Neil. 2017. *Egypt in a Time of Revolution.* New York, NY: Cambridge University Press.

Ketchley, Neil, and Thoraya El-Rayyes. 2019. "Unpopular Protest: Mass Mobilization and Attitudes to Democracy in Post-Mubarak Egypt." *University of Oslo Working Paper.* https://www.academia.edu/40074527/Unpopular_Protest_ Mass_Mobilization_and_Attitudes_to_Democracy_in_Post-Mubarak_Egypt_ forthcoming_Journal_of_Politics_ (retrieved October 1, 2019).

Kingstone, Peter, Joseph K. Young, and Rebecca Aubrey. 2013. "Resistance to Privatization: Why Protest Movements Succeed and Fail in Latin America." *Latin American Politics and Society* 55(3): 93–116.

Kinzo, Maria D'Alva G. 1988. *Legal Opposition Politics under Authoritarian Rule in Brazil: The Case of the MDB, 1966–79.* New York, NY: Springer.

Kriseova, Eda. 1993. *Vaclav Havel: The Authorized Biography.* New York, NY: St. Martin's Press.

Kuran, Timur. 1991. "Now out of Never: The Element of Surprise in the East European Revolution of 1989." *World Politics* 44(1): 7–48.

Lakier, Genevieve. 2007. "Illiberal Democracy and the Problem of Law: Street Protest and Democratization in Multiparty Nepal." In *Contentious Politics and Democratization in Nepal*, ed. Mahendra Lawoti. Thousand Oaks, CA: Sage Publications, 251–72.

Lamounier, Bolivar. 1989. "Authoritarian Brazil Revisited: The Impact of Elections on the Abertura." In *Democratizing Brazil: Problems of Transition and Consolidation*, ed. Alfred C. Stepan. New York, NY: Oxford University Press, 43–79.

Lamounier, Bolivar, and O. A. Neto. 2005. "Brazil." In *Elections in the Americas: A Data Handbook*, ed. D. Nohlen. New York, NY: Oxford University Press, 163–252.

Landman, Todd. 2005. *Protecting Human Rights: A Comparative Study*. Washington, DC: Georgetown University Press.

Langland, Victoria. 2013. *Speaking of Flowers: Student Movements and the Making and Remembering of 1968 in Military Brazil*. Durham, NC: Duke University Press.

Larmer, Miles. 2016. *Rethinking African Politics: A History of Opposition in Zambia*. Abingdon-on-Thames, UK: Routledge.

Lauth, Hans-Joachim. 2000. "Informal Institutions and Democracy." *Democratization* 7(4): 21–50.

Laver, Michael, Kenneth Benoit, and John Garry. 2003. "Extracting Policy Positions from Political Texts Using Words as Data." *American Political Science Review* 97(2): 311–31.

Lawson, George. 2004. *Negotiated Revolutions: The Czech Republic, South Africa and Chile*. Farnham, UK: Ashgate Publishing.

LeBas, Adrienne. 2011. *From Protest to Parties: Party-Building and Democratization in Africa*. New York, NY: Oxford University Press.

Lecomte-Tilouine, Marie. 2004. "Ethnic Demands within Maoism: Questions of Magar Territorial Autonomy, Nationality, and Class." In *Himalayan "People's War": Nepal's Maoist Rebellion*, ed. Michael Hutt. London, UK: Hurst & Company, 112–35.

Lee, Francis L. F. 2006. "Collective Efficacy, Support for Democratization, and Political Participation in Hong Kong." *International Journal of Public Opinion Research* 18(3): 297–317.

Leech, Beth L. 2002. "Asking Questions: Techniques for Semistructured Interviews." *PS: Political Science & Politics* 35(4): 665–68.

Leeson, Peter T., and Andrea M. Dean. 2009. "The Democratic Domino Theory: An Empirical Investigation." *American Journal of Political Science* 53(3): 533–51.

Levitsky, Steven, and Lucan A. Way. 2010. *Competitive Authoritarianism: Hybrid Regimes after the Cold War*. New York, NY: Cambridge University Press.

Li, Eric. 2014, October 6. "The Umbrella Revolution Won't Give Hong Kong Democracy. Protesters Should Stop Asking for It." *The Washington Post*. https://www.washingtonpost.com/posteverything/wp/2014/10/06/the-umbrella-revolution-wont-give-hong-kong-democracy-protesters-should-stop-calling-for-it/?noredirect=on&utm_term=.59500f29391f (retrieved August 17, 2018).

Lichbach, Mark Irving. 1998. *The Rebel's Dilemma*. Ann Arbor, MI: University of Michigan Press.

Lieberman, Evan S. 2005. "Nested Analysis as a Mixed-Method Strategy for Comparative Research." *American Political Science Review* 99(3): 435–52.

Linz, Juan J. 1973. "The Future of an Authoritarian Situation or the Institutionalization of an Authoritarian Regime: The Case of Brazil." In *Authoritarian Brazil: Origins, Policies, and Future*, ed. Alfred C. Stepan. New Haven, CT: Yale University Press, 233–54.

Linz, Juan J. 1978. *The Breakdown of Democratic Regimes: Crisis, Breakdown, and Reequilibration*. Baltimore, MD: The Johns Hopkins University Press.

Linz, Juan J., and Alfred Stepan. 1996. *Problems of Democratic Transition and Consolidation: Southern Europe, South America, and Post-Communist Europe*. Baltimore, MD: Johns Hopkins University Press.

Lipset, Seymour Martin. 1959. "Some Social Requisites of Democracy: Economic Development and Political Legitimacy." *American Political Science Review* 53(1): 69–105.

Lipset, Seymour Martin. 1960. *Political Man: The Social Bases of Politics*. New York, NY: Doubleday.

Lopez-Calva, Luis F, and Sonia Rocha. 2012. *Exiting Belindia? Lessons from the Recent Decline in Income Inequality in Brazil*. Washington, DC: The World Bank. https://openknowledge.worldbank.org/bitstream/handle/10986/12808/701550ESW0P1230ICooInequalityBrazil.pdf?sequence=1 (retrieved February 11, 2020).

Lukes, Steven. 1986. *Power*. New York, NY: NYU Press.

Lyons, Terrence. 2016. "From Victorious Rebels to Strong Authoritarian Parties: Prospects for Post-war Democratization." *Democratization* 23(6): 1026–41.

Magaisa, Alex. 2019. "Zimbabwe: An Opportunity Lost." *Journal of Democracy* 30(1): 143–57.

Mainwaring, Scott. 1986. *The Catholic Church and Politics in Brazil*. Stanford, CA: Stanford University Press.

Mainwaring, Scott. 1988. "Political Parties and Democratization in Brazil and the Southern Cone." *Comparative Politics* 21(1): 91–120.

Mainwaring, Scott. 1989. "Grassroots Popular Mobilization and the Struggle for Democracy: Nova Iguacu." In *Democratizing Brazil: Challenges of Transition and Consolidation*, ed. Alfred C. Stepan. New York, NY: Oxford University Press, 168–204.

Mainwaring, Scott. 1999. *Rethinking Party Systems in the Third Wave of Democratization: The Case of Brazil*. Stanford, CA: Stanford University Press.

Malupenga, Amos. 2009. *Levy Patrick Mwanawasa: An Incentive for Posterity*. Grahamstown, South Africa: NICS (pty), Ltd.

Mampilly, Zachariah Cherian. 2012. *Rebel Rulers: Insurgent Governance and Civilian Life during War*. Ithaca, NY: Cornell University Press.

Maoz, Zeev, and Errol A. Henderson. 2013. "The World Religion Dataset, 1945–2010: Logic, Estimates, and Trends." *International Interactions* 39(3): 265–91.

Marcus, Richard R. 2004. "Political Change in Madagascar: Populist Democracy or Neopatrimonialism by Another Name?" *Institute for Security Studies Papers* 2004(89): 20.

Markoff, John, and Silvio R. Duncan Baretta. 1990. "Economic Crisis and Regime Change in Brazil: The 1960s and the 1980s." *Comparative Politics* 22(4): 421–44.

Marshall, Monty G., Ted Robert Gurr, and Keith Jaggers. 2016. *Polity IV Project: Political Regime Characteristics and Transitions, 1800–2015*. Vienna, VA: Center for Systemic Peace.

Martinez-Lara, Javier. 1996. *Building Democracy in Brazil: The Politics of Constitutional Change, 1985–95*. New York, NY: Springer.

Marx, Karl. 1977. *A Contribution to the Critique of Political Economy*. Moscow, USSR: Progress Publishers. (Original work published 1859)

May, Todd. 2015. *Nonviolent Resistance: A Philosophical Introduction*. Hoboken, NJ: John Wiley & Sons.

Mbao, Melvin L. M. 1998. "Human Rights and Discrimination: Zambia's Constitutional Amendment, 1996." *Journal of African Law* 42(1): 1–11.

Mbikusita-Lewanika, Akashambatwa. 2003. *Hour for Reunion: Movement for Multi-party Democracy, Conception, Dissension, and Reconciliation*. Lusaka, Zambia: African Lineki Courier.

McAdam, Doug. 1982. *Political Process and the Development of Black Insurgency, 1930–1970*. Chicago, IL: University of Chicago Press.

McCracken, Grant. 1988. *The Long Interview*. Newbury Park, CA: Sage.

McFaul, Michael. 2002. "The Fourth Wave of Democracy and Dictatorship: Noncooperative Transitions in the Postcommunist World." *World Politics* 54(2): 212–44.

McKeown, Timothy J. 2004. "Case Studies and the Limits of the Quantitative Worldview." In *Redesigning Social Inquiry: Diverse Tools, Shared Standards*, ed. Henry E. Brady and David Collier. Lanham, MD: Rowman & Littlefield Publishers, 139–68.

McMann, Kelly, et al. 2016. "Strategies of Validation: Assessing the Varieties of Democracy Corruption Data." *Varieties of Democracy Working Papers* 24. https://papers.ssrn.com/sol3/papers.cfm?abstract_id=2727595 (retrieved February 11, 2020).

Mechkova, Valeriya, Anna Lührmann, and Staffan I. Lindberg. 2017. "How Much Democratic Backsliding?" *Journal of Democracy* 28(4): 162–69.

Mikecz, Robert. 2012. "Interviewing Elites." *Qualitative Inquiry* 18(6): 482–93.

Milam, William B. 2007. "Bangladesh and the Burdens of History." *Current History: Philadelphia* 106(699): 153–60.

Mill, John Stuart. 1967. *A System of Logic: Ratiocinative and Inductive*. London, UK: Longmans.

Mills, Terence, and Kerry Patterson. 2006. *Palgrave Handbook of Econometrics*. New York, NY: Palgrave Macmillan.

Mitchell, Michael J., and H. Wood. 1998. "Ironies of Citizenship: Skin Color, Police Brutality, and the Challenge to Democracy in Brazil." *Social Forces* 77(3): 1001–20.

Mohamedou, Mohammad-Mahmoud Ould, and Timothy D. Sisk, eds. 2016. *Democratisation in the 21st Century: Reviving Transitology*. Milton Park, UK: Taylor & Francis.

Moisés, José Alvaro. 1979. "Current Issues in the Labor Movement in Brazil." *Latin American Perspectives* 6(4): 51–70.

Moore, Barrington. 1966. *Social Origins of Dictatorship and Democracy: Lord and Peasant in the Making of the Modern World*. Boston, MA: Beacon Press.

Morris, Zoë Slote. 2009. "The Truth about Interviewing Elites." *Politics* 29(3): 209–17.

Mouffe, Chantal. 1999. "Deliberative Democracy or Agonistic Pluralism." *Social Research* 66(3): 745–58.

Mouffe, Chantal. 2013. *Agonistics: Thinking the World Politically*. London, UK: Verso Books.

Mounk, Yascha. 2018. *The People vs. Democracy: Why Our Freedom Is in Danger and How to Save It*. Cambridge, MA: Harvard University Press.

Muller, Edward N., and Mitchell A. Seligson. 1987. "Inequality and Insurgency." *American Political Science Review* 81(2): 425–51.

Munck, Gerardo L., and Richard Snyder. 2007. "Visions of Comparative Politics: A Reply to Mahoney and Wibbels." *Comparative Political Studies* 40(1): 45–47.

Muñoz Acebes, Cesar. 2016. *"Good Cops Are Afraid": The Toll of Unchecked Police Violence in Rio de Janeiro*. New York, NY: Human Rights Watch.

Murdie, Amanda. 2009. "The Impact of Human Rights NGO Activity on Human Rights Practices." *International NGO Journal* 4(10): 421–40.

Naruemon, Thabchumpon. 2016. "Contending Political Networks: A Study of the 'Yellow Shirts' and 'Red Shirts' in Thailand's Politics." *Southeast Asian Studies* 5(1): 93–113. https://doi.org/10.20495/seas.5.1_93 (retrieved October 1, 2019).

National Democratic Institute. 1997. *The November 18, 1996 National Elections in Zambia: A Post-election Assessment Report*. Washington, DC: National Democratic Institute. https://www.ndi.org/sites/default/files/870_zm_report_111896.pdf (retrieved August 22, 2017).

Ndulo, Muna B., and Robert B. Kent. 1996. "Constitutionalism in Zambia: Past, Present and Future." *Journal of African Law* 40(2): 256–78.

Nelson, Sara. 1996. "Constructing and Negotiating Gender in Women's Police Stations in Brazil." *Latin American Perspectives* 23(1): 131–48.

Nepal Ministry of Peace and Reconciliation. 2005. "12-Point Understanding Reached between the Seven-Party Alliance and Nepal Communist Party (Maoists)." Kathmandu. http://peacemaker.un.org/sites/peacemaker.un.org/files/NP_051122_12%20Point%20 Understanding.pdf.

Nepstad, Sharon Erickson. 2011. *Nonviolent Revolutions: Civil Resistance in the Late 20th Century*. New York, NY: Oxford University Press.

Nepstad, Sharon Erickson. 2013. "Mutiny and Nonviolence in the Arab Spring: Exploring Military Defections and Loyalty in Egypt, Bahrain, and Syria." *Journal of Peace Research* 50(3): 337–49.

Nepstad, Sharon Erickson, and Clifford Bob. 2006. "When Do Leaders Matter? Hypotheses on Leadership Dynamics in Social Movements." *Mobilization: An International Journal* 11(1): 1–22.

Neu, Kara Kingma. 2018. *Defections and Democracy: Explaining Military Loyalty Shifts and Their Impact on Post-protest Political Change* (Unpublished dissertation). Denver, CO: University of Denver.

Nylen, William. 2000. "The Making of a Loyal Opposition: The Workers' Party (PT) and the Consolidation of Democracy in Brazil." In *Democratic Brazil: Actors, Institutions, and Processes*, ed. Peter Kingstone and T. J. Power. Pittsburgh, PA: University of Pittsburgh Press, 126–43.

O'Donnell, Guillermo A. 1996. "Illusions about Consolidation." *Journal of Democracy* 7(2): 34–51.

O'Donnell, Guillermo A. 2002. "In Partial Defense of an Evanescent 'Paradigm.'" *Journal of Democracy* 13(3): 6–12.

O'Donnell, Guillermo, and Philippe C. Schmitter. 1986. *Transitions from Authoritarian Rule: Tentative Conclusions about Uncertain Democracies*. Baltimore, MD: Johns Hopkins University Press.

O'Donovan, Michael. 2004. "The Administration of Elections in Zambia." In *Elections and Democracy in Zambia*, ed. Claude Kabemba. Johannesburg, South Africa: Electoral Insitute for Sustainable Democracy in Africa, 25–40.

Ogura, Kiyoko. 2008. *Seeking State Power: The Communist Party of Nepal (Maoist)*. Berlin: Berghof Research Center for Constructive Conflict Management.

Olivares, Eduardo. 2011. "Transition to Democracy in Brazil: The Actual Role of the Social Movement 'Diretas Ja.'" University of California, San Diego Working Paper. https://s3.amazonaws.com/academia.edu.documents/8934034/Paper_ Figueiredo_ Diretas%20Ja_ 2011.pdf?response-content- disposition=inline%3B%20filename%3DTransition_to_Democracy_in_ Brazil_The_Ac.pdf&X-Amz-Algorithm=AWS4-HMAC-SHA256&X- Amz-Credential=AKIAIWOWYYGZ2Y53UL3A%2F20200211%2 Fus-east-1%2Fs3%2Faws4_request&X-Amz-Date=20200211T203330Z&X- Amz-Expires=3600&X-Amz-SignedHeaders=host&X-Amz-Signature=683a b267d72d138fe6f4b18eb35f712d11dfa31158cbbc12525671483f6d9f42 (retrieved November 4, 2019).

Pakulski, Jan, Judith S. Kullberg, and John Higley. 1996. "The Persistence of Postcommunist Elites." *Journal of Democracy* 7(2): 133–47.

Pandey, Nishchal N. 2010. *New Nepal: The Fault Lines*. Singapore: Institute of South Asian Studies.

Pang, Eul-Soo, and Laura Jarnagin. 1985. "A Requiem for Authoritarianism in Brazil." *Current History* 84(499): 61–89.

Parker, Phyllis R. 1979. *Brazil and the Quiet Intervention, 1964.* Austin, TX: University of Texas Press.

Pauwels, Teun. 2011. "Measuring Populism: A Quantitative Text Analysis of Party Literature in Belgium." *Journal of Elections, Public Opinion and Parties* 21(1): 97–119.

Paxton, Pamela, Melanie M. Hughes, and Nicholas E. Reith. 2015. "Extending the INGO Network Country Score, 1950–2008." *Sociological Science* 2: 287–307.

Pemstein, Daniel, Stephen A. Meserve, and James Melton. 2010. "Democratic Compromise: A Latent Variable Analysis of Ten Measures of Regime Type." *Political Analysis* 18(4): 426–49.

Pemstein, Daniel, Kyle L. Marquardt, Eitan Tzelgov, Yi-ting Wang, and Farhad Miri. 2015. "The Varieties of Democracy Measurement Model: Latent Variable Analysis for Cross-National and Cross-Temporal Expert-Coded Data." *Varieties of Democracy Institute Working Paper* 21. https://gupea.ub.gu.se/bitstream/2077/41350/4/gupea_2077_41350_4.pdf (retrieved 14 February 2020).

Petrova, Marina G. 2019. "What Matters Is Who Supports You: Diaspora and Foreign States as External Supporters and Militants' Adoption of Nonviolence." *Journal of Conflict Resolution* 63(9): 2155–79.

Pettman, Jan. 1974. "Zambia's Second Republic—The Establishment of a One-Party State." *The Journal of Modern African Studies* 12(2): 231–44.

Pevehouse, Jon C. 2002. "With a Little Help from My Friends? Regional Organizations and the Consolidation of Democracy." *American Journal of Political Science* 46(3): 611–26.

Pevehouse, Jon C. 2005. *Democracy from Above: Regional Organizations and Democratization.* New York, NY: Cambridge University Press.

Pfaff-Czarnecka, Joanna. 2004. "High Expectations, Deep Disappointmet: Politics, State and Society in Nepal after 1990." In *Himalayan "People's War": Nepal's Maoist Rebellion*, ed. Michael Hutt. London, UK: Hurst & Company, 166–91.

Pinckney, Jonathan. 2014. *Winning Well: Civil Resistance Mechanisms of Success, Democracy, and Civil Peace.* University of Denver Master's Thesis. https://digitalcommons.du.edu/etd/517/ (retrieved February 14, 2020).

Pinckney, Jonathan. 2016. *Making or Breaking Nonviolent Discipline.* Washington, DC: ICNC Press.

Pinckney, Jonathan. 2018. *When Civil Resistance Succeeds: Building Democracy after Popular Nonviolent Uprisings.* Washington, DC: ICNC Press.

Pinckney, Jonathan, Charles Butcher, and Jessica Maves Braithwaite. 2018. "Durability and Diversity: Uncovering the Organizational Roots of Democratization." Paper presented at the Annual Meeting of the American Political Science Association, San Francisco, CA.

Pishchikova, Kateryn, and Richard Youngs. 2016. "Divergent and Partial Transitions: Lessons from Ukraine and Egypt." In *Democratisation in the 21st*

Century: Reviving Transitology, ed. Mohammed-Mahmoud Mohamedou and Timothy Sisk. Abingdon-on-Thames, UK: Taylor & Francis, 49–68.

Power, Timothy J. 1988. "Political Landscapes, Political Parties, and Authoritarianism in Brazil and Chile." *International Journal of Comparative Sociology: Leiden* 29: 251–63.

Proksch, Sven-Oliver, and Jonathan B. Slapin. 2010. "Position Taking in European Parliament Speeches." *British Journal of Political Science* 40(3): 587–611.

Przeworski, Adam. 1991. *Democracy and the Market: Political and Economic Reforms in Eastern Europe and Latin America*. New York, NY: Cambridge University Press.

Przeworski, Adam, Michael E. Alvarez, Jose Antonio Cheibub, and Fernando Limongi. 2000. *Democracy and Development: Political Institutions and Well-Being in the World, 1950–1990*. New York, NY: Cambridge University Press.

Przeworski, Adam, and Henry Tuene. 1970. *The Logic of Comparative Social Inquiry*. New York, NY: Wiley.

Putnam, Robert D., Robert Leonardi, and Raffaella Y. Nanetti. 1994. *Making Democracy Work: Civic Traditions in Modern Italy*. Princeton, NJ: Princeton University Press.

Rabushka, Alvin, and Kenneth A. Shepsle. 1972. *Politics in Plural Societies*. Redwood City, CA: Stanford University Press.

Rakner, Lise. 1992. *Trade Unions in Processes of Democratization: A Study of Party Labour Relations in Zambia*. Bergen, Norway: Chr. Michelsen Institute.

Rakner, Lise. 2003. *Political and Economic Liberalisation in Zambia 1991–2001*. Stockholm, Sweden: Nordic Africa Institute.

Reynolds, Andrew. 1999. *Electoral Systems and Democratization in Southern Africa*. New York, NY: Oxford University Press.

Riker, William H. 1962. *The Theory of Political Coalitions*. New Haven, CT: Yale University Press.

Ritter, Daniel P. 2015. *The Iron Cage of Liberalism: International Politics and Unarmed Revolutions in the Middle East and North Africa*. New York, NY: Oxford University Press.

Roberts, Adam, and Timothy Garton Ash. 2009. *Civil Resistance and Power Politics: The Experience of Non-violent Action from Gandhi to the Present*. New York, NY: Oxford University Press.

Roberts, Adam, Michael J. Willis, Rory McCarthy, and Timothy Garton Ash. 2016. *Civil Resistance in the Arab Spring: Triumphs and Disasters*. New York, NY: Oxford University Press.

Robinson, James A. 2006. "Economic Development and Democracy." *Annual Review of Political Science* 9(1): 503–27.

Robinson, William I. 1996. *Promoting Polyarchy: Globalization, US Intervention, and Hegemony*. New York, NY: Cambridge University Press.

Rodrigues, Maria Guadalupe Moog. 2002. "Indigenous Rights in Democratic Brazil." *Human Rights Quarterly* 24(2): 487–512.

Rohlfing, Ingo. 2008. "What You See and What You Get: Pitfalls and Principles of Nested Analysis in Comparative Research." *Comparative Political Studies* 41(11): 1492–514.

Roka, Hari. 2004. "The Emergency and Nepal's Political Future." In *Himalayan "People's War": Nepal's Maoist Rebellion*, ed. Michael Hutt. London, UK: Hurst & Company, 243–60.

Roll, Stephan. 2016. "Managing Change: How Egypt's Military Leadership Shaped the Transformation." *Mediterranean Politics* 21(1): 23–43.

Rosenn, Keith S., and Richard Downes, eds. 1999. *Corruption and Political Reform in Brazil: The Impact of Collor's Impeachment*. Coral Gables, FL: North-South Center Press.

Ross, Michael. 2006. "Is Democracy Good for the Poor?" *American Journal of Political Science* 50(4): 860–74.

Ross, Michael L. 2012. *The Oil Curse: How Petroleum Wealth Shapes the Development of Nations*. Princeton, NJ: Princeton University Press.

Rothman, Franklin, and Pamela Oliver. 1999. "From Local to Global: The Anti-Dam Movement in Southern Brazil, 1979–1992." *Mobilization: An International Quarterly* 4(1): 41–57.

Rueschemeyer, Dietrich, Evelyne Huber Stephens, and John D. Stephens. 1992. *Capitalist Development and Democracy*. New York, NY: Cambridge Polity.

Rustow, Dankwart A. 1970. "Transitions to Democracy: Toward a Dynamic Model." *Comparative Politics* 2(3): 337–63.

Sa, Antonio. 2014. *The Citizen's Constitution: A Study of the Constitution Making Process in the Transition to Democracy in Brazil* (Unpublished dissertation). The New School.

Samuels, David, and Fernando Luiz Abrucio. 2000. "Federalism and Democratic Transitions: The 'New' Politics of the Governors in Brazil." *Publius: The Journal of Federalism* 30(2): 43–61.

Sanders, James B. T., J. Doyne Farmer, and Tobias Galla. 2018. "The Prevalence of Chaotic Dynamics in Games with Many Players." *Scientific Reports* 8(1): 4902.

Sandoval, Salvador A. M. 1993. *Social Change and Labor Unrest in Brazil Since 1945*. Boulder, CO: Westview Press.

Sarles, Margaret J. 1982. "Maintaining Political Control through Parties: The Brazilian Strategy." *Comparative Politics* 15(1): 41–72.

Schaffer, Howard B. 2002. "Back and Forth in Bangladesh." *Journal of Democracy* 13(1): 76–83.

Schedler, Andreas. 1998. "What Is Democratic Consolidation." *Journal of Democracy* 9(2): 91–107.

Schedler, Andreas. 2002. "The Menu of Manipulation." *Journal of Democracy* 13(2): 36–50.

Schneider, Ronald M. 1991. *Order and Progress: A Political History of Brazil*. Boulder, CO: Westview Press.

Schock, Kurt. 2005. *Unarmed Insurrections: People Power Movements in Nondemocracies.* Minneapolis, MN: University of Minnesota Press.

Schrodt, Philip A., Deborah J. Gerner, Omur Yilmaz, and Dennis Hermreck. 2005. "The CAMEO (Conflict and Mediation Event Observations) Actor Coding Framework." Paper presented at the Annual Meeting of the American Political Science Association, Washington, DC. http://eventdata.parusanalytics.com/papers.dir/APSA.2005.pdf (retrieved February 11, 2020).

Schumpeter, Joseph A. 1942. *Capitalism, Socialism and Democracy.* Abingdon-on-Thames, UK: Routledge.

Sekhon, Jasjeet S. 2011. "Multivariate and Propensity Score Matching Software with Automated Balance Optimization: The Matching Package for R." *Journal of Statistical Software* 42(7): 1–52.

Sharma, Sudhindra, and Pawan Kumar Sen. 2005. *Waging Nonviolent Struggle: 20th Century Practice and 21st Century Potential.* Boston, MA: Porter Sargent.

Sharma, Sudhindra, and Pawan Kumar Sen. 2006. *Nepal Contemporary Political Situation III.* Kathmandu, Nepal: Interdisciplinary Analysts..

Sharma, Sudhindra, and Pawan Kumar Sen. 2008. *Nepal Contemporary Political Situation—V.* Kathmandu, Nepal: Interdisciplinary Analysts.

Sharp, Gene. 1973. *The Politics of Nonviolent Action.* Boston, MA: Porter Sargent.

Shrestha, Min Bahadur, and Shashi Kant Chaudhary. 2013. "The Economic Cost of General Strikes in Nepal." *NRB Economic Review* 26(1): 1–23. https://www.nrb.org.np/ecorev/pdffiles/vol26-1_art1.pdf (retrieved September 8, 2018).

Sigdel, Anil. 2014. "Human Rights Norms vs. Peace Process: The Agenda of Truth and Reconciliation Commission in Nepal's Peace Process." *The International Journal of Civic, Political, and Community Studies* 11(3): 1–13.

Simmons, Beth A., Frank Dobbin, and Geoffrey Garrett. 2006. "Introduction: The International Diffusion of Liberalism." *International Organization* 60(4): 781–810.

Simutanyi, Neo. 1996. "The Politics of Structural Adjustment in Zambia." *Third World Quarterly* 17(4): 825–39.

Sishuwa, Sishuwa. 2012. "Review: Rethinking African Politics. A History of Opposition in Zambia by Miles Larmer." *The Journal of Modern African Studies* 50(2): 363–65.

Skar, Harald Olav. 2008. *Between Boy Scouts and Paramilitary Storm Troops: The Young Communist League of Nepal.* Oslo, Norway: Norsk Utenrikspolitisk Institutt (NUPI).

Skidmore, Thomas E. 1988. *The Politics of Military Rule in Brazil, 1964–85.* New York, NY: Oxford University Press.

Skocpol, Theda. 1979. *States and Social Revolutions: A Comparative Analysis of France, Russia and China.* New York, NY: Cambridge University Press.

Solingen, Etel. 2009. *Nuclear Logics: Contrasting Paths in East Asia and the Middle East.* Princeton, NJ: Princeton University Press.

Souza Pinheiro, Alvaro de. 1995. *Guerrilla in the Brazilian Amazon*. Fort Leavenworth, KS: Foreign Military Studies Office.

Spradley, James P. 1979. *The Ethnographic Interview*. Long Grove, IL: Waveland Press.

Starr, Harvey. 1991. "Democratic Dominoes: Diffusion Approaches to the Spread of Democracy in the International System." *Journal of Conflict Resolution* 35(2): 356–81.

Stepan, Alfred. 1988. *Rethinking Military Politics: Brazil and the Southern Cone*. Princeton, NJ: Princeton University Press.

Stepan, Alfred, ed. 1989. *Democratizing Brazil: Problems of Transition and Consolidation*. New York, NY: Oxford University Press.

Stepan, Alfred C. 1989. "Introduction." In *Democratizing Brazil: Problems of Transition and Consolidation*. New York, NY: Oxford University Press, vii–xvii.

Stepan, Alfred C. 2012. "Tunisia's Transition and the Twin Tolerations." *Journal of Democracy* 23(2): 89–103.

Stradiotto, Gary A., and Sujian Guo. 2010. "Transitional Modes of Democratization and Democratic Outcomes." *International Journal on World Peace* 27(4): 5–40.

Strasheim, Julia. 2017. "The Politics of Institutional Reform and Post-conflict Violence in Nepal." *GIGA Working Papers* 296. https://www.giga-hamburg.de/en/system/files/publications/wp296_strasheim.pdf (retrieved February 11, 2020).

Strasheim, Julia. 2018. "A False Promise of Political Stability in Nepal?" *South Asia @ LSE*. http://eprints.lse.ac.uk/89130/1/southasia-2018-03-19-a-false-promise-of-political-stability-in.pdf (retrieved August 10, 2018).

Subedi, D. B., and Prakash Bhattarai. 2017. "The April Uprising: How a Nonviolent Struggle Explains the Transformation of Armed Conflict in Nepal." *Journal of Peacebuilding & Development* 12(3): 85–97.

Svensson, Isak, and Mathilda Lindgren. 2011. "Community and Consent: Unarmed Insurrections in Non-democracies." *European Journal of International Relations* 17(1): 97–120.

Svolik, Milan W. 2008. "Authoritarian Reversals and Democratic Consolidation." *American Political Science Review* 102(2): 153–68.

Svolik, Milan W. 2012. *The Politics of Authoritarian Rule*. New York, NY: Cambridge University Press.

Tarrow, Sidney. 2004. "Bridging the Quantitative-Qualitative Divide." In *Rethinking Social Inquiry: Diverse Tools, Shared Standards*, ed. Henry E. Brady and David Collier. Lanham, MD: Rowman & Littlefield Publishers, 171–80.

Teorell, Jan. 2010. *Determinants of Democratization: Explaining Regime Change in the World, 1972–2006*. New York, NY: Cambridge University Press.

Teorell, Jan, Michael Coppedge, Svend-Erik Skaaning, and Staffan I. Lindberg. 2016. "Measuring Electoral Democracy with V-Dem Data: Introducing a New Polyarchy Index." *Varieties of Democracy Institute Working Paper* https://gupea.ub.gu.se/bitstream/2077/42070/6/gupea_2077_42070_6.pdf (retrieved 14 February 2020).

Thabchumpon, Naruemon. 2016. "Contending Political Networks: A Study of the 'Yellow Shirts' and 'Red Shirts' in Thailand's Politics." *Southeast Asian Studies* 5(1): 93–113.

Thapa, Deepak. 2004. "Radicalism and the Emergence of the Maoists." In *Himalayan "People's War": Nepal's Maoist Rebellion*, ed. Michael Hutt. London, UK: Hurst & Company, 21–37.

Thoreau, Henry David. 2016. *Civil Disobedience*. Peterborough, ON: Broadview Press.

Thurber, Ches. 2018. "Ethnic Barriers to Civil Resistance." *Journal of Global Security Studies* 3(3): 255–70.

Thurber, Ches. 2019. "Social Ties and the Strategy of Civil Resistance." *International Studies Quarterly* 63(4): 974–86.

Tilly, Charles. 1978. *From Mobilization to Revolution*. Boston, MA: Routledge.

Toft, Monica Duffy. 2010. "Ending Civil Wars: A Case for Rebel Victory?" *International Security* 34(4): 7–36.

Tolstoy, Leo. 1894. *The Kingdom of God Is within You: Christianity Not as a Mystic Religion but as a New Theory of Life*. New York, NY: The Cassell Publishing Co.

Trimberger, Ellen Kay. 1978. *Revolution from Above: Military Bureaucrats and Development in Japan, Turkey, Egypt, and Peru*. Piscataway, NJ: Transaction Publishers.

Tucker, Joshua A. 2007. "Enough! Electoral Fraud, Collective Action Problems, and Post-communist Colored Revolutions." *Perspectives on Politics* 5(3): 535–51.

Tufekci, Zeynep. 2017. *Twitter and Tear Gas: The Power and Fragility of Networked Protest*. New Haven, CT: Yale University Press.

Upreti, Bishnu Raj. 2008. "Resistance Movements in Conflict Transformation and Social Change." In *Nepal: Transition to Transformation*, ed. Kailash Nath Pyakuryal, Bishnu Raj Upreti, and Sagar Raj Sharma. Kathmandu, Nepal: NCCR North to South, 15–48.

Valença, Márcio Moraes. 2002. "The Politics of Giving in Brazil: The Rise and Demise of Collor (1990–1992)." *Latin American Perspectives* 29(1): 115–52.

Valenzuela, J Samuel. 1990. "Democratic Consolidation in Post-transitional Settings." Helen Kellogg Institute for International Studies Working Paper 38. https://kellogg.nd.edu/sites/default/files/old_files/documents/150_0.pdf (retrieved February 11, 2020).

van Donge, Jan Kees. 1995. "Zambia: Kaunda and Chiluba—Enduring Patterns of Political Culture." In *Democracy and Political Change in Sub-Saharan Africa*, ed. J. A. Wiseman. New York, NY: Routledge, 193–219.

van Donge, Jan Kees. 2008. "The Plundering of Zambian Resources by Frederick Chiluba and His Friends: A Case Study of the Interaction between National Politics and the International Drive towards Good Governance." *African Affairs* 108(430): 69–90.

Verba, Sidney, Norman H. Nie, and Jae-On Kim. 1987. *Participation and Political Equality: A Seven-Nation Comparison*. Chicago, IL: University of Chicago Press.

https://scholar.google.com/scholar_lookup?title=Participation+and+Political+ Equality:+A+Seven+Nation+Comparison&publication+year=1978&author=Ve rba+Sidney&author=Nie+Norman+H.&author=Kim+Jae-on (retrieved August 6, 2018).

Vinthagen, Stellan. 2015. *A Theory of Nonviolent Action: How Civil Resistance Works.* London, UK: Zed Books Ltd.

Wampler, Brian, and Leonardo Avritzer. 2004. "Participatory Publics: Civil Society and New Institutions in Democratic Brazil." *Comparative Politics* 36(3): 291–312.

Weber, Max. 1978. *Economy and Society.* Berkeley, CA: University of California Press.

Weffort, Francisco. 1989. "Why Democracy?" In *Democratizing Brazil: Problems of Transition and Consolidation*, ed. Alfred C. Stepan. New York, NY: Oxford University Press, 327–50.

Weinstein, Jeremy M. 2006. *Inside Rebellion: The Politics of Insurgent Violence.* New York, NY: Cambridge University Press.

Weizenmann, Pedro Paulo. 2019. "'Tropical Trump'? Bolsonaro's Threat to Brazilian Democracy." *Harvard International Review* 40(1): 12–14.

Wenman, Mark. 2013. *Agonistic Democracy: Constituent Power in the Era of Globalisation.* New York, NY: Cambridge University Press.

Weyland, Kurt. 1995. "Social Movements and the State: The Politics of Health Reform in Brazil." *World Development* 23(10): 1699–712.

Whelpton, John. 2005. *A History of Nepal.* New York, NY: Cambridge University Press.

Whitehead, Laurence, Guillermo A. O'Donnell, and Philippe C. Schmitter. 1989. *Transitions from Authoritarian Rule: Latin America.* Baltimore, MD: Johns Hopkins University Press.

Wood, Elisabeth Jean. 2000. *Forging Democracy from Below: Insurgent Transitions in South Africa and El Salvador.* New York, NY: Cambridge University Press.

World Integrated Trade Solutions. 2017. "Nepal Exports, Imports, and Trade Balance by Country and Region 2017." The World Bank. https://wits.worldbank.org/ CountryProfile/en/Country/NPL/Year/LTST/TradeFlow/EXPIMP (retrieved 14 February, 2020).

Zakaria, Fareed. 1997. "The Rise of Illiberal Democracy." *Foreign Affairs* 76: 22.

Zartman, I. William. 2015. *Arab Spring: Negotiating in the Shadow of the Intifadat.* Athens, GA: University of Georgia Press.

Zirker, Daniel. 1986. "Civilianization and Authoritarian Nationalism in Brazil: Ideological Opposition within a Military Dictatorship." *Journal of Political and Military Sociology* 14: 263–76.

Zirker, Daniel. 1993. "The Military Ministers and Political Change in Post-authoritarian Brazil." *Canadian Journal of Latin American and Caribbean Studies* 18(35): 87–110.

Zunes, Stephen, Sarah Beth Asher, and Lester Kurtz. 1999. *Nonviolent Social Movements: A Geographical Perspective.* Hoboken, NJ: Wiley-Blackwell.

Index

For the benefit of digital users, indexed terms that span two pages (e.g., 52–53) may, on occasion, appear on only one of those pages.